AF564646

STRATEGIC REBALANCING

China and US Engagement with South Asia

STRATEGIC REBALANCING

China and US Engagement with South Asia

Anand Kumar

Copyright © Manohar Parrikar Institute for Defence Studies and Analyses,
New Delhi, 2024

All rights reserved. No part of this publication may be reproduced, stored in a retrieval system, or transmitted in any form or by any means, electronic, mechanical, photocopying, recording or otherwise, without the prior written permission of the Publisher.

First published in 2024 by

PENTAGON PRESS LLP
206, Peacock Lane, Shahpur Jat
New Delhi-110049, India
Contact: 011-26490600

Typeset in AGaramond, 11.5 Point
Printed by Aegean Offset Printers, Greater Noida

ISBN 978-81-971986-1-8 (HB)

Disclaimer: The views expressed in this book are those of the authors and do not necessarily reflect those of the Manohar Parrikar Institute for Defence Studies and Analyses, or the Government of India.

www.pentagonpress.in

Contents

Preface

The geopolitical landscape of the 21st century is increasingly defined by the intricate interplay of global powers and regional dynamics. Among the most consequential relationships shaping our contemporary world is the strategic triangle involving the United States, China, and South Asia. "Strategic Rebalancing: China and US Engagement with South Asia" delves into this complex nexus, offering a comprehensive analysis of how China's rise influences American policies and strategic decisions in the South Asian context.

South Asia, with its burgeoning economies, demographic weight, and strategic maritime corridors, stands at the crossroads of significant geopolitical interests. The United States, with its longstanding interest in the region, finds its traditional approaches challenged and reshaped by China's expanding influence. Beijing's ambitious Belt and Road Initiative, robust economic partnerships, and strategic investments in infrastructure and military capabilities present both opportunities and challenges for American engagement in South Asia.

This book explores these dynamics through a multi-faceted lens, examining historical precedents, economic interdependencies, security considerations, and diplomatic manoeuvres. By providing a detailed account of China's role as a critical factor in the US-South Asia engagement, this work aims to enhance our understanding of the broader geopolitical implications and the shifting balance of power in the region.

The impetus for this book arises from a recognition of the need for a nuanced and informed perspective on the triangular interactions between the US, China, and South Asia. Policymakers, scholars, and strategic analysts will find this work an invaluable resource for navigating the complexities of this evolving geopolitical environment. Through rigorous analysis and thoughtful insights, the book hopes to contribute to the ongoing discourse on how the United States can effectively engage with South Asia in the face of China's growing presence and influence.

I am reminded of the adage that the only constant in international relations is change. As we explore the shifting dynamics of power and influence in South Asia, it is my hope that this book will serve as a guide for understanding and navigating the intricate web of relationships that define our world today.

ANAND KUMAR

Acknowledgements

Writing a book is a journey that one does not undertake alone. I owe a debt of gratitude to many individuals and institutions whose support, guidance, and encouragement have been invaluable throughout this process. While space constraints may not allow me to acknowledge everyone individually, and some have expressed a desire to remain anonymous due to the sensitive nature of their professions, this volume would not have been possible without the help of colleagues and friends.

First and foremost, I extend my deepest appreciation to the Manohar Parrikar Institute for Defence Studies and Analyses (MP-IDSA). The intellectual environment and resources provided by MP-IDSA have been instrumental in shaping my research and writing. The comments received from anonymous referees were of immense value and significantly enhanced the quality of this book. I am especially grateful to my colleagues for their insightful discussions, constructive feedback, and unwavering support.

Special thanks go to the University of Dar-Es-Salaam (UDSM), where I had the privilege of serving as a visiting professor and ICCR Chair (Indian Ocean Studies). The rich academic environment and the opportunity to engage with fellow scholars significantly enriched my perspectives and research.

I would also like to express my gratitude to Vivek Kaushik, Associate Editor at MP-IDSA, for rigorously overseeing the development of this book. Special thanks are also due to Ms. Priyanka Sarkar for her professional and timely copy-editing of the manuscript. Mr. Rajan Arya and the staff of Pentagon Press LLP played an essential role in publishing this volume on time. Their professionalism and dedication to excellence have made this book possible.

To my friends and family, your unwavering support and patience have been a constant source of strength. Thank you for your understanding and for always believing in me, even during the most challenging times of this journey. My wife Nisha and children Yashi and Shaurya had to bear with my irregular schedules while this book was being written. This book is dedicated to them.

Finally, I acknowledge the numerous scholars, practitioners, and readers who have engaged with my work over the years. Your feedback, critiques, and encouragement have been vital in refining my ideas and strengthening my resolve to contribute to the field of South Asian studies.

This book is a culmination of the collective efforts of many, and I am profoundly grateful to each of you. Thank you for being a part of this journey with me.

ANAND KUMAR

CHAPTER 1

Introduction

The emergence of China as a major world power has prompted the United States to reassess its global security interests, including its engagement in South Asia. China's rapid economic growth, expanding military capabilities, assertive behaviour in the region, and growing influence are seen by the US as potential challenges to its own strategic interests and regional stability.

Since the end of the Second World War, the US's engagement in South Asia has undergone changes in response to evolving geopolitical dynamics in the region and the global landscape. During the Cold War, the US sought allies and partners to counter the Soviet Union, which led to a closer relationship with Pakistan. Pakistan leveraged its alliance with the US to balance against India, albeit with a subordinate status. During this period, China, which began as a rival of the US, later became a partner of the US along with Pakistan to counterbalance the Soviet Union. After the end of the Cold War, the US became increasingly concerned about the nuclearization of the South Asian subcontinent due to its implications for global security. Though this nuclearization was a result of China's connivance with Pakistan and US indifference towards Pakistani efforts to acquire nuclear weapons.

With the onset of the twenty-first century, the US found itself compelled to increase its engagement with South Asia following the tragic events of the 9/11 attacks and the increasing influence of China in the Indo-Pacific region. The aftermath of 9/11 prompted a significant shift in US foreign policy towards the South Asian region, which had long been grappling with terrorism. This pivotal event necessitated US involvement in counterterrorism efforts within the Afghanistan-Pakistan (Af-Pak) region. By collaborating with countries such as Pakistan and Afghanistan, the US aimed to combat terrorist organizations and promote stability in the area. However, despite substantial investments of resources and personnel, Pakistan's inconsistent actions posed challenges and hindered the progress of US counterterrorism efforts.

The US also faced the growing assertion of China in the Pacific and Indian Ocean. The US has been a dominant Pacific power. Moreover, it has important military assets and treaty commitments in East Asia and the Western Pacific. However, China's expansionist ambitions have raised concerns among US allies, as it has asserted expansive territorial claims in the region. With China emerging as the world's largest trading nation and a major economic power, its core interests have extended into the Indian Ocean. China has bolstered its presence in the region, establishing a military base in Djibouti and gaining control of a port in Sri Lanka. These developments have fueled unease among both India and the US regarding Chinese intentions. The rise of a more assertive China presents a substantial challenge, prompting the US to prioritize the Indo-Pacific region in its strategic agenda.

Recognizing the significant geopolitical developments in the Indo-Pacific, the US shifted its strategic focus to the region, and its Indo-Pacific strategy aims to counterbalance China's influence and uphold a free and open order in the region. Consequently, the US has intensified its engagement with South Asian countries, particularly India, as a key partner in this approach. It seeks to maintain a favourable balance of power to prevent China from becoming overly dominant.

China has used it's the Belt and Road Initiative (BRI) projects to expand its influence in South Asia. It has also leveraged its expanding military-industrial complex to support and arm its allies so that Chinese overseas interests could be protected. Beijing seeks a new form of 'Great Power Relations' with the US, urging recognition of its primacy in Asia. On the other hand, the US now seeks to persuade South Asian nations to diversify their economic partnerships beyond China. It encourages them to engage with various partners, including the US, so that their dependence on China could be reduced and a more balanced economic engagement could be fostered.

This book argues that historically, US interests in South Asia have been subservient to its broader global objectives. Initially, American policymakers viewed South Asia as strategically significant for maintaining control over Gulf oil reserves and for containing the Soviet Union and China. However, with the nuclearization of the Indian subcontinent, South Asia became a crucial component of the global security agenda. Subsequently, the tragic events of 9/11 propelled the US into a prolonged engagement with the region, as combating terrorism became its foremost priority. Now, amidst the emergence of China as an assertive global power, containing its rise has become the primary focus of the US foreign policy. Consequently, the US's strategic attention is shifting towards the Indo-Pacific region and South Asia has once again become a tool in its effort to maintain a balance of power in its favour in the region.

Dynamic Interplay: China, the US, and South Asia

The relationship between China, the US, and South Asia holds significant implications for global politics and security dynamics due to several reasons. South Asia is strategically located at the crossroads of major global trade routes, making it crucial for regional stability and economic prosperity. Its geopolitical significance is further amplified by its proximity to the Indian Ocean, a vital maritime corridor for global commerce. As such, any developments in South Asia have far-reaching consequences for international trade and security.

China's rapid economic ascent and expanding influence in South Asia has altered the traditional power dynamics in the region. With its ambitious BRI, China has invested heavily in infrastructure projects across South Asia, enhancing connectivity and economic ties. This has enabled China to assert itself as a major player in the region, challenging the influence traditionally held by the US and other Western powers.

South Asia is beset by myriad security challenges, including nuclear proliferation, terrorism, and regional conflicts. The presence of nuclear-armed states such as India and Pakistan, coupled with longstanding territorial disputes, adds a layer of complexity to the security landscape. China's involvement in South Asia, particularly its close relationship with Pakistan and its military expansion in the Indian Ocean, has further exacerbated regional tensions and raised concerns among US and Indian policymakers about stability and security.

The strategic competition between China and the US for influence in South Asia has become increasingly pronounced. Both powers seek to cultivate closer ties with countries in the region to advance their geopolitical interests and secure access to key resources. This competition manifests in various forms, including economic assistance, military cooperation, and diplomatic initiatives, and has the potential to shape the future trajectory of South Asian politics.

Understanding the dynamics of the relationship between China, the US, and South Asia is therefore imperative to grasp the broader shifts in global power dynamics and security architecture. It provides insights into the evolving strategic calculations of major powers, the drivers of regional conflict and cooperation, and the potential risks and opportunities for international stability. Moreover, given the interconnected nature of today's world, developments in South Asia have ripple effects that extend far beyond the region, underscoring the importance of a comprehensive understanding of these dynamics for policymakers and analysts alike.

Research Questions and Objectives

This book delves into the intricate relationship between China's rise and US engagement with South Asia, addressing several key questions. First, it explores how China's rise as a major power has influenced US involvement in South Asia. Additionally, it investigates the significance of South Asia in the broader strategic calculations of the US. Finally, it examines how evolving geopolitical dynamics shape American strategies in the region.

The research examines the historical evolution of US engagement in South Asia, analysing pivotal events and policy decisions that have shaped its approach over time. It seeks to analyse the evolution of US interests in the region, particularly in response to shifts in global geopolitics and the emergence of China as a major player.

This study identifies and analyses specific strategic interests of the US in South Asia, evaluating the extent to which these interests have been influenced by China's presence and actions. It investigates security dynamics in South Asia, focusing on nuclear proliferation, terrorism, and regional conflicts. The research critically assesses the US role in addressing these challenges and its interactions with China in this context.

Moreover, the study meticulously examines economic interactions between the US, South Asia, and China, including trade relations, investment flows, and infrastructure projects. It explores how economic factors shape US engagement and responses to China's initiatives like the BRI.

Furthermore, the research rigorously analyses military cooperation and competition between the US, South Asia, and China, assessing implications for regional stability and US-China strategic competition. Diplomatic relations between the US, South Asian countries, and China are evaluated, including diplomatic initiatives, alliances, and multilateral forums. The study analyses the role of diplomacy amidst growing Chinese influence.

Lastly, the research meticulously investigates responses of South Asian countries to US engagement and China's presence, examining how they navigate relationships with both powers and the implications for regional dynamics.

Theoretical Framework

The theoretical framework guiding this analysis will draw from a combination of realism and constructivism. Realism will provide insights into the power dynamics and strategic interests driving the interactions between China, the US, and South Asia. Meanwhile, constructivism will illuminate the role of norms, identities, and perceptions in shaping the evolving relationships among these actors. By integrating these theoretical perspectives, we aim to offer a nuanced understanding of the complex dynamics at play in this geopolitical region.

The concept of balance of power has also been prominently used in the study as the world is now witnessing a reemergence of the great power competition. In this great power competition both China and the US are trying to keep the balance of power in the Indo-Pacific in their favour. States generally engage in two primary types of balancing to safeguard their security. The first is known as 'internal balancing,' which involves a state's efforts to increase its relative power through various means. This includes strengthening its military capabilities, promoting economic growth, and implementing policies that enhance its overall power in relation to other nations.

The second type is called 'external balancing,' which aims to increase a state's relative power by forming alliances with other nations against a common perceived threat. This approach recognizes the inherent uncertainty in international politics, where today's ally could become tomorrow's competitor, leading states to adopt a more dynamic strategy by combining both internal and external balancing methods.

In essence, states recognize the anarchic nature of world politics and understand that their security cannot solely rely on alliances, as the interests of allies may change over time. Consequently, they adopt a pragmatic approach, combining internal efforts to strengthen their own capabilities with external efforts to build cooperative alliances, thus ensuring a more comprehensive and flexible security stance.

With the rise of great-power politics in the Indo-Pacific region, the major powers in the area are actively pursuing internal balancing strategies to bolster their relative power and security. Beijing's foreign policy, characterized by its projection of power, has motivated other major players to focus on enhancing their military capabilities, strengthening their economic prowess, and making strategic decisions that provide them with a competitive edge. This dynamic power competition has led to significant increases in defense spending and military upgrades in countries like Australia and Japan.

Geo-political setting of the South Asia Region

The geopolitical setting of the South Asia region is characterized by a complex interplay of various factors. India, as the largest and most populous country in South Asia, plays a central role in the region's geopolitics. Its size, growing economy, military capabilities, and political influence contribute to shaping the dynamics of the region.

The colonial legacy of British imperialism has left an indelible mark on South Asia, shaping its contemporary borders and political landscape. Many of the region's states were once a part of the British colonial empire, and the term 'South Asia' itself emerged in the post-colonial era. Ongoing disputes, such as the longstanding rivalry between India and Pakistan over Kashmir, continue to shape regional alliances, security policies, and military strategies, often leading to tensions and sporadic conflicts.

South Asia, as a region is characterized by its fractious nature. South Asian nations have connections with neighbouring regions, and the region exhibits significant influences of religious and ethnic factors. It is home to indigenous religions as well as those that arrived from outside. Ethnic overlaps and connections, such as Pashtoon, Baloch, and Tamil communities, are prevalent in the region.

South Asia has witnessed various internal conflicts and the rise of extremist groups, posing security challenges within and beyond the region. These conflicts have shaped the geopolitical landscape and regional security dynamics. Wars have taken place between India and Pakistan. Violence has been witnessed in the ongoing conflict in Afghanistan since 1979.[1] The Pakistan Army committed serious atrocities during the liberation war of Bangladesh. The region has also seen emergence of various separatist and terrorist movements, such as Sikh separatism, the Sri Lanka Tamil issue, Maoist issues in Nepal and India, insurgencies in northeastern India and Jammu and Kashmir, the Taliban insurgency, and the Baloch issue. However, the overall level of violence in South Asia due to insurgencies and terrorism is currently decreasing.

The ongoing instability in Afghanistan carries profound implications for the region's geopolitics, as the withdrawal of US forces and the resurgence of the Taliban raise uncertainties and potential security challenges for neighbouring countries.[2] Both India and Pakistan have vested interests in shaping Afghanistan's future, with India seeking regional stability and Pakistan aiming to secure strategic depth in the country.

The countries in South Asia are asymmetric in size, with India being significantly larger than all other countries in the region combined. India is also the only country that shares a geographical border with all other South Asian countries and occupies a central position, enhancing its geopolitical significance. Smaller countries in the region often feel the weight of this asymmetry and seek means to balance their larger neighbour.

South Asia hosts several regional organizations, notably the South Asian

Association for Regional Cooperation (SAARC). However, these institutions encounter significant hurdles in achieving substantial regional integration and cooperation, largely due to political discord and bilateral disputes among member states.[3] Limited interconnectivity, restricted regional trade, and minimal people-to-people contact further hinder progress, compounded by a general lack of mutual trust among South Asian nations.

Pakistan's historical role as a counterbalance to India's dominance was diminished with the separation of Bangladesh in 1971, prompting Pakistan to pursue nuclear weapons as a means of restoring strategic equilibrium. Unlike ASEAN and the European Union, where shared security perceptions prevail, South Asian nations often perceive threats emerging from within the region itself. India has endeavoured to address disputes with its smaller neighbours through bilateral negotiations. Yet these nations occasionally seek mediation from multilateral institutions or extra-regional powers, leveraging external intervention to bolster their positions.

The Indian Ocean plays a pivotal role in South Asia's geopolitics, with major powers like India, China, and the US vying for influence and control over sea routes, ports, and trade networks. This competition carries far-reaching implications for security, energy transportation, and trade dynamics in the region.[4]

Security dynamics in South Asia are intricate, with India assessing its position vis-à-vis China while Pakistan evaluates itself in comparison to India. China's emergence as a significant player in South Asia further complicates the security equation, with smaller nations sometimes leveraging the 'China card' to counterbalance India's influence.[5] China's BRI has substantially expanded its economic footprint in the region, sparking concerns in India and engendering a complex dynamic involving China, India, and other South Asian countries.

Prospects for a substantial improvement in India-Pakistan relations remain bleak in the short term, as the Pakistan army benefits from perpetuating adversarial ties with India to justify its existence and influence domestically. Strategically, China has positioned itself to advance its own interests in South Asia, with Pakistan increasingly reliant on Chinese support and perceived as more amenable to Chinese influence.

India faces formidable challenges in competing with China due to a widening military and economic gap between the two countries.[6] Despite starting from similar points, China has outpaced India in several key areas, exacerbating India's struggle to match China's assertiveness and influence in the region.[7] While some South Asian nations may seek to balance their relationships, there is a growing trend of pursuing closer diplomatic and economic ties with China, often on terms dictated by Beijing.

South Asia's Significance in Global Geopolitics

South Asia holds significant strategic importance for various reasons. It is strategically located, serving as a crucial bridge between the Middle East, Central Asia, and the Indo-Pacific region. It is adjacent to vital sea lines of communication, such as the Strait of Malacca, through which a significant amount of global trade flows. Control over these sea routes provides access to important markets and resources.

The region's proximity to the Middle East, a major energy-producing region, makes it a vital transit route for energy resources. The transportation of oil and natural gas from the Middle East to energy-consuming countries in the Indo-Pacific region, including China, Japan, and South Korea, relies on the stability and security of South Asian countries.

Moreover, South Asia shares borders with China and Central Asia. These regions can gain access to the Indian Ocean through Afghanistan, Iran, Pakistan, or even Myanmar via the Irrawaddy Corridor. For landlocked countries in Central Asia and parts of China, the Indian Ocean offers a shorter and more convenient route for trade and maritime access compared to the South China Sea.

Economically, South Asia is experiencing notable growth, driven by the emergence of robust middle-class consumers in nations like India and Bangladesh. This burgeoning consumer base has attracted significant interest from external actors keen on tapping into the region's economic potential. As South Asian economies continue to mature, they offer lucrative prospects for trade, investment, and broader economic collaboration on the global stage.

However, South Asia's geopolitical landscape is also shaped by the presence of nuclear powers, namely India and Pakistan, embroiled in a longstanding and tense rivalry centered on the Kashmir dispute. Both countries possess nuclear weapons and have been engaged in an arms race, developing long-range ballistic missiles. While there have been no indications of intentions to use these weapons beyond their regional context, the presence of nuclear capabilities adds to the strategic complexities and concerns in South Asia.

Recent Geo-Political Shifts in South Asia

In recent years, South Asia has witnessed significant geopolitical shifts, reshaping the dynamics of the region. Following the US withdrawal from Afghanistan, the strategic importance of the Afghanistan-Pakistan (Af-Pak) region has dwindled in the eyes of the West, leading to diminished interest from Western powers. This withdrawal has strained the already fragile relationship between Afghanistan and Pakistan, marked by border disputes and allegations of cross-border terrorism.

Pakistan's strategic significance has also waned, as its relevance was previously bolstered by its role in US military operations against the Taliban. Pakistan used the Afghan card not only to remain strategically important to the US but also to ensure parity with India in the US South Asia policy.[8] However, Pakistan is now concerned about its decreasing strategic relevance and perceives the US as using it.

Pakistan has become increasingly reliant on China. The situation has worsened after its economic downslide. The two countries have deepened their economic and strategic ties, with China investing heavily in Pakistan's infrastructure and economic projects.[9] China also views Afghanistan as an opportunity for economic engagement, further strengthening its relationship with both Pakistan and Afghanistan.

In contrast, India has pursued a 'neighbourhood first policy,' actively engaging with its neighbouring countries, except Pakistan, to enhance regional cooperation and connectivity.[10] India has made efforts to resolve land and maritime border disputes with Bangladesh, resulting in improved relations and growing trade between the two countries. People-to-people contacts have also intensified.

India's strategic focus has also shifted eastward, as it seeks to enhance connectivity with Southeast Asian nations through Myanmar.[11] Northeast India presents a geostrategic opportunity for India to enhance its connectivity with Southeast Asian countries. This move aligns with India's Act East Policy, which aims to strengthen economic and strategic ties with Southeast Asian nations.

India's sustained economic growth has further bolstered its regional influence, attracting foreign investment and facilitating trade opportunities. This economic prowess allows India to pursue its national interests, including investments in infrastructure and military capabilities, thereby enhancing its strategic position in South Asia and beyond.

However, there is a growing competition for influence and control of the Indian Ocean, with countries like India, China, Pakistan, and the US vying for strategic advantages. The Chinese People's Liberation Army Navy (PLAN) has expanded its naval capabilities and presence in the region, although the US still maintains superior capabilities. India, recognizing the need to counter Chinese expansionism, has also been bolstering its maritime forces. It has acquired nuclear-powered submarines.

China's increasing presence in the Indian Ocean is partly driven by the need to protect its vulnerable energy supply lines. It has been expanding its maritime activities and establishing military bases in the Indian Ocean Region (IOR), such as in Djibouti. This presence allows China to project power, safeguard its interests, and potentially challenge the influence of other countries, including India.

China has taken several initiatives to improve its position in South Asia. It is also keen to address its 'Malacca Dilemma,' which is described as the threat of a naval blockade of vital Chinese sea lines of communication in the Indian Ocean. The China-Pakistan Economic Corridor (CPEC), a part of the BRI, aims to enhance connectivity between China and Pakistan. While facing challenges, the completion of CPEC could benefit Pakistan and potentially address China's 'Malacca dilemma' by providing an alternate route for its energy imports.

Despite their strategic competition, India and China have engaged in various ways, including expanding bilateral trade and pursuing diplomatic dialogues. According to Chinese customs data, India's bilateral trade with China reached a record high of $135.98 billion in 2022. However, this growth has also led to increasing trade deficits for India, surpassing $100 billion for the first time.[12] Both nations have demonstrated maturity in managing their differences, while also acknowledging the importance of maintaining cooperation.

However, there are growing concerns about China's increasingly assertive actions. China has been establishing its own regional organizations and initiatives that bypass involvement from the US. Through platforms like the Shanghai Cooperation Organisation (SCO) and the Asian Infrastructure Investment Bank (AIIB), China has significantly bolstered its influence in Central Asia and offers borrowing opportunities for South Asian nations. These initiatives potentially constrain India's strategic options and influence in the region.

However, India is also making its own efforts to counter Chinese influence. In response to China's growing presence, India has been leveraging its soft power while also bolstering its relationships with neighbouring countries like Bangladesh, Maldives, Sri Lanka, and Nepal. To exert pressure on China, India has been forging closer partnerships with countries and entities in proximity to China, such as Japan, Vietnam, ASEAN, and BIMSTEC. Moreover, India is actively modernizing its military capabilities and acquiring advanced weapons systems.

India's neighbours, while recognizing the need to maintain relationships with India, also seek to hedge their strategic bets by engaging with China. While India's soft power and historical ties provide influence in the region, China's self-interested activities and growing assertiveness are becoming sources of concern for some countries.

India's Growing Concern About China

India's apprehensions regarding China's expanding influence in South Asia have grown significantly, particularly due to China's deepening ties with Pakistan. China has not openly supported Pakistan in past conflicts with India, such as the wars in 1965, 1971, and the Kargil incursion in 1999. However, Pakistan has increasingly leaned towards China hoping that the latter will invest in its infrastructure and limited alternatives. China's efforts to strengthen relationships with other South Asian nations have also raised concerns in India.

In addition to maritime competition in the Indian Ocean, India and China grapple with an unresolved border and territorial dispute. Spanning 3,440 kilometers (2,100 miles), the disputed border is characterized by rugged terrain, including rivers, lakes, and snow-covered peaks, making it susceptible to shifting demarcation lines. This ambiguity has led to frequent face-to-face encounters and standoffs between soldiers at various points along the border. Both countries are also engaged in a race to develop infrastructure along this contested Line of Actual Control.[13]

The persistent border issue has resulted in intermittent tensions and military standoffs between India and China, complicating their strategic relationship. Moreover, China's close alliance with Pakistan raises the specter of a potential two-front conflict for India, further exacerbating security concerns in the region.

Even with the resolution of their territorial dispute, China and India are likely to maintain a competitive relationship within the Asia-Pacific region. Beyond territorial issues, several other factors contribute to the strained and uneasy nature of their relationship.[14] These include China's alliances with India's South Asian neighbours, particularly its military ties with Pakistan and Myanmar; ongoing tensions in Tibet and Kashmir; disputes over Sikkim; concerns about terrorism; the dynamics of multi-polarity and discussions around UN Security Council expansion; their respective relationships with the US and Russia; the presence of power imbalances; China's perceived encroachments into what India considers its sphere of influence, such as Beijing's plans for naval presence in the Indian Ocean, countered by India's efforts to bolster strategic ties with Vietnam and Japan; and more recently, issues related to nuclear proliferation and missile development.

A prominent aspect of Beijing's strategy in South Asia has been its focus on India, with military ties with India's neighbouring countries taking precedence in its policy agenda. China's overarching goal in its Asian strategy has been to thwart the emergence of a formidable competitor, preventing the rise of a peer rival in Asia-Pacific that could challenge China's position as the predominant power in the region, often referred to as the 'Middle Kingdom.'[15]

US Aims for a Manageable South Asia

The US views South Asia primarily through the lens of its global interests, rather than considering it as a region of primary focus. Instead, South Asia is seen as a component of broader global strategies. The aim of US policy in the region is to maintain a level of manageability so that issues in South Asia do not become overwhelming distractions from broader global priorities.

Policy formation toward South Asia involves various actors within the US government, including the President, the State Department, and the Pentagon, among others. Decision-making is influenced by a combination of strategic interests, regional dynamics, and domestic political considerations, resulting in a multifaceted approach.

The President, as the chief architect of US foreign policy, holds ultimate authority in shaping and directing policy toward South Asia. However, the President receives advice from a range of sources, including the State Department, which implements foreign policy and conducts diplomacy with foreign governments. The State Department's analysis of regional trends and issues informs policy recommendations to the President.

The Pentagon, responsible for US military affairs, also plays a significant role in shaping South Asia policy, particularly regarding security and defence matters. It advises the President on military strategy and operations in the region, coordinating closely with the State Department to align military and diplomatic efforts.

Additionally, other entities such as the National Security Council, the Intelligence Community, and Congress provide further guidance and influence policy decisions.[16] Domestic interest groups also contribute to shaping policies.

Decision-making in Washington is characterized by decentralization, power diffusion, and multidimensional bargaining. Priorities may shift over time and are subject to change based on evolving circumstances. Consequently, US actions in South Asia may not always align perfectly with its long-term national interests, but rather focus on maintaining an acceptable level of stability in the region.[17]

The overarching goal of US policy in South Asia is to prioritize stability over accommodating various interests or fostering extensive international cooperation to shape regional dynamics according to US interests. This approach seeks to ensure that the region remains manageable and does not pose significant challenges to US security or strategic objectives.

Shifting Global Priorities of US and South Asia

The US has continually adjusted its partnerships in South Asia to safeguard its global interests. This strategy dates back to the Cold War era, where the US aimed to form a security alliance with Pakistan to counter the Soviet Union. Following the Cold War, preventing nuclear proliferation in the region became paramount, yet efforts failed to prevent India and Pakistan from acquiring nuclear weapons in 1998. Concerns over potential conflict, particularly over Kashmir, heightened, prompting increased US attention on South Asia.

The 9/11 attacks prompted a reassessment of regional partnerships, with Pakistan designated as a non-NATO ally and the development of the Afghanistan-Pakistan (Af-Pak) strategy to combat terrorism. However, Pakistan's ambiguous stance in the war against terrorism has posed challenges to US efforts.

Since 2008, the US has significantly transformed its policy towards India in response to the rise of China as an assertive power. There is now a bipartisan consensus in the US that a stronger India is in its national interest. The US sees India's ability to balance China in Asia and the broader Indo-Pacific region as a natural response to China's rise and a preferable alternative to other costly options.

The 2017 National Security Strategy marked the explicit articulation of US interests in the region. US interests in the region include countering terrorist threats that affect the security of the US homeland and its allies, preventing cross-border terrorism that could lead to military and nuclear tensions, and averting the risk of nuclear weapons, technology, and materials falling into the hands of terrorists. The US seeks a presence in the region proportionate to the threats it faces and aims for a stable and self-reliant Afghanistan while desiring Pakistan to refrain from destabilizing behaviour.[18]

Although the most recent version of the National Security Strategy published in 2022 does not explicitly mention South Asia, it identifies the People's Republic of China (PRC) as the most significant geopolitical challenge, particularly in the Indo-Pacific region.[19] The strategy acknowledges that the PRC's actions have global implications beyond the region.

The US perceives itself as a global power with global interests and recognizes that turmoil or dominance by a hostile power in one region can have detrimental effects on American interests elsewhere. The US aims to establish a free, open, prosperous, and secure international order. To achieve this objective, it intends to invest in its sources and tools of power, build strong coalitions with other nations, and modernize and strengthen its military.

As part of its strategy, the US seeks to collaborate with India, the world's largest democracy and a major defence partner, both bilaterally and multilaterally, to foster a free and open Indo-Pacific region.[20] The US aims to support the development of a stronger India that can act as a geostrategic balancer against China.

Meanwhile, India's strategic outlook has evolved and its relationship with the US has improved. It is shaped by several factors, including the dissolution of the Soviet Union and the rise of China. While India continues to value its strategic autonomy, there has been a significant improvement in its relations with the US driven by mutual interests in countering China's assertiveness.

China's gradual advancement of its strategic interests has not yet compelled India and the US to forge a formal strategic alliance. Nonetheless, China's emergence as a significant strategic, military, and economic rival poses substantial concerns for both nations. China's rapid military modernization, assertive foreign policies, and expansive economic initiatives have established it as a formidable competitor across multiple domains.

The escalating assertiveness of China in both the Western Pacific Ocean and the Indian Ocean has led to a convergence of strategic interests between India and the US. This has led to increased collaboration and alignment between India and the US in safeguarding their respective interests.

Realignment of US Policies in South Asia

The evolving dynamics in South Asia, particularly the rise of a more assertive China, have prompted a significant realignment of US policies towards both India and Pakistan. While recognizing the importance of both countries in the region, the US tailors its approach based on factors such as strategic alignment, counterterrorism efforts, and regional dynamics.

The US-India relationship has witnessed remarkable growth and is poised to strengthen further. India is viewed as a strategic partner, crucial for maintaining a balance of power in the face of China's growing influence in the region and the Indo-Pacific. The US now believes that India is on its way to becoming a major global power and that collaboration with the US will help India achieve its vital geopolitical goals on the global stage.[21] A bipartisan consensus in the US has emerged, emphasizing the need to bolster ties with India across various domains, including defense, counterterrorism, trade, and investment. Joint military exercises, technology transfers, and intelligence sharing underscore the deepening strategic alignment between the two nations.

In contrast, the US-Pakistan relationship is more complex. While the US acknowledges Pakistan's role in counterterrorism efforts, tensions persist due to concerns over Pakistan's support for extremist groups. The US has urged Pakistan to take more decisive action against terrorism. Pakistan, in turn, has expressed frustration with what it perceives as inconsistent US policies in the region.

The de-hyphenation of India and Pakistan in US policy began during the George W. Bush administration and evolved further under the Obama administration. Separate initiatives and dialogues, such as the Af-Pak strategy and US-India strategic and commercial dialogue, underscore this shift. The US has sought to distinguish between its engagements with India and Pakistan, recognizing their distinct interests and priorities in the region.

While the US respects India's tradition of strategic autonomy and does not expect it to form a formal alliance, it also acknowledges Pakistan's concerns regarding US policies, particularly related to democratic initiatives and its approach towards India. To enhance the effectiveness of its South Asia policy, the US maintains separate policy baskets for India and Pakistan, recognizing the need for nuanced approaches tailored to each country's specific context and interests.

China's Unease Over US Policy Shifts in South Asia

The relegation of Pakistan's importance in the region has not been appreciated by their 'all-weather friend,' China. Chinese officials believe that the US is treating Pakistan as a partner of last resort. They are engaging Pakistan because they think that Pakistan has the potential to endanger their security.[22] The Chinese also blame US for its present troubles, which they claim are a result of the US counterterrorism policies over the past two decades.

In contrast, the US approach towards India is based on positive expectations, given the immense potential for cooperation between the two countries. The US views India as a valuable friend sharing common values, respect for the rule of law, and a mutual desire for a similar world order. Chinese analysts also believe that the US's issues with India are largely tactical, while its engagement with Pakistan is seen as temporary and a result of having no better option. There's apprehension in Beijing that this approach could elevate India's role in South Asia, where China is also expanding its influence, potentially altering regional dynamics.

Overview of Chapters

This book is divided into eight chapters. The first chapter provides an introduction to the book's themes and objectives. Chapter 2 traces the historical trajectory of US-South Asia relations, particularly during the Cold War era, where geopolitical dynamics influenced US priorities in the region. Chapter 3 examines the challenges posed by nuclear proliferation in South Asia and the longstanding Kashmir dispute, while also delving into the evolving nature of US engagement with the region post-9/11. Chapter 4 analyses the rise of China as a major global power and its impact on traditional US dominance, reshaping the geopolitical landscape.

Chapter 5 explores China's growing influence in South Asia, particularly in infrastructure and security spheres, and its implications for regional dynamics, including India's position. Chapter 6 investigates the formulation and implementation of the US Indo-Pacific Strategy (IPS) in response to

China's assertive posture, examining its objectives and implications for regional stability. Chapter 7 assesses US efforts to engage with smaller South Asian nations to counterbalance Chinese influence, exploring the varying degrees of engagement and strategic implications. The last chapter concludes by synthesizing key insights from preceding chapters and arguing that US engagement with South Asia is intricately linked to its global priorities, reflecting evolving geopolitical realities.

Methodology

This research work employs a multifaceted methodology to investigate the intricate dynamics of China's involvement in South Asia and its ramifications for US engagement with the region.

First, it undertakes a thorough historical analysis, delving into the diplomatic, economic, and military interactions between China, the US, and South Asian nations throughout history. By scrutinizing key historical events, treaties, agreements, and conflicts, the study elucidates the historical underpinnings that have shaped the evolving relationships among these actors.

Additionally, interviews were conducted with a diverse array of stakeholders, including policymakers, diplomats, scholars, and experts from the US, China, and South Asia. These interviews provided invaluable insights and perspectives on China's role in US engagement with the region, shedding light on stakeholders' perceptions, attitudes, and policy preferences regarding China's influence and its implications for US-South Asia relations.

Furthermore, the research incorporates a comprehensive literature review of existing scholarship, academic articles, policy papers, and government reports pertaining to China's involvement in South Asia. This extensive review serves as the groundwork for the study, enriching its analysis with a nuanced understanding of the existing discourse on the subject.

Moreover, the study employs a comparative analysis to juxtapose the approaches of the US and China towards South Asia. By examining areas of convergence, divergence, and competition in their respective strategies and priorities, the research evaluates the effectiveness of US engagement strategies vis-à-vis China's growing influence in the region. Furthermore, it assesses the implications of these dynamics for regional stability and US and Indian national interests, providing valuable insights for policymakers and scholars alike.

Contemporary Relevance

In today's geopolitical landscape, the themes explored in this book hold significant contemporary relevance. With the resurgence of great power competition, particularly between the US and China, understanding the dynamics of their engagement in South Asia is paramount. China continues to assert its influence across the region through ambitious infrastructure projects and strategic partnerships. Hence, the US is compelled to recalibrate its approach to maintain its interests and alliances. Additionally, the nuclear proliferation concerns and unresolved disputes in South Asia persist as potential flashpoints with global implications. Moreover, the evolving Indo-Pacific strategy reflects Washington's strategic manoeuvering in response to China's expanding footprint. As smaller South Asian nations navigate their relationships with these major powers, the strategic choices they make could significantly shape the regional balance of power. Therefore, this book's insights into the historical context and contemporary challenges are invaluable for policymakers, scholars, and observers seeking to comprehend and navigate the complexities of South Asia's geopolitical landscape in the twenty-first century.

NOTES

1 Charlotte Greenfield, 'Over 1,000 Afghan civilians killed in blasts, violence since August 2021, UN says,' Reuters, 27 June 2023 at https://www.reuters.com/world/asia-pacific/over-1000-afghan-civilians-killed-blasts-violence-since-august-2021-un-2023-06-27/ last accessed on 12 June 2024.

2 Jennifer Hansler, Kylie Atwood, 'US State Department report details damning failings around chaotic Afghanistan withdrawal,' CNN, 30 June 2023 at https://edition.cnn.com/2023/06/30/politics/state-deparment-afghanistan-withdrawal-report/index.html last accessed 13 June 2024 Also see 'Threat of terrorism rising in Afghanistan and Region: UN Report,' *The Times of India*, 11 June 11, 2023 at https://timesofindia.indiatimes.com/india/threat-of-terrorism-rising-in-afghanistan-and-region-un-report/articleshow/100909918.cms?from=mdr last accessed on 13 June 2024.

3 V.V. Desai, 'The Political Economy of Regional Cooperation in South Asia,' ADB Working Paper on Regional Economic Integration, No. 54, July 2010 at https://www.adb.org/sites/default/files/publication/28528/wp54-political-economy-south-asia.pdf last accessed on 13 June 2024.

4 Rivalry between America and China has spread to the Indian Ocean, *The Economist*, 10

April 2023 at https://www.economist.com/asia/2023/04/10/rivalry-between-america-and-china-has-spread-to-the-indian-ocean?gclid=CjwKCAjwqZSlBhBwEiwAfoZUINHTSIymVKCGdRYX-7Tbt29Ee2d2panfgiIMatbg7AltkLTxf97v3hoCL3YQAvD_BwE&gclsrc=aw.ds last accessed on13 June 2024.

5 Harsh V. Pant, 'China's clout grows in South Asia, but can India raise its game?', *South China Morning Post*, 19 January 2018 at https://www.scmp.com/comment/insight-opinion/article/2129480/chinas-clout-grows-south-asia-can-india-raise-its-game last accessed on 13 June 2024.

6 Cameron Abadi, 'What Accounts for the Economic Gap Between China and India?', *Foreign Policy*, 4 October 2022 at https://foreignpolicy.com/2022/10/04/china-india-economic-gap-tooze/ last accessed on 13 June 2024.

7 Subhash Chandra Garg, 'India's GDP gap with US, China is widening alarmingly,' *Deccan Herald*, 04 July 2023 at https://www.deccanherald.com/opinion/india-s-gdp-gap-with-us-china-is-widening-alarmingly-1233747.html, last accessed on13 June 2024. Please also see Vivek Katju, 'Bridging the power gap with China', *Hindustan Times*, 09 September 2020 at https://www.hindustantimes.com/analysis/bridging-the-power-gap-with-china/story-4OalcjuIms94RUIiHIR4AN.html last accessed on 13 June 2024.

8 SD Pradhan, 'Pakistan's search for strategic relevance to US', *The Times of India*, 22 March 2021, at https://timesofindia.indiatimes.com/blogs/ChanakyaCode/pakistans-search-for-strategic-relevance-to-us/ last accessed on 13 June 2024.

9 Uzair Younus, 'With Pakistan's economy in freefall, Chinese economic and military influence is likely to grow in the country', Atlantic Council, 9 March 2023 at https://www.atlanticcouncil.org/blogs/southasiasource/with-pakistans-economy-in-freefall-chinese-economic-and-military-influence-is-likely-to-grow-in-the-country/ last accessed on13 June 2024 also see 'Pakistan's dependence on China for economic well-being going to increase: Expert,' ANI, 7 February 2022 at https://www.aninews.in/news/world/asia/pakistans-dependence-on-china-for-economic-well-being-going-to-increase-expert20220207182521/ last accessed on 13 June 2024.

10 'India tries to ensure ties across the world, except with China, Pakistan: Jaishankar,' ANI, 30 April 2023 at https://www.aninews.in/news/world/asia/india-tries-to-ensure-ties-across-the-world-except-with-china-pakistan-jaishankar20230430210026/ last accessed on 13 June 2024.

11 MEA, 'Act East Policy', Press Information Bureau, Government of India, 23 December2015, at https://pib.gov.in/newsite/printrelease.aspx?relid=133837 last accessed on 13 June 2024.

12 Ananth Krishnan, 'India's imports from China reach record high in 2022, trade deficit surges beyond $100 billion', *The Hindu*, at https://www.thehindu.com/news/international/indias-imports-from-china-reach-record-high-in-2022-trade-deficit-surges-beyond-100-billion/article66372861.ece last accessed on 13 June 2024.

13 BBC, 'India-China dispute: The border row explained in 400 words', 14 December 2022 at https://www.bbc.com/news/world-asia-53062484 last accessed on 13 June 2024.

14 J. Mohan Malik, 'South Asia in China's Foreign Relations,' *Pacifica Review*, Vol. 13, No. 1, February 2001, p. 77.

15 Ibid., p. 74.

16 Glenn Hastedt, 'Presidents, Advisers, and Future Directions of American Foreign Policy,' in Steven W. Hook and James M. Scott (ed.) *U.S. Foreign Policy Today: American Renewal?*, Washington: CQ Press, 2011, pp. 16-35.

17 Yang Xiaoping, 'Managing Leadership in the Indo-Pacific,' *China Quarterly of International Strategic Studies*, vol. 3, No. 4, p. 469.

18 The White House, 'National Security Strategy of the United States of America', December 2017, p. 60 at https://trumpwhitehouse.archives.gov/wp-content/uploads/2017/12/NSS-Final-12-18-2017-0905.pdf last accessed on 13 June 2024.

19 The White House, 'National Security Strategy of the United States of America', October 2022, pp. 10-11 at https://www.whitehouse.gov/wp-content/uploads/2022/10/Biden-Harris-Administrations-National-Security-Strategy-10.2022.pdf last accessed on 13 June 2024.

20 Ibid., p. 38.

21 The White House, 'National Security Strategy of the United States of America', December 2017, p. 56 at https://trumpwhitehouse.archives.gov/wp-content/uploads/2017/12/NSS-Final-12-18-2017-0905.pdf last accessed on 13 June 2024.

22 Yang Xiaoping, 'Managing Leadership in the Indo-Pacific', *China Quarterly of International Strategic Studies*, vol. 3, No. 4, p. 471.

CHAPTER 2

Historical Evolution of US-South Asia Relations

The US-South Asia relationship has witnessed significant transformation over several decades. Until the 1990s, the US did not perceive South Asia as a single entity. It was not a priority in terms of US strategic interests. In the initial post-independence decades, India and Pakistan did not factor into American strategic considerations directly. They were viewed within the context of US policies towards China or the Soviet Union, influencing American responses to the region's political developments.

Intermittent engagement commenced with Pakistan as the US sought allies and friends to counter communism and the Soviet Union during the Cold War. Additionally, Pakistan was considered crucial for maintaining control over Gulf Oil.[1] During the Cold War era, British and American policymakers harboured suspicions toward the Indian National Congress and its leader, Jawaharlal Nehru. They supported Pakistan to impede the rise of India, based on an assumption that India was fragile and prone to disintegration. In contrast, Pakistan, with its Islamic identity, was viewed as a desirable ally with natural immunity against communism.

This dynamic shifted significantly when India and Pakistan conducted nuclear tests in 1998. The US then prioritized nuclear proliferation, India-Pakistan tensions, and the Kashmir dispute in its approach to the region. The 1999 Kargil war further underscored the importance of the region, leading to the hyphenation of India and Pakistan. Both countries were perceived as inextricably intertwined and in perpetual competition with each other. Consequently, other countries in the region, such as Afghanistan, Bangladesh, Nepal, Bhutan, and Sri Lanka, were often overlooked. The issues relating to their national economies and domestic political dynamics were poorly understood. The US also showed little interest in the broader strategic context of the region and the role of China in it.

A crucial shift occurred with the 9/11 attacks. Washington recognized the potential for India's economic and political emergence on a broader Asian canvas. India, primarily due to its burgeoning economy, began to be integrated into the institutional and commercial structures of East Asia, led by ASEAN. This integration also gave rise to the term 'Indo-Pacific,' unequivocally positioning India as a part of Asia. Meanwhile, other states like Pakistan and Afghanistan continued to be perceived as part of the Greater Middle East, signifying the Muslim world west of India.

Confusion about South Asia persisted within the US bureaucracy.[2] During the counter-insurgency era post-9/11, South Asia became synonymous with AfPak, marginalizing India and other smaller South Asian nations. There were concerns that AfPak might lead to the re-hyphenation of India and Pakistan as President Obama initially tried to link the Afghan problem to dispute in Kashmir.

The rise of an assertive China after 2008 altered the dynamics of US engagement with South Asia. India was enlisted as a partner to contain China, especially in the Indo-Pacific region. Simultaneously, the US maintained contact with Pakistan to prevent it from aligning completely with China. The US intensified its relationships with other South Asian countries to maintain a balance of power in its favour in the broader Indo-Pacific region, especially in South Asia.

American and British Motives behind Embracing Pakistan

When the British were preparing to depart from India, Pakistan did not exist as a nation but rather as an idea rooted in the concept of a separate Muslim-majority state. The security concerns surrounding South Asia mainly revolved around the status of India, which was seen as the dominant regional power. Within the ranks of British colonial rulers, there were varying opinions, with some favouring a united Muslim India while others supported the idea of an independent Pakistani state. Still, others recognized that in the event of a partition, the larger India would emerge as the dominant regional power. From a strategic standpoint, British policymakers envisioned a scenario where both India and Pakistan would require some form of military alliance, possibly entailing a continued British presence in the region for an extended period. The underlying assumption was that both nations would maintain a degree of dependence on their former colonial power.[3]

For the British, the creation of an independent Pakistan held potential advantages for their own interests. British strategists considered Pakistan a more reliable ally because of their suspicions towards the Indian National Congress and its leader, Jawaharlal Nehru. They saw it as a way to maintain their influence over the region and to safeguard their far-flung territories in Southeast Asia. Pakistan's strategic location was also seen as significant in terms of controlling the vital energy resources in the Middle East.

Over time, the US emerged as a potentially influential power in the region, taking over from Britain. The US recognized the strategic value of West Pakistan's location as a bulwark against communism and a potential base for bombers on the southern flank of the Soviet Union. As a result, close ties were forged between the West, particularly the US, and Pakistan's nascent army. Both American and British officials praised Pakistan for its well-trained army, strong martial tradition, strategic location, and willingness to collaborate with the West.[4] Although initially small, the Pakistan Army became a conduit for Western influence in the region.

Pakistan's Emergence as a Cold War Ally

During the Cold War, the US pursued a global policy of containment, and Pakistan emerged as a Cold War ally through various alliances and military support. Pakistan was recruited into alliance systems with the ostensible purpose of simultaneously boosting both western Asia and south-east Asian security while making south Asia itself less vulnerable to communist penetration.[5] The alliance between the US and Pakistan began in the 1950s when the US turned to Pakistan for support, particularly after India chose non-alignment. The US saw Pakistan as a valuable ally due to its geographical proximity to both communist powers and its assumption that Islam conferred a natural immunity to communism. Pakistan became a member of the Baghdad Pact (CENTO) in 1952. On 25 February 1954, the US announced its plan to initiate a substantial military aid programme for Pakistan. On 2 May 1954, the two countries formally signed a Mutual Defence Assistance Agreement. Pakistan later became a member of the Southeast Asia Treaty Organization (SEATO). These alliances aimed to block communist advances in their respective regions.

The US provided substantial military assistance to Pakistan, which had a significant impact on the regional military balance. Pakistan received modern weapons such as tanks, armoured vehicles, jet bombers, and engineering equipment from the US. This aid elevated the political influence and prestige of the Pakistani military and strengthened Pakistan's favourable image among US military and political leaders.

Between 1954 and 1965, Pakistan received substantial military aid from the US, including over $630 million in grant military assistance for weapons, $619 million for defence support assistance, and $55 million worth of equipment purchased on a cost or concessional basis. In comparison, India received relatively less military assistance during the same period. India purchased over $50 million in military equipment, and after the Sino-Indian war in 1962-1965, it received over $90 million worth of grant military assistance, mainly consisting of communication and transport equipment, some hardware, and support for arms production facilities.[6]

Pakistan drew several conclusions from the new situation. With the realization that they were no longer the exclusive recipients of US military support in the region, they anticipated the loss of the material leverage that had balanced their position. Moreover, they harboured doubts about the political dimension. Pakistan had long been apprehensive that the US, if given a choice, would prioritize India, relegating Pakistan to a secondary status in its strategic calculations. Even if this assumption proved unfounded, it was evident that the US's preoccupation with countering Communist China overshadowed any sense of obligation it may have felt under their alliance to support Pakistan against India.[7] Thus, Pakistan found itself in need of a new means to balance power. Sensing an opportunity, the Communist Chinese sought to capitalize on Pakistan's animosity towards India and its growing disillusionment with the US.

Dissatisfaction with the US arms transfer policy grew in both India and Pakistan after the 1962 India-China war. Pakistan began turning to China for support, and China reciprocated.[8] India aimed for self-sufficiency and diversified its sources of weaponry. Pakistan's growing bilateral relationship with China was seen as an irritant by Washington, further straining US-Pakistan relations.[9] All grant programmes for military assistance were terminated after the India-Pakistan war in 1965.

Following the 1965 war, prevailing sentiment in the US leaned towards a policy of low priority or disengagement concerning the permanent role of the US in South Asia. This stance was reinforced by several factors. Politically, there was a belief that maintaining a low profile would serve US interests, as the existing situation was deemed satisfactory. Some argued that the Soviets had assumed responsibility for Indian security, which could help contain Chinese pressure, though this strained Sino-Soviet relations, which was seen as advantageous from the American perspective.[10] Economically, South Asia was viewed as having little value or significance, with minimal trade, investment, or other economic ties. The region's development challenges were seen as immense, rendering even substantial US assistance insufficient. Moreover, there was a lack of popular support within the US for such massive efforts.

Militarily, criticism arose over the use of supplied arms by India and Pakistan against each other. Pressure mounted within Congress and among the public to address this practice. In March 1966, the Foreign Minister of Pakistan announced that the embargo on American military assistance had forced his government to turn to China for arms procurement.[11] Since the 1960s, China has forged robust economic, political, and military bonds with Pakistan. Beijing has played a crucial role as Islamabad's supporter at the United Nations Security Council, serving as a vital supplier of military hardware, contributing to Pakistan's nuclear weapons programme, and extending billions of dollars in economic assistance and investments.[12]

The US arms transfer policy had profound effects on the domestic politics of Pakistan. It strengthened the position of the military and increased defence expenditure. In Pakistan, there was a perception that US military assistance enabled them to negotiate with India on a near-equal basis, countering their sense of national inferiority.[13] However, the political elevation of the military had negative consequences for its professional competence, resulting in a decline in capabilities compared to India from 1965 to 1971.

The US arms transfer policy also affected India, as it forced the latter to seek weapons from other sources and invest in their domestic arms industry.[14] India viewed the US programme as misguided or malevolent and believed it disrupted US-India relations. The arms transfers symbolized US support for Pakistan. It placed a heavy burden on India, which had to match it from other sources. It far outweighed whatever limited assistance US was giving to India.

However, these alliances and military support succeeded in turning Pakistan into a Cold War ally of the US. It also affected the regional military balance. Through these efforts US wanted to influence the regional dynamics in support of its larger objective of containing communism and the Soviet Union.

Changing Nature of Pakistan's Cold War Alliances

Pakistan's initial motivation for entering into a Cold War alliance with the US was primarily driven by the desire to acquire weapons and political support to balance India. Its primary objective was to seek parity with India in South Asia.[15] Pakistan was a nominal ally in the broader context of containing the Soviet Union, and it was not an ally of the US against China. Pakistan's alliance with the US could be characterized as a 'bandwagoning' alliance. Pakistan joined CENTO (Central Treaty Organization) and SEATO (Southeast Asia Treaty Organization) to nominally oppose communism, receiving significant economic and military aid in return.[16]

However, this alliance was not robust enough to prevent Pakistan from developing closer ties with China. The US itself later recognized China as a lesser communist threat than the Soviet Union, and Pakistan played a role in facilitating the US-China relationship. It facilitated Henry Kissinger's visit to Beijing in July 1971. This visit proved crucial in reshaping Cold War dynamics and led to a major realignment of global powers.

Kissinger's visit to Beijing marked the recognition by the US that the communist movement was not monolith. It acknowledged that, despite being a communist nation, China had its own concerns about Soviet power and could potentially serve as a counterbalance. Actually, both China and the US were looking for counterweight against Moscow between 1970 and 1978.[17] The visit paved the way for improved relations between the US and China, eventually culminating in the normalization of diplomatic relations in 1979. This development had far-reaching implications for global geopolitics, challenging the previous binary framework of the Cold War.

While Pakistan's contributions to the broader objectives of containing the Soviet Union and China may not have been substantial, its role in facilitating Kissinger's visit to Beijing had a profound impact. It not only reshaped Cold War dynamics but also prompted the US to reevaluate its approach toward communist powers. In this way, Pakistan inadvertently hastened the end of the Cold War.

Subsequently, Pakistan's bandwagoing alliance transformed into a strategic alliance with China directed against India.[18] While the US did not view India as a strategic threat, Pakistan and China developed a closer partnership. China initially saw India as a tool of the West, but it appreciated Pakistan's decision to distance itself from the US. Pakistan became a sort of alliance partner with China and supported US efforts to counter the Soviets in Afghanistan. At this stage, a true balancing alliance emerged, with China, Pakistan, and the US joining hands against the Soviets.

Interestingly, Pakistan did not play a balancing role against the Soviets until it left CENTO and SEATO. However, Pakistan's decision to leave those alliances later proved to be a blessing as it served as a bridge between the US and China. Pakistan's role during the Cold War was primarily to counter India, but it played a significant role in facilitating the American-Chinese alliance.

Thus, Pakistan's alliances during the Cold War started as bandwagoning with the US, then transformed into a strategic alliance with China against India. This transformation played a part in hastening the end of the Cold War, while Pakistan pursued its objective of achieving parity with India in the region.

Rupture in alliance in 1971

The US-Pakistan alliance had already started to fray in the early 1960s when Pakistan turned to China for assistance, while the US backed India in its war with China. This divergence in interests created a strain in the alliance. The alliance became dormant until it was briefly revived in 1970-1972 when Pakistan facilitated the US opening to China. The US supported Pakistan during this period to demonstrate to China that it could be relied upon. However, once the objective of establishing relations with China was achieved, both countries went their separate ways.

The disintegration of East Pakistan and the emergence of Bangladesh in 1971 further strained the US-Pakistan alliance. Pakistan felt betrayed as it received no substantial military support from either the US or China during the conflict. Despite the US showing a tilt in favour of Pakistan, it had limited material impact. There is minimal evidence to suggest that US support deterred India from launching attacks on West Pakistan. This sense of disillusionment regarding the efficacy of alliances for ensuring security prompted Pakistan to reevaluate its dependence on the US.

Zulfikar Ali Bhutto, who came to power after the war, pursued a policy to lessen Pakistan's dependence on the US. Diplomatically, Bhutto emphasized Pakistan's Muslim identity and strengthened ties with countries like Saudi Arabia and Iran. Pakistan became a key member of the Organization of Islamic Cooperation (OIC), and Bhutto withdrew Pakistan from the SEATO and severed military links with the West. Pakistan also joined the non-aligned movement.

In terms of military strategy, Bhutto reversed the previous policy of relying on conventional US military and economic aid and instead pursued the development of nuclear weapons.[19] The nuclear programme was initiated in the mid-1970s and resulted in Pakistan acquiring nuclear weapons within a decade.[20] Bhutto's successor, General Zia ul-Haq, continued the nuclear programme.

The acquisition of nuclear weapons provided Pakistan with a deterrent capability, allowing it to provoke and probe India while avoiding direct conflict. However, going nuclear also came at a price. It became a sticking point in Pakistan's relationship with its Western allies, who were concerned about nuclear proliferation and the stability of the region.

Revival of a Defunct Alliance

After the loss of East Pakistan and the development of Pakistan's nuclear programme, the Carter administration imposed sanctions on Pakistan. However, the dynamics of the relationship quickly changed due to significant events. The Soviet invasion of Afghanistan in December 1979 played a pivotal role, with Islamabad providing vital support for anti-Soviet operations.

The ongoing war in Afghanistan compelled the US to waive legislative restrictions on providing aid to countries like Pakistan, despite concerns over their unverifiable nuclear programme. During this period, other US interests took a backseat as Pakistan accepted President Reagan's offer of $3.2 billion in economic and military assistance in 1981. However, the introduction of the Pressler amendment in 1985 imposed restrictions on economic and military assistance to Pakistan, unless the president certified annually that Pakistan did not possess a nuclear explosive device and that the proposed US assistance programme would significantly reduce the risk of Pakistan acquiring such a device. Nevertheless, a second economic and military assistance package worth $4 billion was announced in 1986.

Driven by the perception that Jihadi fighters were the most effective anti-Soviet forces, the Reagan administration displayed little concern for the consequences of supporting them. The religious fervour exhibited by these fighters appealed to US officials, influencing their decisions and policies. However, with the withdrawal of Soviet forces in 1989, the US stopped providing waivers, indicating a shift in priorities.

Benefits to Pakistan from its Cold War Alliances

Pakistan enjoyed several benefits from its Cold War alliances, particularly with the US and other allied countries. One of the key advantages was the significant economic and military assistance provided by the US. Pakistan received financial aid, grants, and military equipment through various assistance programmes. Although an embargo was imposed on Pakistan during the Indo-Pakistan War in 1965, it was later lifted in 1975, allowing for resumption of aid.

Through its alliances, Pakistan had the opportunity to enhance its military capabilities and knowledge. Pakistani officers benefited from interactions with American and other allied military forces. Many Pakistani officers received training in the US, which contributed to their professional development. Similarly, foreign officers trained in Pakistan, referred to as 'allied officers,' further strengthened military ties.

Pakistan also received diplomatic support from the US and Britain on the Kashmir issue. These countries backed Pakistan's position in the United Nations and provided diplomatic assistance.[21] In times of crises between India and Pakistan, the US and Britain often intervened to prevent large-scale war and facilitate negotiations over the Kashmir dispute. Their involvement aimed to promote a peaceful resolution and avoid further escalation.

However, it is important to note that while the US and Britain supported Pakistan diplomatically, they did not provide a formal commitment under CENTO or SEATO in the event of a war. The interventions and diplomatic support varied in their success in achieving lasting peace between India and Pakistan, with mixed outcomes.

India's Potential as a Major Power and Counterbalance Recognized since 1965

India's potential as a major power and counterbalance was recognized in US since the 1965 war. In the 1950s, the debate in US was about the political and military importance of India and Pakistan. In that Pakistan was chosen as a preferred partner. The focus of this debate however shifted in 1970s and integrity of Pakistan became a major concern. Now the possibility of emergence of India as a great power became a subject of vigorous debate.

Although the 1965 war did not demonstrate India's strategic dominance, it did demonstrate the Indian military's capacity to rebuild and regenerate itself. With its technological advancements and superior manpower, India showed that it was only a matter of time before it would attain a prominent position in the region. The main obstacle to this was the substantial external support provided to Pakistan. As the original communist threat diminished, the prospects of a comprehensive arms programme for Pakistan waned, leading American policymakers to reevaluate its significance.

Even prior to 1965, India had the potential to receive greater assistance from the US due to its status as the only regional power with military nuclear capabilities. Indian elites were more inclined toward military assistance from the West rather than the Soviet Union. Despite its chaotic yet resilient and robust political system, India possessed the military and political capacity to dominate South Asia. However, the US approached its support cautiously, uncertain whether such a policy would be reciprocated by the Indian government.

Since 1967, American policymakers have reached a consensus on key propositions regarding US interests in South Asia. It became evident that Pakistan could no longer achieve strategic superiority in the subcontinent, even with significant external arms suppliers. This was confirmed by the 1971 war, leading the US to publicly acknowledge India's sub-continental preeminence and its attainment of great power status. However, Pakistan was still strong enough to be used to put pressure on India.

American policymakers historically did not prioritize South Asia independently but rather viewed it primarily through the lens of East-West relations.[22] The primary US interests in the South Asian region were not solely based on direct relationships with individual countries, but from the role the regional states play vis-a-vis other regions and powers, especially the USSR and China.[23] The impact of the region on other significant American interests held greater importance. Nuclear proliferation and the integrity of Pakistan were other concerns that warranted reasonable consideration. Preserving the integrity of Pakistan, as a former US ally, was important for regional stability. Regional stability reduced the possibility of external intervention and entanglement for the US.

Recognizing that India and Pakistan were unlikely to cooperate in joint defence efforts, it made sense for an external power to leverage India as the dominant regional power to counterbalance any major external threat, while using Pakistan as a means to exert pressure on India. This is what US seems to be doing now with the emergence of assertive China as a major threat.

This perception of American interests implied a reduction in arms transfers to the region, although it did not exclude them entirely. A complete arms transfer ban would have disproportionately affected Pakistan, which heavily relied on US support.

Consequences of US-Pakistan Partnership During the Cold War

Pakistan's decision to adopt an adversarial stance towards its larger neighbour, India, led it to seek an external patron to support this position. Consequently, Pakistan developed a close relationship with the US and aligned itself with the Western bloc during the Cold War.

This alliance exhibited a transactional nature, as the aid provided by the US was tied to specific issues and strategic calculations. The alliance experienced periods of active cooperation followed by periods of relative disengagement, primarily because the two countries did not share a strong strategic congruence. The US sought Pakistan as an ally to counter Soviet influence, while Pakistan aimed to gain resources and political support in its regional rivalry with India.

Pakistan's Cold War alliances had profound political, economic and ideological consequences on the country. The Pakistani military emerged as a major beneficiary of these alliances. Both the country's Western allies and the state itself favoured anti-communist Islamic forces.[24] This preference for Islamic forces over left and liberal factions restricted the development of ideological and social diversity in Pakistan, which could have countered the rise of Islamic extremism.

Pakistan's political system remained underdeveloped and influenced by its feudal origins. This was encouraged by Pakistan's allies and close friends, who found it more convenient to engage with military and establishment elites. Criticism of political repression was absent from the discourse of Pakistan's allies and close friends, allowing undemocratic practices to persist.

Pakistan's constitutional state faced continuous challenges. The country's elite and its foreign supporters whitewashed the failure to establish constitutional normalcy. The compromise on constitutional processes was justified on the basis of external pressures and internal turmoil. Pakistan relied on borrowed power but didn't use it to reform its social and political institutions.

The military assumed a dominant role in Pakistan, justifying its intervention in strategic and moral terms. It positioned itself as the guardian of Pakistan's sovereignty, claiming to possess the best understanding of national defence and security requirements. The military believed that regional peace could only be achieved through a military balance with India, and Pakistan needed to possess significant military capabilities to compel India to acknowledge its legitimacy and the two-nation theory.

American aid played a significant role in strengthening Pakistan's army and had a profound impact on the regional military balance. The transfer of arms altered the dynamics between India and Pakistan. India kept struggling to match the increasing military capabilities of its neighbour solely through the deployment of larger numbers of soldiers. The US effectively enhanced Pakistan's military power through its arms transfer policy.

Prior to 1962, US weapons were seen as an asset for Pakistan and a problem for India. In the early 1960s, a true dependency relationship began to take shape between the US and Pakistan. The scale of the arms programme was disproportionately large for the region and served as a symbolic message of support from the US to Pakistan.[25] This extensive arms programme played a crucial role in the modernization of the Pakistani army, equipping it with advanced weaponry and capabilities.

Pakistan's alliances enabled it to hold its ground against India and compete with it militarily. By staying afloat, Pakistan defied Indian predictions of its failure. These alliances also facilitated Pakistan's nuclear programme, as the US either turned a blind eye or actively supported it.

Both India and Pakistan made concerted efforts to influence the US policy process during this period. Recognizing the significance of American support, they sought to shape the direction of US policy in the region to serve their respective interests.

Regarding the central dispute of Kashmir, Pakistan raised the issue to prove that Muslims could not live peacefully or safely in India. However, capturing Kashmir required borrowing more power from its alliances, which was not available. Later, General Pervez Musharraf engaged in serious discussions with India over the Kashmir issue, but by then, India's stance toward Pakistan had become more rigid.

The civilian rulers of Pakistan frequently displayed personalistic and autocratic tendencies. Their actions were closely monitored by the military, which eventually ousted them from power. Only a few politicians dared to oppose military rule, as most either found a place within the new system or quietly withdrew from politics without any objection from their Cold War allies.

The American aid and security alliance with Pakistan played a significant role in strengthening the Pakistan military, but several other factors have also contributed to the imbalance between the civil and military institutions in the country. Since its creation, Pakistan has faced distortions in the functioning of its state, with the military assuming a dominant role. This phenomenon has persisted throughout the nation's history due to various reasons, including the absence of genuine democracy and the concentration of power in the hands of key figures.

The founder of Pakistan, Muhammad Ali Jinnah, exhibited an authoritarian streak during his time as the first Governor General, centralizing vast amounts of power. This trend continued under his prime minister, Liaquat Ali Khan, who held multiple positions of responsibility and suppressed political parties that were perceived as divisive. Over time, the capital's shift from Karachi to Islamabad further increased the military's influence, as the General Headquarters of the Pakistan army was already located in Rawalpindi, Punjab, where the army had strong roots.

The army's self-definition as the defender of Pakistan against external threats, particularly India, was fueled by a sense of paranoia and hysteria. Armed conflicts over Kashmir added to the military's prominence, leading to its dominance in Pakistan's state affairs. Feudal interests aligned with the predominantly Punjabi army and civil servants, forming a loosely termed 'establishment' that co-opted other groups, including religious and ambitious political factions, to maintain control.

The justification of absence of democracy in Pakistan by its foreign allies further bolstered the military's position. The army's leadership exercised both direct and indirect control over the state, using clever methods to maintain its hold without overtly taking over the government. Civilian leaders, including some who later opposed the army's influence, were complicit in its machinations to control power at various points in time. Public criticism of the army from politicians has been rare due to this power dynamic.

The judiciary, with some exceptions, has often aligned itself with the army, further enabling its control over the state. A notable instance was the

Federal Court's endorsement of Governor General Ghulam Muhammad's dismissal of the first constituent assembly in 1954, using the "doctrine of necessity" to justify the move.

The army has meticulously controlled the national narrative in Pakistan, restricting civilian leaders from pursuing their policies, particularly concerning security and foreign affairs. Although not explicitly mentioned in the constitution, the military remains the supreme institution in the country. It wields significant influence over critical national issues, claims a priority over national resources, and continues to interfere in constitutional governance with impunity, quashing dissenting voices. While the army has not overtly taken over the government in recent times, it possesses the means to maintain its firm grip on power. This strong control of army over Pakistani polity has not allowed the relationship between India and Pakistan to improve.

The economic impact of the US-Pakistan relationship has been mixed. The adversarial relationship between Pakistan and India has contributed to Pakistan becoming a security state, prioritizing defence against external threats over welfare. As a result, a substantial portion of national resources is allocated to defence spending, with the armed forces, particularly the army, receiving a significant share of the budget. The burden of heavy debt and substantial defense expenditure leaves limited resources for other government activities, including development.

Unfortunately, Pakistan's education budget is the lowest among South Asian countries, hindering progress in the education sector. One consequence of the US-Pakistan partnership was the collapse of Pakistan's educational system, with Islamic schools replacing traditional ones. The US could have focused more attention on Pakistan's uneven economic development, crumbling educational infrastructure, and the rise of Islamic radicalism. However, these issues were often regarded as 'soft' and received less emphasis compared to concerns about Pakistan's nuclear programme.

Economic growth in Pakistan coincided with periods of high aid flows, but assistance was not conditioned on serious economic and social reforms. The absence of 'tough love' hindered the prospect of long-term sustainable progress.

Pakistan's economy heavily relies on external aid and borrowing, leading to a dependence on an external patron. The country faces numerous challenges, including low economic growth, high inflation, inadequate foreign exchange reserves, poor resource mobilization, high fiscal deficit, reliance on foreign aid, a heavy debt burden, and a significant allocation of resources to defence and debt servicing.

The external sector of Pakistan's economy faces challenges such as an adverse balance of trade and payments, with exports underperforming. To bridge the resource gap and maintain external stability, Pakistan has consistently relied on external aid, borrowing, and IMF bailouts. In the past, the US has been a significant provider of aid, while China has recently extended loans to support Pakistan's foreign exchange reserves.

The economic problems in Pakistan are deeply rooted in both its external posture and internal functioning. The policy of confrontation with India, the concentration of benefits among influential groups, and economic mismanagement all contribute to these challenges. To sustain its economy and pursue its ambitions regarding India, Pakistan seeks an external patron willing to support its economic endeavors.[26] While historically under the tutelage of the US, Pakistan established relations with China in the 1960s based on their shared animosity towards India. Pakistan subsequently became the country which was taking financial assistance from both US as well as China.

A shift in strategy could have greatly benefited Pakistan following the end of the Cold War. Instead of prioritizing more weapons for Pakistan army, the immediate post-Cold War period called for a focus on economic liberalization and capital infusion through integration into the global economy. Pakistan required rapid economic development and essential social reforms to address the concentration of wealth among a limited Punjabi elite, which included landed, bureaucratic, and military factions. This elite's political dominance relied heavily on control over the military apparatus, perpetuated in part by American South Asia policy over the past four decades. Additionally, settling differences with India over Kashmir was crucial. Unfortunately, these vital changes did not materialize, leading to a worsening of Pakistan's economic woes.[27]

Over the years, Pakistan's perception of its relationship with the US has undergone a significant shift. Initially seen as a staunch, reliable, and strong Muslim ally of the West, Pakistan now considers itself a victim of the partnership. There is a prevailing sentiment that Pakistan has endured the consequences of its cooperation with the West without receiving sufficient compensation in return.

The army also became wary of the US because of the episodic nature of the alliance. While military training programmes enhanced understanding of US society and strategic policies, they did not necessarily create a pro-American leadership within the Pakistani military.

Despite being a key partner, the US remains highly unpopular in Pakistan. While the Pakistani elite may admire the American way of life and often send their children to the US for study and work, they are also critical of the US government. They believe that Pakistan did not receive its due in terms of economic and military aid and support, particularly concerning its rivalry with India. Additionally, they express discontent over policies imposed by the US, such as involvement in the Afghan Jihad, which they view as having been harmful in the long run, despite Pakistan's willingness to be part of those policies at the time.

Religious-minded individuals and extremists in Pakistan regard the US as an enemy of Islam. Many perceive the War on Terror as a war against Islam, fostering a sense of animosity towards the US. An incident in 1979, when the US embassy in Islamabad was burned down due to a rumour that it had bombed a mosque in Mecca, exemplifies the deep-rooted suspicions and tensions between the two nations.

Pakistan's view of its relationship with the US has transformed over time, with a growing sense of disillusionment and a belief that the country has not received fair treatment or adequate support from its American ally. This sentiment is shared by various segments of Pakistani society, including the elite and religious groups, contributing to a complex and often strained relationship between the two countries.

During the Cold War, Pakistan gained parity with India through its partnership with US, but it came at a price. The lack of focus on critical issues had long-term impact on Pakistan's development and stability.

NOTES

1 Lloyd I. Rudolph and Susanne Hoeber Rudolph, 'The Making of US Foreign Policy for South Asia: Offshore Balancing in Historical Perspective,' *Economic and Political Weekly*, 25 February–3 March 2006, Vol. 41, No. 8, pp. 704-05.

2 Dhruva Jaishankar, 'Does "South Asia" Exist?', *Foreign Policy*, 26 November, 2013 at https://foreignpolicy.com/2013/11/26/does-south-asia-exist/ last accessed on 14 June 2024.

3 Stephen Cohen, 'Pakistan and the Cold War,' *Superpower Rivalry and Conflict: The Long Shadow of the Cold War on the 21st Century*, Chandra Chari (ed.), Routledge, 2010, pp. 74-75.

4 Robert J. McMahon, 'United States Cold War Strategy in South Asia: Making a Military Commitment to Pakistan,' 1947-1954, *The Journal of American History*, December 1988, Vol. 75, No. 3, pp. 823-824.

5 Harold A. Gould, 'Bill Clinton's Moribund South Asia Policy', *Economic and Political Weekly*, 23 November, 1996, Vol. 31, No. 47, p. 3079.

6 Stephen Cohen, 'US weapons and South Asia: A policy analysis,' *Pacific Affairs*, Vol. 49, No. 1, Spring, 1976, p. 50.

7 Thomas Perry Thornton, 'South Asia and The Great Powers,' *World Affairs*, New Delhi: Sage Publications, March 1970, Vol. 132, No. 4, p. 351.

8 Yun Sun and Hannah Haegeland, 'China And Crisis Management In South Asia,' *Investigating Crises: South Asia's Lessons, Evolving Dynamics, and Trajectories*, Hannah Haegeland (ed.), Michael Krepon, Sameer Lalwani and Yun Sun, Stimson Center, Washington DC, 2018, p. 169 at https://www.stimson.org/wp-content/files/InvestigatingCrisesChina.pdf last accessed on 14 June 2024.

9 Iftikhar H. Malik, 'The Pakistan-U.S. Security Relationship: Testing Bilateralism,' *Asian Survey*, March 1990, Vol. 30, No. 3, p. 293.

10 Stanley A. Kochanek, 'US Foreign Policy in South Asia,' *Pakistan Horizon*, July-October 1993, Vol. 46, No. ¾, July-October 1993, pp. 20-21.

11 Zubeida Hasan, '"United States Arms Policy in South Asia, 1965-1967,' *Pakistan Horizon*, Second Quarter, 1967, Vol. 20, No. 2, p. 128.

12 Jeff M. Smith, 'South Asia: A New Strategy,' *Backgrounder, The Heritage Foundation*, No. 3721, August 29, 2022, p. 8 at http://report.heritage.org/bg3721 last accessed on 14 June 2024.

13 Stephen Cohen, 'US weapons and South Asia: A policy analysis,' *Pacific Affairs*, Vol. 49, No. 1, Spring, 1976, p. 54, also see, Paul Kreisberg, 'The United States, South Asia and American Interests', *Journal of International Affairs*, Summer/Fall 1989, Vol. 43, No. 1, Summer/Fall 1989, p. 86.

14 Robert G. Wirsing, 'The Arms Race in South Asia: Implications for the United States,' *Asian Survey*, March 1985, Vol. 25, No. 3, pp. 265-291.

15 Lloyd I. Rudolph and Susanne Hoeber Rudolph, 'The Making of US Foreign Policy for South Asia: Offshore Balancing in Historical Perspective,' *Economic and Political Weekly*, 25 February-3 March 2006, Vol. 41, No. 8, p. 705.

16 Stephen Cohen, 'Pakistan and the Cold War,' *Superpower Rivalry and Conflict: The Long Shadow of the Cold War on the 21st Century*, Chandra Chari (ed.), New Delhi: Routledge, 2010, p. 82.

17 Paul H. Kreisberg, 'The US and China in the 1990s', *Contemporary Southeast Asia*, June 1988, Vol. 10, No. 1, p. 57.

18 Stephen Cohen, 'Pakistan and the Cold War,' *Superpower Rivalry and Conflict: The Long Shadow of the Cold War on the 21st Century*, Chandra Chari (ed.), New Delhi: Routledge, 2010, p. 82.

19 Stephen Cohen, 'Pakistan and the Cold War,' *Superpower Rivalry and Conflict: The Long Shadow of the Cold War on the 21st Century*, Chandra Chari (ed.), New Delhi: Routledge, 2010, p. 78.

20 Steven R. Weisman, 'Report of Pakistani A-Bomb Causes a Stir in The Region', *New York Times*, 2 March 1987, https://www.nytimes.com/1987/03/02/world/report-of-pakistani-a-bomb-causes-a-stir-in-the-region.html last accessed on 14 June, 2024.

21 Stephen Cohen, 'Pakistan and the Cold War,' *Superpower Rivalry and Conflict: The Long Shadow of the Cold War on the 21st Century*, Chandra Chari (ed.), New Delhi: Routledge, 2010, p. 77.

22 Paul Kreisberg, 'The US, South Asia and American Interests,' *Journal of International Affairs*, Summer/Fall 1989, Vol. 43, No. 1, p. 83.

23 Stephen Cohen, 'US weapons and South Asia: A policy analysis,' *Pacific Affairs*, Vol. 49, No. 1, Spring, 1976, p. 67.

24 Stephen Cohen, 'Pakistan and the Cold War,' *Superpower Rivalry and Conflict: The Long Shadow of the Cold War on the 21st Century*, Chandra Chari (ed.), New Delhi: Routledge, 2010, p. 80.

25 Stephen Cohen, 'US weapons and South Asia: A policy analysis,' *Pacific Affairs*, Vol. 49, No. 1, Spring, 1976, p. 55.

26 Sharat Sabharwal, *India's Pakistan Conundrum: Managing a Complex Relationship*, New Delhi: Routledge, 2022, pp. 27-29.

27 Harold A. Gould, 'Bill Clinton's Moribund South Asia Policy', *Economic and Political Weekly*, 23 November 1996, Vol. 31, No. 47, p. 3084.

CHAPTER 3

Post-Cold War Challenges

During the Cold War between the US and the Soviet Union, winning the global conflict took precedence over other major concerns. As a result, the South Asia region, including countries like India, Pakistan, and Afghanistan, did not receive significant priority in US foreign policy until the 1990s. While the US had made substantial investments in the region, its attention was relatively limited. Policy-making often revolved around strategic considerations primarily focused on other regions such as the Middle East and Asia Pacific. The geopolitical dynamics and complexities of South Asia were overshadowed by the more immediate and perceived critical issues elsewhere.

The Bureau of South Asia Affairs was created through a congressional legislation on 24 August 1992. It was because of this bureau that for the first time, South Asia was seen as a single entity by the American policy makers. The views on the region began to shift in the 1990s due to various factors, including the evolving perception of India and the continuous rise of China. The prospects of India disintegrating diminished, and its effective management of coalitions became evident despite the complexity of its federal system.

With the end of the Cold War and the collapse of the Soviet Union in 1991, the US' rationale for acting as an offshore balancer in South Asia diminished. Nevertheless, issues such as nuclear programs and the complications surrounding the Kashmir dispute remained core concerns in US-Pakistan relations. Additionally, the US had to confront the problem of terrorism following the devastating events of 9/11.[1] These factors prompted a reevaluation of US policy towards South Asia.

Nuclear Proliferation became a Core Concern

Historically, South Asia hadn't received significant priority, as the US lacks vital interests there compared to regions like the Persian Gulf, the Caribbean, or East Asia, where factors such as oil, proximity, or extensive trade shape American interests. The region lacks essential resources or major markets crucial to US interests. However, there was a growing recognition that the US should devote more attention to South Asia for several compelling reasons.[2]

First, the region is home to a massive population. Moreover, its geographical location between the oil-rich Persian Gulf and the economically vibrant East Asia region adds to its significance. Additionally, the presence of nuclear weapons and ballistic missiles in both Pakistan and India heightens the strategic importance of South Asia. Consequently, the US gradually increased its focus on the region, acknowledging the necessity of addressing the intricate dynamics between India and Pakistan while understanding the broader implications of regional stability for global security.

Recognizing the potential dangers of nuclear proliferation, the US encouraged both India and Pakistan to seek a regional solution to address this threat. However, Pakistan always felt aggrieved, arguing that it disproportionately bore the consequences of US anti-proliferation policies.[3]

During the Clinton administration, nuclear issues received substantial emphasis, with concerns expressed regarding the nuclear programmes of both India and Pakistan. Primary fears included the potential use of nuclear weapons in crises, regional instability, and the transfer of nuclear technology to non-state actors or rogue groups. Actually, the nuclear proliferation concern surrounding Pakistan was linked with military sales. The US justified its extensive military aid program to Pakistan as a strategic measure aimed at preventing Pakistan from pursuing nuclear capabilities. Arms transfers were presented as a means to incentivize Pakistan to maintain its status as a non-nuclear state.[4]

Despite these efforts, both India and Pakistan conducted nuclear tests in 1998, defying expectations and further complicating non-proliferation objectives. Notably, Pakistan's nuclear programme received assistance from both Western countries and China. Western nations occasionally turned a blind eye to Pakistani scientists acquiring nuclear technology by circumventing regulations or engaging in outright theft. China played a significant role by providing nuclear design assistance, and there were technological exchanges between Pakistan and China.[5]

When China joined the Nuclear Suppliers Group (NSG) in 2004, it justified its cooperation with Pakistan's Chashma nuclear power reactors as a pre-existing commitment, allowing it to be covered under the 'Grandfather clause.' Consequently, Pakistan continued to receive nuclear technology and material from China, while India had to seek special dispensation from the NSG and the International Atomic Energy Agency (IAEA).

These developments underscored the limitations of pursuing non-proliferation goals without a comprehensive understanding of the regional dynamics and interests at play.[6] It became evident that India and Pakistan were able to resist external pressures, illustrating the challenges and impracticality of achieving nuclear disarmament in South Asia.

These developments highlighted the need for a more nuanced approach that considered the unique complexities of the region. Subsequently, the focus shifted towards managing the risks associated with nuclear capabilities rather than seeking outright disarmament. The US and the international community began to engage in diplomatic efforts aimed at promoting confidence-building measures, encouraging dialogue, and establishing frameworks for nuclear risk reduction in South Asia.

Focus Shifts to the Kashmir Issue

The rise of a separatist movement in Kashmir in 1989 raised Pakistan's aspirations and eventually led to the Kargil conflict in 1999. As efforts to prevent the nuclearization of South Asia proved unsuccessful, the US shifted its focus to the long-standing Kashmir dispute, widely believed to be a key factor driving the nuclear arms race in the region.

The Kashmir issue was recognized by US officials and intelligence analysts as the world's most probable flashpoint for a nuclear war. However, it became clear that the dispute extended beyond mere territorial disagreements. It involved defining competing national identities: India as a secular state and Pakistan as an Islamic one. This intricate dynamic made external mediation in the Kashmir issue exceedingly challenging. Pakistan insisted on a plebiscite that would lead to Kashmir's accession to Pakistan, disregarding alternative solutions.

In February 1999, a glimmer of hope for regional reconciliation emerged when Indian Prime Minister Atal Bihari Vajpayee visited Pakistan. However, these hopes were shattered by the eruption of intense fighting during the Kargil conflict later that year. The conflict erupted when Pakistani forces infiltrated the Kargil district of Jammu and Kashmir. Adding further complexity and uncertainty to the region, Pakistan's fragile democracy was subsequently overthrown in October 1999 by a military coup led by General Pervez Musharraf.

These developments underscored the deep-rooted challenges and complexities of the Kashmir issue, making a resolution through external mediation increasingly elusive. The US recognized the limitations of its influence and turned its attention to promoting dialogue and confidence-building measures between India and Pakistan, aimed at mitigating tension and fostering regional stability.

Role of US in the Kargil Crisis

During the Kargil Crisis of 1999, the US played a significant role, intervening diplomatically to help resolve the conflict between India and Pakistan. During this crisis, the US demanded that Pakistan withdraw its forces from the Line of Control (LoC) in Kargil and urged India to refrain from crossing the LoC or launching attacks on Pakistan elsewhere. The US was able to exert influence in this situation because it had established close dialogue with both India and Pakistan.

The Kargil Crisis highlighted that US intervention did not necessarily go against Indian interests. This experience fostered a new level of trust in bilateral relations and raised hopes for a more substantial relationship with the US.[7] The Clinton Administration played a decisive role in the conflict by pressuring Pakistan to end its aggression, demonstrating a distinct approach in dealing with India and Pakistan.

The US viewed India as an emerging power on the global stage and a potential partner. India also viewed the US agenda as being positive during the Kargil Crisis. In contrast, Pakistan perceived US policy objectives as directed against its support of the Taliban, involvement in narcotics trafficking, and religious extremism.

A Positive Shift in US-India Relations

During the 1990s, the US underwent a significant change in its approach towards South Asia. Now a positive shift took place in the US-India relations, which stemmed from a recognition of India's economic prowess, regional influence, and shared interests between the two countries.

Despite a period of democratic rule in Pakistan, the country faced challenges. Its institutions deteriorated, and its military continued to meddle in politics. In contrast, the US began acknowledging India's economic, diplomatic, and military prominence in the region, leading to a shift in focus.

During President Clinton's second term, the need for a special relationship with Pakistan diminished. Instead, the Clinton administration started according recognition to India's dominant position. This was evident in President Clinton's successful visit to India in March 2000.[8] India's economic reforms, sustained growth, expanding middle class, and investment opportunities made it an attractive market and partner for the US.

The changing economic landscape of India, coupled with its increasing global visibility, played a significant role in the positive shift in US-India relations. Despite lingering differences, both countries shared common interests, such as investment, technology exchange, and India's critical role in software and computer products. India also appreciated the balanced and effective diplomacy of the US during regional crises. Besides, India's growing diaspora and strategic importance enhanced its visibility within the US.

Furthermore, it became evident that India and Pakistan were not comparable entities. While India did not match China's level of influence, it held significant influence in the Asian sphere. However, recognizing India's importance did not imply neglecting Pakistan, particularly as a nuclear-armed state. Both India and the US were status quo powers, and despite ongoing differences, they were able to find common ground.

US-China Relations in the 1990s

In the 1980s and 1990s, China underwent a significant pro-market transformation driven by internal dynamics. During this era, Francis Fukuyama made a bold prediction that these economic changes would inevitably pave the way for democratic reforms and global harmony. He envisioned that Chinese students, business-people, and tourists exposed to Western ideals would catalyze reformist movements upon their return, ultimately leading to democratic triumph.

While the shift to a market-oriented economy did lift millions out of poverty, the anticipated democratic progress failed to materialize following the Cold War. In fact, in some instances, democratic principles regressed. The Tiananmen Square massacre, far from marking the demise of Chinese authoritarianism, underscored the determination of the Communist Party elite to safeguard their political dominance amidst economic liberalization.[9]

Contrary to expectations, Chinese political landscape in the late twentieth and early twenty-first centuries was not shaped by embracing Western democracy. Instead, it witnessed a resurgence of nationalism and a forceful reinterpretation of historical narratives, illustrating a divergence from Fukuyama's anticipated trajectory.[10]

Post-Cold War, the original motivation behind China-US rapprochement waned. The aftermath of the Tiananmen Square protests saw the US and other governments impose measures against China's human rights violations, including suspending high-level official exchanges and imposing economic sanctions. Despite these actions, the Bush administration maintained a less critical stance towards Beijing, hoping for normalized relations. However, the Tiananmen events disrupted the US-China trade relationship, leading to decreased US investor interest and tourism.

During this period, China encountered three primary challenges. First, there was the risk to China's political autonomy and domestic stability due to its significant economic interdependence with the US. Second, China reassessed its strategic environment and devalued the importance of the US in the regional balance of power. Underlying the first two issues was the third one, the rise of Chinese nationalism, which gradually became the most controversial and problematic aspect of China's American policy.[11] Deng Xiaoping, acknowledging US hegemony, adopted a low-profile foreign policy focused on domestic development.

In 1992, Bill Clinton criticized his predecessor George H.W. Bush for prioritizing trade over human rights issues in China. His administration linked China's most favoured nation trading status to human rights progress but eventually delinked it despite China's lack of compliance. The influential lobbying power of corporate entities heavily invested in the Chinese economy consistently compelled the Clinton administration to separate trade considerations from human rights concerns.[12] Congressional pressure led Clinton to approve arms sales to Taiwan, further straining relations.

Tensions between the US and China peaked in 1993 over the Taiwan Strait Crisis, with military manoeuvers by both sides. However, tensions gradually eased, leading to improved bilateral relations, marked by high-level visits and progress on various issues, including human rights and trade.

Despite challenges like the US bombing of the Chinese embassy in Belgrade in 1999, leading to widespread outrage in China, both countries reached agreements on compensation and began repairing relations. However, accusations of espionage by a Chinese-American scientist in mid-1980s but only detected in mid-1990s further strained ties. American officials alleged that by the mid-1990s, China had built and tested small bombs, a breakthrough accelerated by the theft of American nuclear secrets from Los Alamos National Laboratory in New Mexico.[13]

US-South Asia Relations in the Post-9/11 Era

The relationship between the US and South Asian states underwent significant changes in the post-9/11 era following the attacks on the World Trade Center and Pentagon. The US had to reevaluate its policy towards Pakistan, leading to a shift in the broader dynamics of South Asia.

President Bush lifted many sanctions on Pakistan and designated it a major non-NATO ally, which entitled Pakistan to purchase certain military equipment at reduced prices. Pakistan once again served as a support base for the Afghan war and was considered a partner in tracking down al-Qaeda and Taliban leaders who had fled to Pakistan. The US initiated a substantial military and economic assistance programme, providing Pakistan with $1 billion for the use of its facilities. However, allegations later surfaced that Pakistan was supporting both sides of the conflict.

India was keen to join US militarily in its war against terror. However, the US chose Pakistan instead. The US saw Pakistan's geographic access to the main theatre of war in Afghanistan and its intimate knowledge of the Taliban as advantageous. India, on the other hand, was viewed as an emerging power and a counterbalance to China.

The events of September 11 challenged the Clinton administration's policy of treating Pakistan as a failing and pariah state, and the Bush administration restored Pakistan to its role as a frontline state. The US rewarded the Musharraf government with large-scale military and economic assistance, and it appeared that the US was resuming its role as an offshore balancer.[14]

However, there was a difference this time, as the US sought to enlist both India and Pakistan in the war against terror. Some US officials, like Ashley J. Tellis, attempted to persuade India to join forces with Pakistan as a US ally.

Despite incremental progress, disagreements persisted between India and the US on certain issues. India's independent actions occasionally diverged from the US and the global agenda of the Bush administration. The US prioritized its global security interests over India's pursuit of energy independence. Their approaches towards Iran differed as well, with the US seeking to punish Iran and potentially change its regime, while India had its own interests. India also continued its arms purchase relationship with Russia.

Nevertheless, the India-US relationship showed signs of advancement, with both countries establishing a new framework for defence cooperation in 2005, signifying a growing strategic partnership.[15] India's ability to navigate a multipolar world became evident.

US Starts Engaging with Other South Asian Countries

Prior to the events of 9/11, there were already discussions about engaging with smaller South Asian nations.[16] However, in the aftermath of 9/11, the scope of US involvement in South Asia expanded beyond counterterrorism efforts. The US began to look at deeper conflicts in the region, promote regional stability, and encourage economic integration. Under the pressure of Washington Consensus for globalization and privatization, most countries of the region adopted liberal economic policies. It led to increased trade between India and Bangladesh. Besides, trade between India and Sri Lanka also increased.

US policy towards South Asia since 9/11 represented a fundamental change in the extent and quality of US engagement in the region. South Asian leaders eagerly sought US engagement in their regional and internal disputes, recognizing the importance of South Asian security as a global issue. However, the unintended consequences of US strategies during the Cold War era, such as the rise of religious extremism and international terrorism, posed challenges to regional stability.

The US also acknowledged the importance of addressing conflicts beyond India and Pakistan, including Sri Lanka, Nepal, and Bangladesh. The US became more directly involved in the civil war in Sri Lanka and the threat of Maoist insurgency in Nepal. There was a realization that defeating terrorism required dealing with failing states, and the US adopted a strategy to root out the forces of extremism and encourage conflict resolution.

The events of 11 September had led to a globalization of South Asian security, which in turn increased consultations between the US and India regarding sub-continental security issues. Previously, India had aimed to maintain its exclusive role in managing conflicts and prevent other major powers from encroaching on what it considered its sphere of influence. Protecting this sphere of influence had been a crucial national security priority for India, even though it couldn't completely prevent China and Pakistan from exerting their influence in the region.

Before 11 September, India would have opposed an expanded US military and diplomatic presence in its immediate neighbourhood, despite seeking and expecting improved relations with the US. However, the shifting international landscape made India recognize the potential of the US to act as a stabilizing force. India understood that its own regional interests were not at odds with current US priorities, but rather aligned with them.[17] Consequently, the challenge for New Delhi and Washington was to move beyond mere consultation and develop substantive political and security cooperation to address issues like failing states, political moderation, regional conflict resolution, and the defeat of regional extremism.

India exhibited a willingness to shed its accumulated mistrust of Washington and actively sought stronger bilateral ties with the US. It was prepared to collaborate with the US to promote peace and prosperity in the region. The events of 11 September and the changing dynamics in South Asia created opportunities for partnerships between India, the US, and other regional actors.

NOTES

1 Zhang Guihong, 'US security policy towards South Asia after September 11 and its implications for China: A Chinese perspective,' *Strategic Analysis*, Vol. 27, No. 2, Apr-Jun 2003, p. 165.

2 Lawrence E. Grinter, 'The United States and South Asia: New Challenges, New Opportunities,' *Asian Affairs: An American Review*, Summer, 1993, Vol. 20, No. 2, p. 101.

3 Iftikhar H. Malik, 'The Pakistan-U.S. Security Relationship: Testing Bilateralism', *Asian Survey*, March, 1990, Vol. 30, No. 3, p. 293.

4 Stanley A. Kochanek, 'US Foreign Policy in South Asia,' Pakistan Horizon, July-October 1993, Vol. 46, No. 3/4, p. 23.

5 Sharat Sabharwal, *India's Pakistan Conundrum: Managing a Complex Relationship*, New Delhi: Routledge, 2022, p. 180.

6 Stephen P. Cohen, 'A New Beginning in South Asia,' The Brookings Institution, Policy Brief, No. 55, January 2000 at https://www.brookings.edu/articles/a-new-beginning-in-south-asia/ last accessed on 15 June 2024.

7 C. Raja Mohan, 'A Paradigm Shift Toward South Asia?,' *The Washington Quarterly*, Winter 2002-03, 26:1, p. 151.

8 Lloyd I Rudolph, Susanne Hoeber Rudolph, 'The Making of US Foreign Policy for South Asia: Offshore Balancing in Historical Perspective,' *Economic and Political Weekly*, 25 February – 3 March 2006, Vol. 41, No. 8, p. 705.

9 Michael Patrick Cullinane and Alex Goodall, *The Open Door Era*, Edinburgh, Scotland, Edinburgh University Press, 2017, pp. 176-178.

10 Ibid., p. 178.

11 Xiaoxiong Yi, 'China's U.S. Policy Conundrum in the 1990s: Balancing Autonomy and Interdependence,' *Asian Survey*, August 1994, Vol. 34, No. 8, p. 675.

12 Harold A. Gould, 'Bill Clinton's Moribund South Asia Policy', *Economic and Political Weekly*, 23 November 1996, Vol. 31, No. 47, p. 3084.

13 James Risen and Jeff Gerth, "Breach at Los Alamos: A special report.; China Stole Nuclear Secrets for Bombs, U.S. Aides Say," *The New York Times*, 6 March, 1999 at https://www.nytimes.com/1999/03/06/world/breach-los-alamos-special-report-china-stole-nuclear-secrets-for-bombs-us-aides.html last accessed on 15 June 2024.

14 Lloyd I Rudolph, Susanne Hoeber Rudolph, 'The Making of US Foreign Policy for South Asia: Offshore Balancing in Historical Perspective,' *Economic and Political Weekly*, 25 February--3 March 2006, Vol. 41, No. 8, p. 706.

15 Lloyd I Rudolph, Susanne Hoeber Rudolph, 'The Making of US Foreign Policy for South Asia: Offshore Balancing in Historical Perspective,' *Economic and Political Weekly*, 25 February – 3 March 2006, Vol. 41, No. 8, p. 707.

16 US Relations with South Asia, Testimony of Teresita C. Schaffer, Director for South Asia, Center for Strategic & International Studies to the Asia-Pacific Subcommittee, House International Relations Committee, October 20, 1999 at https://csis-website-prod.s3.amazonaws.com/s3fs-public/legacy_files/files/attachments/ts991020_schaffer.pdf last accessed on 15 June 2024.

17 C. Raja Mohan, 'A Paradigm Shift toward South Asia,' *The Washington Quarterly*, Winter 2002-03, p. 154-155.

CHAPTER 4

Shifts in Global Security Paradigm

The global security landscape began to shift at the turn of the century marked by emergence of China as a major power driven by aspirations of global influence. This has significantly altered the global security dynamics, challenging the traditional dominance of the US. The economic growth of Asian countries, particularly China, has shifted the global economic centre, influencing the geopolitical landscape.

China experienced significant growth after Deng Xiaoping implemented a new economic policy in December 1978, known as the Open Door Policy, which allowed foreign businesses to operate in the country. This policy propelled China into becoming a major economic power by the end of the twentieth century. Additionally, China's membership in the World Trade Organization (WTO) further accelerated its already high growth economy and transformed it into a major trading nation. As China's economic interests expanded, so did its core interests, leading to a more assertive military and economic posture aimed at defending its expanding interests and attaining great power status.

China's assertiveness became particularly apparent following the global financial crisis of 2008. While most major economies were significantly impacted, China emerged relatively unscathed.[1] This success prompted a shift in China's foreign policy from a stance of 'hide and bide' to 'seize and lead.' China's current objectives include reestablishing dominance in Asia, asserting territorial claims, and reshaping the regional order.[2]

China also sought to engage with the US as a major global power, no longer content with playing a secondary role. It aimed to challenge the US-led global order and establish a Sino-dominated order in its place. While aware that this transformation would not occur overnight, China has endeavoured to increase its influence within existing world bodies during this transitional period.

China's assertive behaviour has been most evident in the South China Sea, where it has made expansive territorial claims. Under the leadership of Xi Jinping, China's ambitions have grown further. The country has taken unilateral actions and displayed a reluctance to adhere to rule-based systems.

These Chinese claims and actions have led to tensions with smaller countries in the region, including Japan. The East Asia and Western Pacific regions, where the US maintains important military assets and treaty commitments, are also areas of concern. The US is apprehensive that China's increasing assertiveness could potentially lead to a major conflict in the region. Therefore, the US aims to collaborate with other regional countries to establish a safe, secure, prosperous, free, and open Indo-Pacific region. The security focus of the US has now shifted to the Indo-Pacific after its withdrawal from Afghanistan.

In response to China's growing assertiveness, the US has developed its own IPS, incorporating the Quadrilateral Security Dialogue (Quad). Leveraging its improved relationship with India and engaging other South Asian nations, the US aims to maintain a favourable balance of power. Recognizing that China's expanding influence in South Asia undermines the strategic interests of both India and the US, they have joined forces with other democratic allies to uphold a free and open Indo-Pacific region.

China Challenges US Dominance through Maritime Expansion

China's emergence as a major power has driven its efforts to extend influence and safeguard interests. The primary area of competition between the US and China remains East Asia and the Western Pacific, where the US maintains significant military assets and treaty commitments. China seeks to challenge the US' position by leveraging its strengthened maritime presence.

Traditionally a coastal power, China's expanding economic interests have prompted a shift towards maritime orientation and a desire to project power into the Indian Ocean. Chinese military planning is aligned with this objective, involving the modernization of the People's Liberation Army (PLA) through the expansion of submarine fleets and aircraft carriers, extending beyond the capture of Taiwan.

China seeks to reduce its reliance on US naval powers to secure crucial sea lanes for oil transportation that pass through the Indian Ocean.[3] It aims to bolster its own naval capabilities at strategic chokepoints along the sea routes from the Persian Gulf to the South China Sea. Bases like Sanya on Hainan Island, which house submarines, strengthen China's naval presence.

These objectives of China led to changes in China's military doctrine, moving away from Mao Zedong and Zhou Enlai's 'People's War' doctrine, which primarily focused on land-based forces. China now sought to become a maritime power capable of defending its overseas interests. The 2006 Defence White Paper of the Chinese navy emphasized the development of sea-based forces, with strategic objectives focused on expanding offshore defensive operations, enhancing integrated maritime operations, and strengthening nuclear counter-attack capabilities.

China's increased emphasis on sea power was reflected in higher budget allocations for its navy. With the second-highest defence expenditure globally, China's navy surpasses the Indian navy both in terms of quality and quantity.

China's military modernization plans, including the development of a blue-water navy and advanced missile capabilities, present a formidable challenge to the US presence and its regional competitors such as Japan and India. Through a combination of trade, investment, military-industrial complex, and strategic alliances, China aims to reassert dominance in Asia, reclaim disputed territories, and reshape the regional order.

Central to China's long-term strategy is the objective of limiting the regional role of the US, marginalizing traditional US allies like Japan, and dictating the resolution of disputes on its own terms.[4] China's strategic vision includes hindering the effectiveness of the US Navy's operations within the first island chain and establishing dominance in the region. However, these efforts have led to escalating tensions and encounters between US and Chinese military forces.

China's Presence in South Asia Constrains India and US

China's presence in the Indian Ocean Region (IOR) is driven by its high dependence on the Malacca Straits for energy supply, which makes it vulnerable to economic coercion during conflicts with major powers like the US. To mitigate this vulnerability, China is investing in infrastructure to sustain alternative trade routes.[5] Since 2008, China has been striving to establish a naval presence in the IOR to facilitate economic activities and protect its strategic interests, under the pretext of countering terrorism and piracy. Construction began on China's first overseas quasi-military base in Djibouti in 2017, primarily serving as a naval logistics facility. China is also exploring the feasibility of a naval base at Gwadar port.

China has successfully pursued diplomatic ties with South Asian states. It has implemented a number of projects under the Belt and Road Initiative (BRI). It has invested in the construction of container ports, including the acquisition of a 99-year lease on the Hambantota port. This maritime expansion in India's periphery can be seen as an attempt to contain India and challenge US military power.

While China may not seek naval domination of the Indian Ocean due to India's geographical advantages, it aims to play a greater role in the region. China's presence in the Indian Ocean expands its strategic depth in India's vicinity and limits the maneuverability of the Indian navy. This growing maritime strength also serves to confine India within South Asia, with support from key allies like Pakistan, as the Sino-Indian relationship remains largely competitive.

In response to China's expanding presence in the IOR, India has been strengthening its relationships with strategic partners. India, along with Japan and the US, has expressed a collective intention to support strategic port development in the Indo-Pacific. India has also signed agreements with Singapore and the US to share logistics and actively collaborates with Canberra, Washington, and Tokyo in the political and military realms to address China's power projection in the Indo-Pacific. However, it is unlikely that this coalition will develop into a formal treaty alliance in the near future.

The Complex Rivalry between India and China

The rivalry between China and India in South Asia has had far-reaching implications for the region and the global order. This complex competition spans multiple domains, including geopolitics, economics, technology, ideology, and soft power, and is evident at bilateral, regional, and global levels.

The historical Sino-Indian border conflict in 1962 marked a turning point in India's approach to balancing China. While the US attempted to forge closer ties with China in 1971 through Pakistan, this move pushed India closer to the Soviet Union. However, the dynamics have since evolved dramatically.

The longstanding boundary dispute is a major source of tension between the two countries. With the longest non-demarcated border in the world, China and India have competing territorial claims in areas like Aksai Chin and Arunachal Pradesh. The 1962 war and subsequent skirmishes have left a historical burden on their relationship. The boundary dispute has resurfaced since 2013, leading to several military standoffs, including the 2017 trijunction standoff and the more recent 2020-21 conflict in Ladakh. These incidents have strained the bilateral relationship and eroded trust.

Another point of contention is China's suspicions regarding India's attitude towards Tibet. China has been wary of India's relationship with the Dalai Lama and the Tibetan government-in-exile based in Dharamshala. The Tibetan presence in India, including the deployment of the Special Frontier Force, has been a source of concern for Beijing. Additionally, India objects to China's reluctance to recognize Jammu and Kashmir as part of India and has shown opposition to China's BRI.

The strategic partnership between China and Pakistan has further fueled tensions between China and India. India views China's support for Pakistan, particularly through initiatives like the CPEC which passes through a disputed area as problematic. Delhi thinks that Beijing is enhancing Islamabad's military capabilities and providing diplomatic cover at international institutions. China's deepening ties with other South Asian countries, including Bangladesh, the Maldives, Myanmar, Nepal, and Sri Lanka, through the BRI, have also raised concerns for India, as it perceives China as encroaching on its sphere of influence. This perception has led to India's opposition to the BRI and increased its willingness to work with like-minded partners to counter Chinese influence.

Economic ties between China and India have grown, but so have tensions. India has raised concerns about the trade deficit, lack of market access, intellectual property theft, data security, and China's influence over Chinese companies operating in India. The economic dimension of the rivalry has played a role in India's decision not to join the Regional Comprehensive Economic Partnership in 2019.

At the regional and global levels, China's expanding influence and assertiveness in the IOR and its opposition to India's deepening ties with like-minded partners have added to the rivalry. China's unilateral actions in the South and East China Seas, as well as its borders with Bhutan, India, and Nepal, have raised concerns about Beijing's adherence to international rules and norms. India has sought to counterbalance China's influence by strengthening partnerships with countries like the US, Australia, France, and Japan, with a focus on maintaining a rules-based order in the Indian Ocean.

The differing visions of China and India for the region and their approaches on the global stage have further strained their relationship. China sees Asia in a hierarchical manner with itself at the top, while India advocates for a multipolar Asia.[6] China's resistance to India's aspirations for a permanent seat in the UN Security Council and its efforts to limit India's rise have been sources of contention. India, on the other hand, has cooperated with like-minded partners to counter Chinese influence in international organizations. Additionally, the ideological contrast between the two countries, particularly regarding political systems, has become a sensitive subject. China's efforts to undermine the effectiveness of democracies, including India, have reinforced the rivalry and hindered cooperation during the Covid crisis.

India, as a rising power, is determined not to play second fiddle to China. With a growing economy and population, India holds significant influence in the Asian region. However, it remains cautious of China's expansionist tendencies. Despite increasing economic ties, India maintains wariness of Beijing's intentions, particularly in relation to unresolved issues such as the border, Tibet, Pakistan, and geopolitical rivalries. India perceives China's actions as containment efforts and seeks to strengthen its strategic ties with the US to bolster its position and navigate the challenges posed by China and its neighbour, Pakistan.

Transformation of India–US Ties

A transformation has taken place in the India-US ties due to the need to contain Chinese regional assertiveness. The aim is to handle the threat of terrorism and due to growing economic synergy in the high-tech sector.[7] The US initially wanted a multi-polar Asia, which is not dominated by any single power. A multi-polar Asia with India, China and Japan as three different players would have helped it maintain balance of power in its favour.

To create a strong India under President George W. Bush, the US lifted sanctions imposed on India over its nuclear weapons programme and signed defence (2005) and nuclear (2008) cooperation agreements. President Barack Obama further emphasized the importance of the US-India relationship, considering it the 'indispensable partnership of the 21st century.'[8] Both New Delhi and Washington agreed that China was posing a challenge to the global order. However, China is now not content just being a pole in Asia. It wants a great power status for itself. This desire of China has created friction with the US and both countries are now engaged in an intense rivalry.

The US views China's rivalry with India as destabilizing, but it has also used it as an opportunity to strengthen its partnership with India. The US sees India as a geopolitical counterbalance, economic alternative and democratic contrast to China, which aligns with its interests in countering China's influence.

India, in turn, sees the US as crucial to its strategy of managing China. It has cooperated with the US in various ways, including internal and external balancing. India has found that its ties with the US have given China an incentive to engage with India more seriously. The US has also contributed to enhancing India's military, economic, and technological capabilities, and it is part of India's network of partnerships that help maintain a favorable balance of power in the region.

The US has also worked with India to counter Chinese resistance in international institutions. This has benefitted India in areas such as obtaining waivers, designations, and blocking China-Pakistan efforts related to issues like technology access, counter-terrorism, and Kashmir.

The competition between the US and China has significantly influenced Washington's perspectives and strategies in South Asia. The US now regards the CPEC with skepticism, citing concerns over its costs and lack of transparency. Additionally, there has been a heightened focus on smaller South Asian states by the US, with increased provisions of security and development assistance. This intensified competition between the US and China, coupled with apprehensions regarding Chinese activities in South Asia, has facilitated greater consultation, coordination, and cooperation between the US and India in the region. India, in turn, has demonstrated a growing openness to extra-regional involvement, particularly if it presents viable alternatives to China's initiatives.

India's Cold War-era opposition to the US's forward presence has been buried as it recognizes the value of balancing China's power. The US views India as a strategic partner and a net security provider in the Indian Ocean and beyond. The convergence of interests between the US and India has led to a closer alignment of their strategic aims, particularly in countering China's expansionist moves. India's democratic values, strategic ambitions, and regional influence frustrate China's efforts to establish a Sino-centric order. As the competition between China and the US intensifies, India finds itself in a 'swing state' position, similar to China's role during the Cold War.

India now actively seeks closer ties with the US. India desires American economic and technological assistance to support its rise as a major power and maintain its maritime preeminence in the IOR. India's defense acquisitions from the US have directly enhanced its capabilities vis-à-vis China. Initiatives like the Defence Trade and Technology Initiative (DTTI) aim to deepen defence cooperation and move towards co-development and co-production models.

While the primary area of US-China competition remains in East Asia and the western Pacific, China sees the US, particularly its ties with India, as part of its challenge in South Asia. China sees the US presence in the region as negative, although there have been some instances of cooperation or consultation in response to crises. However, as the rivalry between the US and China intensifies, it could potentially change the dynamics in the region. The traditional security concerns of India, namely Pakistan and China, have now become immediate and long-term concerns for Washington as well.

Despite these major changes, both countries still have some remaining concerns. First, India views the US-Pakistan's military ties as supporting China's strategy to keep India off balance. Trade disputes, barriers, and issues such as intellectual property, H1B visas, and market access have also hindered business ties between the two countries. India is wary of aligning too closely with the US due to the potential backlash from China, which could strengthen its influence over India's smaller neighbors and exacerbate India's security concerns. India values its strategic autonomy and sees itself as a rising great power, not a junior partner to the US. There is also an undercurrent of suspicion in New Delhi that Washington may be a fickle and unreliable partner, with shifting priorities and policies that could negatively affect India's national interests.

On the other hand, Beijing is attempting to woo and coerce India to prevent a closer US-India relationship that could challenge China's comfort. China has promised significant investments in India and has played on India's fears of the US changing its stance on China in the future. India is concerned about the emergence of a US-China condominium where China remains hostile to India, and the US is unavailable as a balancing power. Past instances, such as the Obama administration's silence on the Sino-Indian border dispute and the cancellation of a joint army drill in Arunachal state, have left a lingering sense of doubt among Indian policymakers about US support in times of crisis.

From the US perspective, there are doubts about India's claim to global power. Some believe that India's material basis of power is weak and insecure due to the failure to implement necessary economic reforms. There is a perception that India lacks the economic clout to match China and fulfill the role of a regional security provider. Some American policymakers see an alignment with India as costly and risky, preferring a deal with China for shared hegemony. They argue that the US would not be able to fulfill a commitment to Indian security against China and Pakistan and that an alignment with India presents more risks than benefits.

De-hyphenation of India and Pakistan gets more pronounced under Obama

During President Obama's tenure, India-US relations experienced significant progress despite initial challenges. Obama initially tried to move away from the Bush administration's policy of treating India and Pakistan separately, advocating for an integrated approach in the region. While urging Pakistan to combat extremism and cooperate in counterterrorism efforts, he also encouraged dialogue between India and Pakistan regarding the Kashmir issue. However, India remained cautious of potential US involvement in Kashmir, fearing it could disrupt security cooperation.

Following this, Obama's proposal of a 'Group of Two' (G-2) partnership with China garnered attention but also raised significant concerns. The aim was to collectively address global challenges. However, China's reluctance to participate resulted in a loss of momentum for the idea. It's worth noting that China, which had been eager for great power status, missed out on this opportunity at the time.

The de-hyphenation of India and Pakistan, initiated under Bush, continued under Obama, acknowledging both countries' individual merits. India was recognized as a crucial partner in managing Asia's power balance and addressing global challenges, while Pakistan's role in the war on terror was acknowledged.

Obama's visit to India in 2010 marked a significant milestone, with endorsements for India's bid for a permanent UN Security Council seat and easing export controls on sensitive technology imposed after India's 1998 Pokhran II nuclear tests. Notably, Obama refrained from visiting Pakistan during his presidency, signaling a further separation between India and Pakistan. However, he pushed for India to liberalize its economy and reform its Intellectual Property Rights regime under pressure from US corporations.

India-US relations continued to strengthen, with Obama making history as the first US president to attend India's Republic Day parade and visit the country twice while in office. Modi emerged as a key partner, which was particularly evident during the Paris Accord meeting in December 2015.

During Modi's subsequent visit to the US in June 2016, the Obama administration elevated India's status to that of a major defence partner.

This designation aimed to redefine the growing defence collaboration between the two nations, offering India enhanced cooperation. Although not equivalent to US relationships with NATO allies or Israel, it marked a departure from India's previous position on the periphery of American influence.

India gained access to advanced US defence equipment and technology, with opportunities for co-development and co-production emerging as new areas of cooperation. This evolution underscored the deepening strategic partnership between India and the US, paving the way for closer defence ties in the future.

Shift in Power Dynamics in the Indo-Pacific

The Obama administration faced a significant setback in maintaining American leadership in the Indo-Pacific, particularly concerning China's island reclamation activities in the South China Sea. Despite the region's historical territorial disputes and economic importance, including vast oil, gas, and mineral reserves and critical trade routes, China's aggressive expansion largely went unchecked during Obama's tenure.

Under Xi Jinping's leadership, China began reclaiming land in the South China Sea in 2013 to bolster its strategic and maritime interests. Despite international concerns, the Obama administration's response remained passive, allowing China to steadily tighten its grip on the region. Even Obama's defence secretary, Ash Carter, criticized the administration's leniency, which emboldened China's ambitious expansion efforts.

In 2013, the Philippines filed an arbitration case challenging China's sovereignty claims, but China dismissed the case and refused to participate in the legal proceedings. Despite growing frustration from Southeast Asian nations, the Obama administration did little to counter China's actions, enabling it to reclaim over 3,200 acres of land in the South China Sea by 2015.

While China claimed its activities were peaceful, satellite images revealed militarization of these artificial islands with runways, ports, and military structures. The administration's neutral stance and limited practical actions further underscored its inability to enforce international rulings.

The change in Indian leadership in 2014 brought Narendra Modi to power, leading to joint statements with the US condemning actions in the South China Sea. This marked the first official and on-the-record projection of a joint front against China by India and the US. Reports also surfaced about potential joint patrols in disputed waters.

In 2016, The Hague ruled against China's claims, deeming its island-building efforts unlawful. Despite this, China continued its expansion, signaling a significant shift in power dynamics in the Indo-Pacific. These developments made clear that in the Indo-Pacific there was no country powerful enough to stop China from its misadventures. Despite conducting freedom of navigation operations in the South China Sea, the US maintained a neutral stance towards all parties, and its official policy had limited practical significance in enforcing the UN ruling.

Admiral Harry Harris, during a security conference in India, urged joint efforts with the US, Japan, and Australia through the Quadrilateral Security Dialogue to address regional challenges. He believed such an alliance could have deterred China's aggressive actions earlier and stressed the importance of initiating it, despite its delayed commencement.

Transformative Shifts in India-US Relations under the Trump Presidency

During the Trump presidency, initially, there was a sense of uncertainty in the Modi government. He started by imposing visa restrictions and criticizing India as the 'tariff king.' He also grouped India and China together on trade and accused them of receiving an unfair advantage on climate change, which led to US withdrawal from the Paris climate accord.

However, soon after crucial foreign policy shifts took place, and a more positive foreign policy framework emerged for India after Prime Minister Modi visited the White House in June 2017. There was a revival of the Quad and renaming the Pacific Command as the 'Indo-Pacific' Command. Over a few months in 2018, significant developments took place, such as India's categorization under Strategic Trade Authorization (STA)-1, the first 2+2 dialogue, the signing of COMCASA, and approvals related to CAATSA waivers, Iran oil purchases, and Chabahar.

There were major changes in US policy towards Pakistan and China, two of India's biggest concerns. Trump declared an end to aid to Pakistan, citing its support for terrorists. The US suspended military assistance and sales to Pakistan and played a leading role in Pakistan's grey-listing at the Financial Action Task Force (FATF). The US also offered India moral and military support to counter Chinese aggression, took a stance against China's BRI and 5G telecom push, and pledged a response to China's loans in the Indo-Pacific region.

Under the presidency of Donald Trump, the US's relations with several close allies deteriorated significantly. However, the relationship between the US and India experienced notable improvements during this period. The defence and intelligence cooperation between the two countries reached new heights, with a particular focus on maritime security through various agreements. Bilateral trade also witnessed steady growth. At a personal level, there appeared to be a strong bond between Prime Minister Narendra Modi and President Trump.

One of Donald Trump's campaign promises was to end the war in Afghanistan. He negotiated an agreement with the Taliban in 2020 to withdraw all US forces.[9] India was initially unhappy with Trump's negotiations with the Taliban, but even that served a purpose. The withdrawal of the US from Afghanistan has also removed a factor that previously had hindered closer India-US relations—the support of Pakistan.

Defence cooperation between India and the US significantly improved. There was an increase in equipment sales, joint military exercises, and technological collaboration. Since 2008, the US's defence exports to India grew from zero to a cumulative $20 billion, and it now accounts for 15 per cent of India's military equipment purchases. During the Trump administration, India was able to sign defence agreements with the US that had eluded previous Indian governments. These arrangements promoted the interoperability of the two countries' forces and covered everything from logistics to communications. The Indian armed forces conducted more joint exercises with the US military since 2005 than with all other countries' militaries combined. The annual Malabar naval exercise, which initially involved India and the US, expanded to include Japan and was expected to include Australia after a 13-year hiatus.[10]

Economic ties also strengthened between India and the US. In 2019, the US surpassed China to become India's largest trading partner. While India's trade with China declined in 2019, reaching $84 billion, its trade with the US increased to $143 billion. India ranked as the ninth-largest goods trading partner of the US, and US exports to India in goods and services supported around 200,000 jobs.

However, the Trump Administration also showed its disregard for the world order, international institutions, and multilateral cooperation. This made India-US relations occasionally appear transactional. This was in contrast to previous Bush and Obama administrations, which considered India's rise in the interest of the US. There were also some differences over the central issue of China between India and the US. India sought to maintain a delicate balance with Beijing. India's vision for a 'free, open, and inclusive Indo-Pacific,' outlined by Modi in 2018, differs from the American vision, as it includes accommodating China and focuses on uncontroversial issues.

Strengthening the US-India Strategic Partnership to Counter Assertive China

The increasing assertiveness of China has brought about a significant power shift in the Indo-Pacific region, leading to heightened tensions and concerns about regional stability. During the Trump presidency, both India and the US deepened their strategic partnership to address these challenges and counter China's expanding influence, particularly in the Indian Ocean and beyond. China's aggressive diplomatic approach, known as 'Wolf Warrior diplomacy,' targeted not only the US but also India, raising alarm bells in both countries.

India, in particular, voiced concerns about China's growing military presence in the Indian Ocean, its strengthening ties with Pakistan, and its interference in neighbouring countries like Myanmar, Nepal, and Sri Lanka. Additionally, China's opposition to Indian interests in international forums like the United Nations further strained relations between the two Asian giants.

The border tensions between India and China reached a boiling point in April 2020 when China attempted to redefine the Line of Actual Control in the Ladakh region, resulting in a deadly clash in June 2020 that claimed the lives of 20 Indian soldiers and an undisclosed number of Chinese troops.

President Trump, aware of the challenges posed by China, reshaped his administration to align with his strategic vision. His strategy towards China, influenced by his earlier writings in 'The America We Deserve,' focused on addressing issues such as unfair trade practices, intellectual property theft, and the significant trade deficit through negotiations and sanctions.

Trump also sought to cultivate a personal relationship with President Xi Jinping of China to leverage tough sanctions on North Korea. His administration prioritized enhancing communication between the US and Chinese military forces, as outlined in the National Defense Strategy of December 2017.

Furthermore, Trump advocated for a comprehensive approach to challenge China's economic dominance, reform misconduct at the World Trade Organization, and foster a 'free and open Indo-Pacific' region through collaboration with allies and partners.[11] This IPS, formalized during his presidency, aimed to coordinate efforts across various government agencies and enlist support from regional allies.

Recognizing that the challenges in the Indo-Pacific region exceeded the capacity of any single country to address alone, President Trump emphasized cooperation with like-minded allies and partners to tackle common issues. Ahead of his Asia trip in November 2017, he focused on strengthening military alliances with Japan, South Korea, Australia, the Philippines, and Thailand, while also expanding partnerships with Singapore, Taiwan, New Zealand, and Mongolia. Operationalizing the major defense partnership with India was a significant milestone in this strategic approach, following Trump's meeting with Prime Minister Narendra Modi. President Trump also focused on enhancing security relationships with Southeast Asian partners like Vietnam, Indonesia, Malaysia, and sustained engagements with Brunei.

South Asia's Resurgence in US Foreign Policy

The change in global security landscape because of the rise of assertive China has also prompted a strategic recalibration by the US and has given renewed significance to South Asia in US foreign policy. South Asia is important for global geopolitical interests because of its strategic location. It connects the Middle East, Central Asia, and the Indian Ocean. However, China's escalating presence in the region, marked by significant economic investments and strategic collaborations, has heightened concerns about regional stability.

To counterbalance Beijing's expanding influence, the US is strategically aligning with South Asian nations, notably India, to safeguard regional stability. This strategy involves forging security partnerships and alliances to address shared concerns such as counterterrorism and regional security threats, while also curbing China's influence.

During President Trump's administration, concerted efforts were made to cultivate emerging partnerships with countries across South Asia, including Sri Lanka, the Maldives, Bangladesh, and Nepal. This underscores a broader strategy aimed at bolstering US presence and influence in the region.

However, China's assertive presence, exemplified by initiatives like the CPEC, has heightened geopolitical tensions, particularly in Pakistan, where Beijing's investments have bolstered its influence.[12] Additionally, China's expansive BRI projects have extended its reach across various South Asian nations, intensifying competition with the US.

In this landscape, India emerges as a key player, actively seeking to enhance its strategic partnership with the US to counterbalance China's regional dominance and address pressing security concerns. This partnership serves as a linchpin in navigating the evolving geopolitical dynamics of South Asia.

Attempts to Restore American Leadership

The Obama Administration witnessed a significant power shift in the Western Pacific and South China Sea region, highlighting the lack of a country capable of curbing China's assertiveness. While Asia's economic growth brought global benefits, it also drew attention to territorial disputes and challenges to international laws and norms, notably in the South China Sea. These concerns were further exacerbated by China's BRI.

In response to these shifting dynamics, the Indo-Pacific emerged as a geopolitical framework, initially proposed by Japanese Prime Minister Shinzô Abe in 2007 during his address to the Indian parliament. It aimed to strengthen ties among democracies in the Indian and Pacific Oceans to safeguard sea lanes and promote prosperity. Recognizing the interconnectedness and significance of the region, the Indo-Pacific construct encompasses a broader geographical scope, emphasizing economic, security, and diplomatic considerations.

The Indo-Pacific framework seeks to address evolving challenges and opportunities, including the promotion of a rules-based order, freedom of navigation, and shared prosperity. It encourages closer cooperation among nations to tackle maritime security concerns, territorial disputes, and the implications of initiatives like the BRI.

This construct signifies the interconnectedness and growing importance of the Indo-Pacific region in global affairs. With over 65 per cent of global GDP and vital trade routes passing through its waters, the region's economic significance cannot be ignored. Viewing the Indian and Pacific Oceans as a single, continuous area became imperative for effective policy-making, realizing that the interests of countries in both regions are interdependent.

The concept gained traction when President Donald Trump expressed support for it in 2017, leading to widespread adoption by many countries. The US aimed to restore its global leadership, particularly in the Indo-Pacific, and officially announced the IPS during President Trump's Asia trip in November 2017. This strategy focused on economic integration, defence cooperation, and countering China's BRI to maintain US influence in the region.

Japan played a crucial role in the development of the IPS, with like-minded countries such as Australia and India joining forces to counter shared concerns about China. The IPS has been incorporated into US national security and defense strategies and has gained traction among various countries and regional groupings, including ASEAN, France, Germany, and the European Union.

These actors have also launched specific initiatives to complement their Indo-Pacific strategies. The recent launch of the Indo-Pacific Economic Framework for Prosperity (IPEF) by the Biden administration is one such notable initiative. As India holds significant importance in the Indo-Pacific, these strategies and initiatives have direct implications for New Delhi.

NOTES

1 Bonnie S. Glaser, Lyle Morris, 'Chinese Perceptions of U.S. Decline and Power,' The Jamestown Foundation, China Brief, Volume: 9 Issue: 14, 9 July 2009 at https://jamestown.org/program/chinese-perceptions-of-u-s-decline-and-power/ last accessed on 16 June 2024

2 Mohan Malik, 'Balancing Act: The China-India-U.S. Triangle', *World Affairs*, Spring 2016, p. 48.

3 David Brewster, 'An Indian Ocean dilemma: Sino-Indian rivalry and China's strategic vulnerability in the Indian Ocean,' *Journal of the Indian Ocean Region*, Volume 11, Issue 1, 2015, pp. 48-59.

4 Mohan Malik, 'Balancing Act: The China-India-U.S. Triangle', *World Affairs*, Spring 2016, p. 48.

5 Muntazir Ali, 'China as a Factor of Stability in South Asia: Problems and Prospects,' *Pakistan Horizon*, July 2010, Vol. 63, No. 3, pp. 69-70.

6 J. Mohan Malik, 'South Asia in China's Foreign Relations,' *Pacifica Review*, Volume 13, Number 1, February 2001, p. 78.

7 Shivshankar Menon, 'Choices: Inside the Making of India's Foreign Policy,' Penguin Random House India, New Delhi, 2016, pp. 82-83.

8 The White House, Office of the Press Secretary, Remarks by President Obama and Prime Minister Singh in Joint Press Conference in New Delhi, India at https://obamawhitehouse.archives.gov/the-press-office/2010/11/08/remarks-president-obama-and-prime-minister-singh-joint-press-conference last accessed on 16 June 2024

9 Terry Gross, 'Trump's Deal To End War In Afghanistan Leaves Biden With "A Terrible Situation"', NPR, 4 March 2021 at https://www.npr.org/2021/03/04/973604904/trumps-deal-to-end-war-in-afghanistan-leaves-biden-with-a-terrible-situation last accessed on 16 June 2024

10 Shivshankar Menon, 'League of Nationalists: How Trump and Modi Refashioned the U.S.-Indian Relationship', *Foreign Affairs*, September/October 2020 at https://www.foreignaffairs.com/articles/united-states/2020-08-11/modi-india-league-nationalists last accessed on 16 June 2024

11 Michael Pillsbury, 'The Trump Administration's Indo-Pacific Strategy,' in *The Struggle for Power: U.S.-China Relations in the 21st Century*, The Aspen Institute, Washington DC, p. 31.

12 Fatima Raza, 'China in South Asia: CPEC and the Indo-Pacific at the Heart of China-Pakistan Collaboration,' South Asian Voices, Stimson Center, Washington DC, 24 July 2023 at https://southasianvoices.org/china-in-south-asia-pakistans-domestic-upheaval-challenges-china/ last accessed on 16 June 2024

CHAPTER 5

China's Rise and South Asia

India has held sway over South Asia and the IOR since the departure of the British from the region in 1947 due to its central geographic position and strong political, economic, and cultural bonds with neighbouring countries. However, in the past two decades, a subtle geopolitical shift has occurred as a result of increased Chinese involvement in the region, posing a challenge to India's dominance and occasionally its security.

China's economic rise and increased engagement with South Asian nations in infrastructure and security spheres have prompted these countries, especially India's smaller neighbours, to reassess their ties with the larger neighbour. Unlike other major external powers, China enjoys the advantage of close geographical proximity to South Asia and possesses the capability and willingness to provide extensive infrastructural financing. Its relationship with South Asian nations increasingly emphasizes the military dimension.

China's economic and political influence has rapidly expanded across South Asia through investments, trade, military cooperation, and diplomatic and cultural initiatives, enhancing its visibility and altering regional dynamics.

China's Strategic Imperatives in South Asia

China's South Asia policy is largely shaped by its military security concerns with pronounced focus on India and the need to safeguard Tibet, considered China's 'soft strategic underbelly.'[1] China has boundary disputes with India and Bhutan. These disputes stem from the 1947 partition of British India and the 1950 Chinese Occupation of Tibet. While India's borders contracted after the 1947 Partition, China's expanded with the occupation of Tibet in 1950, leading to physical contact and tensions between the two nations.

These unresolved territorial disputes have led to significant conflicts, including a full-scale war in 1962 and near-conflict in 1987. Despite agreements in 1993 and 1996, talks over the past two decades have failed. The territorial disputes have been complicated further by third-party interests, particularly Pakistan's, due to China's historical alliance with the country.

China also aims to prevent the rise of potential regional competitors. It maintains a unique approach to interstate relations, viewing states as either hostile or subordinate. This perspective influences China's alliances and support strategies.

India's perspective differs from China's, historically hoping for joint Sino–Indian leadership against Western influence. However, China's increasing influence in South Asia has strained this vision, with India perceiving it detrimental to its interests.

Both nations desire a multipolar world but disagree on its structure. China envisions an 'inner core' including the US, Russia, and itself. Both countries court the US to balance their relationships, though China remains cautious of India's rising political influence and alignment with the US, fearing it could become a frontline state against China.

China's primary strategic imperative in the Indian Ocean is safeguarding its vital sea lines of communications (SLOCs), particularly those traversing the Strait of Hormuz, encircling the Indian subcontinent, and passing through the Straits of Malacca. The region's geography poses a significant challenge for China, as it is predominantly enclosed and controlled by powers such as India and the US. Consequently, China lacks control over key chokepoints and encounters difficulties in projecting naval power due to the distance and inadequate support facilities.

Given its critical reliance on shipping routes through the Indian Ocean, China has embarked on port construction projects along these vital passages. To address its vulnerabilities, China is employing various strategies, including naval expansion, securing access to Indian Ocean ports, fostering overland transportation links, and cultivating economic and political ties with regional states. However, these efforts only partially mitigate China's strategic weaknesses.

China is also enhancing overland connections to the Indian Ocean through initiatives such as pipelines and economic corridors spanning Myanmar, Pakistan, and the Xinjiang province. Yet, the susceptibility of these connections to interdiction undermines their effectiveness in alleviating China's strategic vulnerabilities. Moreover, China's bid to challenge India's influence in the Indian Ocean adds a maritime dimension to their rivalry.[2]

China also plans to strategically leverage South Asian port cities to stimulate development in its western hinterland, recognizing them as gateways to Gulf countries, Africa, and Europe. To achieve this goal, China has been actively investing in infrastructure projects across nations such as Pakistan, Sri Lanka, and Myanmar. These initiatives not only enhance connectivity between mainland China and South Asia but also extend China's economic reach westward.

President Xi Jinping's BRI stands as a cornerstone for advancing China's commercial and diplomatic interests on a global scale. This initiative is poised to shape Chinese foreign policy in the foreseeable future. President Xi emphasized the importance of South Asia in this context during his address to the Pakistani parliament in April 2015, highlighting the region as a convergence point for the land and maritime silk roads.[3] South Asia thus emerges as a pivotal focus area for China's BRI, encompassing its Maritime Silk Road component, which aims to provide China access to the Indian Ocean via the region, notably benefiting its southwestern provinces.

Beijing's economic aid to South Asian states reinforces its military security objectives. Chinese leaders regularly visit Nepal, Bangladesh, and Sri Lanka to demonstrate involvement and reassure friends in the region that any improvement in India-China relationship would not affect them negatively.

Instruments of Chinese Influence in South Asia

China's growing economic prowess is its primary lever of influence. It proactively uses this tool in the South Asian region. Over the past two decades, China's export-led growth strategy has propelled it to become a prominent exporter of goods to South Asia. However, recognizing the need for diversified influence, China has expanded its toolkit beyond trade and investment. Diplomatic and cultural initiatives now complement its economic endeavors, while efforts to strengthen military ties underscore its multifaceted approach to enhancing influence in the region.

Economic Engagement

In South Asia, geostrategic considerations predominantly shape China's policy rather than the interplay between economics and security. China's economic engagement with South Asia is to supplement its military security goals. China's flagship BRI aims to enhance connectivity and infrastructure development across South Asia, with projects like the China-Pakistan Economic Corridor (CPEC) and the Bangladesh-China-India-Myanmar Economic Corridor (BCIM-EC). BRI projects involve significant investments in ports, railways, highways, and energy infrastructure, fostering economic ties between China and South Asian countries. However, concerns have been raised about debt sustainability, environmental impact and sovereignty issues related to BRI projects.

China has become a major trading partner for South Asian countries, with increasing bilateral trade volumes and investments in diverse sectors. China provides development assistance and loans to South Asian nations, supporting infrastructure development, poverty alleviation, and other socio-economic projects. Soft loans and grants are often used as tools for building diplomatic influence and securing strategic interests in the region.

Military Engagement

China has expanded its military presence and influence in South Asia, particularly through strategic partnerships with countries like Pakistan and closer engagement with others. The development of military infrastructure and joint exercises contribute to China's security footprint in the region.

China is a significant supplier of arms to South Asian countries, including Pakistan, Bangladesh, and Sri Lanka, enhancing its military influence. Defence cooperation agreements, joint exercises, and military training programmes further strengthen China's military ties in the region.

However, China's increasing naval activities in the Indian Ocean, including submarine deployments, raise security concerns for neighbouring countries and contribute to regional dynamics.

Diplomatic Outreach

China engages in diplomatic initiatives to foster positive relations with South Asian nations, participating in regional forums. Multilateral platforms like the SCO, South Asian Association for Regional Cooperation (SAARC), Indian Ocean Region Forum and BRICS provide avenues for diplomatic engagement and cooperation.

Pakistan

China's relations with Pakistan outweigh other bilateral relationships in South Asia. Since its modest and tentative beginnings in 1950, the China-Pakistan relationship has evolved into a robust alliance, characterized by mutual support and cooperation. China provided significant support to Pakistan during various conflicts with India, including wars and disputes over Kashmir. Both nations proudly declare that their bond transcends mere diplomacy, likening it to a connection 'deeper than the oceans, higher than the mountains, and sweeter than honey.'[4] Nurturing a strong and enduring partnership with China occupies a central part in Pakistan's foreign policy agenda.

China views Pakistan as a significant regional partner that helps contain India's regional growth and outreach. The China–Pakistan 'special relationship' is part of China's grand strategy to mould the South Asian security environment. China's *entente cordiale* with Pakistan remains strong, underpinned by nuclear and missile cooperation. China gains military, geopolitical, and regional benefits through its relationship with Pakistan, despite occasional frictions.

Evolution of the Sino-Pakistan Relationship

In the early 1950s, China initially maintained neutrality between India and Pakistan. However, in 1956, the signing of the Treaty of Friendship between Pakistani Prime Minister Huseyn Shaheed Suhrawardy and Chinese Premier Zhou Enlai marked the beginning of a burgeoning relationship between the two nations. The Sino-India Border War of 1962 shifted China's alignment towards Pakistan, and during Pakistan's conflict with India in 1965, China extended diplomatic support to its ally. The early 1970s saw a strengthening of ties as Pakistan played a pivotal role in facilitating improved relations between the US and China.

Following the Tiananmen Square protests in 1989, Pakistan and Cuba stood out as the only two countries to provide crucial official support to the People's Republic of China. However, India's revocation of Article 370 of its constitution in August 2019, which pertained to the special status of Jammu and Kashmir, drew criticism from both Beijing and Islamabad for different reasons. They contested various areas of the Indian state of Jammu and Kashmir: China objected to the inclusion of the Aksai Chin region in the newly established Union Territory of Ladakh, which it presently occupies. India clarified that the constitutional amendment did not change its external boundaries or territorial claims.

Meanwhile, China refrained from criticizing administrative changes introduced by Pakistan in the Gilgit-Baltistan region of Pakistan-occupied Kashmir. India dismissed Chinese criticism, asserting that China had no standing on the issue, as it was purely an internal matter.[5]

Nuclear Collaboration Cements the Foundation of China-Pakistan Relations

China uses its nuclear and missile technology transfers to Pakistan, to resist India's rise and counterbalance Western powers. The nuclear collaboration between China and Pakistan stands as a cornerstone of their bilateral relations. Pakistan's pursuit of nuclear capabilities dates back to the early 1950s when its scientists received training in civilian nuclear technology from the US. However, India's nuclear test in 1974 spurred Pakistan's determination to achieve nuclear parity. In this endeavour, Pakistan sought assistance from China, while the US turned a blind eye as Pakistan was helping it to transfer weapons in Afghanistan during the Soviet Union's invasion of Afghanistan.

China played a significant role in aiding Pakistan's nuclear energy technology development, and by the 1990s, Pakistan intensified its nuclear weapons programme, reportedly acquiring between 7 and 12 nuclear warheads based on Chinese designs and technology, with assistance from Chinese scientists.[6] A pivotal moment came in September 1986 when China and Pakistan signed an agreement to transfer civil nuclear technology.

Following India's nuclear tests in 1998, Pakistan conducted its own tests, believed to have been supported by Beijing. The collaboration between China and Pakistan on nuclear matters was further evident when both nations attempted to block India's exemption at the Nuclear Suppliers Group (NSG) after India applied for membership in May 2016.[7] China has opposed India's entry into the NSG, arguing that only countries that have signed the Non-Proliferation Treaty (NPT) should be allowed membership.

Challenges Emerge in China-Pakistan Economic Relationship

In recent times, Pakistan's economy has been facing significant challenges. While the presence of the US in Afghanistan led to some assistance for Pakistan in exchange for its support in American operations against the Taliban and al-Qaeda, the US withdrawal from Afghanistan and South Asia has left Pakistan seeking alternative solutions for its struggling economy. As a result, Beijing has emerged as the most promising option for Pakistan amidst its economic downturn. This has led to Pakistan's increased economic dependence on Beijing. Beijing claims that it has initiated the CPEC to boost the Pakistani economy. Under this programme, China has invested billions of dollars in Pakistan and has supported Pakistan on global platforms. Many in Pakistan also believe that CPEC could be a game-changer, creating new jobs and bringing economic prosperity to the Pakistani people.

In reality, China has started CPEC for its own strategic and economic gains. CPEC is the first chapter of the Chinese One Belt One Road (OBOR) plan, subsequently referred to as the BRI. In China, many policymakers believe that the country is presently facing a 'middle-income trap,' and BRI could be a tool to overcome it. Chinese President Xi Jinping also favours BRI, viewing it as a means for China to achieve its next stage of development.

Additionally, CPEC projects offers significant strategic advantages to China. The successful implementation of CPEC would elevate China into a major maritime power, providing access to both the Pacific and the Indian Ocean. China also faces the Malacca Dilemma, and the successful implementation of CPEC is likely to reduce its dependence on the Malacca straits. However, the disputed status of Gilgit-Baltistan poses another problem for China. To overcome this, the Chinese have encouraged Pakistan to change its constitutional status.[8]

The CPEC is a vital component of the BRI. It has completed ten years in July 2023. Despite facing criticism, Pakistani officials persist in their support for the project. However, internal weaknesses, planning issues, and implementation gaps within Pakistan have hindered CPEC's ability to fully realize its transformative potential.

China has been considerate towards Pakistan during its economic crisis and has provided help because, in the Chinese scheme of things, Pakistan serves a larger role. China aims to keep Pakistan as an economically and militarily powerful nation to continue creating a two-front situation on the border for India. A tottering Pakistan would not serve this objective. Additionally, Pakistan serves as an important diplomatic conduit with the Muslim world. However, this role of Pakistan is diminishing as the country is perceived as a sponsor of terrorism. This has made several Gulf countries wary of Pakistan. Nonetheless, Pakistan can be useful in dealing with countries like Turkey or Malaysia.

However, the China-Pakistan economic relationship now appears to be in trouble. Rising terrorism, particularly from groups like Tehreek-i-Taliban Pakistan (TTP), threatens Chinese interests in Pakistan, leading to tensions and stalled projects. Pakistan's financial crisis, marked by delayed payments to Chinese companies and uncooperative behavior from officials, has further strained relations.

In this situation, the Chinese are not inclined to show further generosity to Pakistan, which is facing problems of dwindling forex reserves and a massive energy crisis. China is also reluctant to interfere in the messy domestic political situation of Islamabad. The situation has become further complex as China wants Pakistan to fulfill IMF obligations before extending any help, whereas the IMF has raised red flags over the CPEC projects in Pakistan. As Pakistan is simultaneously gripped by social and political problems, some experts advocate for Pakistan to first address its societal issues before fixing its economy.

China could not provide much economic assistance to Pakistan because it was on the Grey List of FATF for some time.[9] However, the removal of Pakistan from the FATF 'Grey List' has made it easier for the country to receive financial aid from the IMF, World Bank, ADB, and the European Union. This might help Pakistan improve its precarious financial situation.

Defence Ties

Since 1962, China has remained a consistent source of military equipment for the Pakistan army, assisting in the establishment and modernization of ammunition factories and providing technological support. Both countries are engaged in multiple projects aimed at enhancing their military capabilities. Recently, the Pakistan Army has integrated Chinese-made VT-4 battle tanks, manufactured by the state-owned armoured vehicle producer Norinco, into its arsenal, deploying them for offensive operations.[10] Additionally, Pakistan has acquired Chinese-made combat drones, bolstering its unmanned aerial vehicle capabilities.

In response to an earlier information-sharing agreement between India and the US, Pakistan and China signed a defence pact in 2020. Pakistan sought this pact as it was concerned about the India-US pact and the advantages it would offer to India in a future conflict over Kashmir.[11] While the specifics of the China-Pakistan pact remain undisclosed, it is believed to involve intelligence sharing regarding Indian border movements.[12]

Following the pact's signing, both nations announced plans for a large-scale joint military exercise named Shaheen IX, building on the success of previous exercises such as Shaheen VIII. This exercise involved approximately 50 warplanes. Both sides also engaged in battle simulations. The increasing frequency of China-Pakistan military exercises underscores the deepening partnership between the two nations. The primary objective of these exercises is to counter Indian and American influence. Historically, this robust defence relationship has also served to check Soviet influence in the region.

While China and Pakistan do not share a formal alliance,[13] their relationship is undergoing significant evolution, particularly in response to increasing Indo-US defence cooperation. The Doklam and eastern Ladakh stand-offs between China and India underscore China's efforts to assert dominance in Asia, prompting increased military aid to Pakistan. Over time, steady growth in defence collaboration has fostered compatibility and operational synergy, with China supplying advanced technology to bolster Pakistan's precision strike capabilities. Additionally, amidst shifting geopolitical dynamics, China is contemplating the utilization of the Gwadar port as a naval base, further solidifying its strategic presence in the region.[14]

Factors Driving China-Pakistan Relationship

The bilateral relationship between China and Pakistan is driven by multiple factors, each contributing to the depth and resilience of their ties.

Structural Explanation

One significant driver of the China-Pakistan relationship lies in their mutual rivalry with India. Since the 1962 war, China has vested considerable interest in Pakistan, recognizing its potential to create a two-front scenario along India's border. A powerful and independent Pakistan serves China's strategic interests in the region.

China Aspires for Asian Leadership

China is increasingly positioning itself as a global powerhouse, but its ambitions for regional dominance are particularly pronounced in Asia. Central to this vision is Pakistan, which plays a pivotal role in China's overarching 'Asian Dream.' China's strategic approach towards Pakistan is also shaped by its aim to mitigate and counterbalance Indian influence, further solidifying its position as a leading force in Asia.[15]

Cold War Politics

Cold War dynamics further solidified the China-Pakistan relationship. Despite being a part of the Western alliance, Pakistan's quick diplomatic recognition of the PRC positioned it as a pivotal ally. China, wary of encirclement by the Soviet Union, cultivated close ties with Pakistan, which played a crucial intermediary role in the 1972 US-China rapprochement.

China's Territorial Integrity

China's concerns over its self-defined borders and territorial integrity also contribute to its alliance with Pakistan. Pakistan's support helps counter separatist movements and mitigates the spread of radical Islamist ideologies, particularly in regions like Xinjiang. Additionally, the settlement of the border dispute between China and Pakistan in 1964 has removed potential conflicts of interest.

Challenging Neighbourhood

China's complex neighbourhood, characterized by potential rivals like Japan, India, and Russia, necessitates strategic partnerships. Pakistan's support helps China balance its main competitor, India, while also providing stability amidst weaker and unstable neighbours like North Korea.

Other Benefits to China

Pakistan has been useful to China as a diplomatic conduit. It has facilitated improved relations with the US and access to organizations like the World Bank. Additionally, initiatives like the CPEC and the port of Gwadar bolster China's geopolitical and geo-economic strategy, offering avenues for energy security and overcoming the Malacca Dilemma.

China indirectly benefited from the US presence in Afghanistan, as US aid and support to Pakistan contributed to stability along China's western border. This enhanced security aligned with China's strategic interests. Though US has subsequently withdrawn from Afghanistan.

Geostrategic Considerations

The evolving Indo-US partnership in South Asia, along with enduring India-Pakistan tensions, shapes China's approach towards the region. Pakistan's recent defence pact with China suggests a desire to counter initiatives like the QUAD alliance. Pakistan's cooperation also holds potential significance in managing the situation in Afghanistan, reflecting the multifaceted nature of China-Pakistan relations.

China Remains Central to Pakistan's Foreign Policy

China remains a cornerstone of Pakistan's foreign policy, retaining a pivotal role in shaping its strategic outlook. Despite facing local opposition to certain initiatives within the CPEC and BRI, China enjoys revered status among Pakistan's political and military echelons. Pakistan views China's involvement in South Asia as a crucial counterbalance to India's regional ambitions.

However, Pakistan's economic fragility and political volatility exacerbate the existing power asymmetry, further cementing China's influence. Moreover, Pakistan's tarnished international reputation, stemming from its association with terrorism, limits its diplomatic leverage. Chinese President Xi Jinping's recent alignment with a BRICS declaration criticizing Pakistan's stance on cross-border terrorism signals a nuanced shift in China's approach.

China now navigates a delicate balance between its robust bilateral ties with Pakistan and its broader multilateral engagements. Despite occasional differences, the enduring all-weather partnership between Pakistan and China remains resilient, with both nations leveraging each other to further their respective agendas in South Asia. Nonetheless, there's a growing apprehension that Pakistan could increasingly become a satellite state for China, given its economic vulnerabilities and political instability.

In the foreseeable future, Beijing will continue to support Pakistan due to its critical importance to China across various fronts. Pakistan plays a vital role in China's energy security, granting access to and bases in the Persian Gulf. It also serves China's military interests by diverting India's attention on its western borders. Geopolitically, Pakistan's strategic location at the crossroads of South Asia, Central Asia, and the Middle East is significant for China. Moreover, Pakistan is crucial for China's national unity and territorial integrity, particularly concerning Tibet and Xinjiang, and for its maritime strategy vis-a-vis India. Pakistan is also valued as a steadfast diplomatically in both regional and international forums, including the Islamic world. Additionally, it serves as a significant buyer and supplier of both conventional and unconventional weaponry for China. Above all, Pakistan remains a crucial bargaining chip in China's relations with both India and the US. Beijing recognizes that Pakistan represents their 'last and best bet' to counter Indian dominance in southern Asia, stretching from the Persian Gulf to the Malacca Straits.

Bangladesh

Despite China's negative role during the liberation war of Bangladesh, it has emerged as a significant partner for the nation in subsequent years. China established diplomatic ties with Bangladesh in 1978 and became a significant economic aid donor, trade partner, and supplier of military hardware. This partnership enjoys bipartisan support from Bangladesh's main political parties, the Awami League and the Bangladesh Nationalist Party (BNP).

Bangladesh holds strategic importance for China within the BRI, particularly due to the Bangladesh-China-India-Myanmar Economic Corridor (BCIM). Additionally, Bangladesh occupies a crucial position along the Twenty-first Century Maritime Silk Road, with its Chittagong port serving as a vital maritime hub in the Indian Ocean. China aims to use Bangladesh for access to the Bay of Bengal and the Indian Ocean.

China has become Bangladesh's largest trading partner, overtaking India in 2015, with bilateral trade exceeding $12.13 billion annually.[16] The economic relationship between China and Bangladesh heavily favours China, with Bangladesh seldom voicing concerns about the imbalance. Despite this, China is regarded as a trusted defence and development partner in Bangladesh. Bangladesh relies significantly on Chinese military hardware procurement. This keeps the influential military establishment in Bangladesh satisfied.

China's defence partnership with Bangladesh grew following its liberation, with Bangladesh perceiving India as a potential threat. Bangladesh aimed to leverage the India-China relationship to its advantage.[17] Furthermore, China benefits from Bangladesh's booming garment industry, which heavily relies on Chinese raw materials.

Chinese President Xi Jinping's visit to Bangladesh in October 2016 marked a significant turning point in bilateral relations, elevating it from a 'comprehensive partnership of cooperation' to a 'strategic partnership of cooperation.' This visit signaled China's economic offensive in Bangladesh, a move aimed at reshaping its own relationship with the country. Despite being a close ally of India in South Asia, Bangladesh saw an opportunity to accelerate its already rapid growth trajectory through enhanced cooperation with China.

Bangladesh's economic success, driven by its thriving garment sector and remittances from its sizable expatriate population, has led to the realization of infrastructural bottlenecks. The shortage of electricity has emerged as the most pressing concern. The country urgently needs to increase power generation capacity and modernize existing plants, presenting an area where China's expertise and resources align with Bangladeshi requirements.

Xi Jinping's visit also sought to promote the BRI, which received praise from the Bangladeshi Prime Minister.[18] She expressed her country's commitment to connecting growth centers within South Asia and fostering economic contiguity between South and Southeast Asia. Bangladesh views initiatives like the BCIM, a part of the BRI, as transformative for underdeveloped regions.

Bangladesh's newfound ambition and confidence, fueled by its rapid economic growth, led to a shift in attitude towards foreign loans. The country, previously cautious in utilizing such resources, appeared more willing to pursue them, even at higher costs. It was felt that with sustained economic growth Bangladesh would be able repay loans.

In line with Bangladesh's aspirations, China offered a substantial $24 billion credit line, the largest from any country, alongside significant trade and investment deals totaling $13.6 billion between the private sectors of both nations. These loans, extended at favorable rates of 2-3 per cent, are anticipated to help Bangladesh break free from its low-level equilibrium trap and achieve middle-income status in the near future. For China, increased infrastructural cooperation presents an opportunity to advance the BCIM and unlock new economic potentials in the region.

China and Bangladesh share significant defence and military ties, characterized by regular military exchanges and China being the largest supplier of military hardware to Bangladesh.

Bangladesh's support for China's request for observer status in the South Asian Association for Regional Cooperation (SAARC) in 2006 underscored its willingness to formalize China's role in the South Asian region. This move indicated a strategic openness to Chinese involvement in regional affairs.

While there has been a prevailing perception in Bangladesh that China refrains from interfering in its internal politics, recent developments suggest a shift in this stance. The Chinese ambassador in Dhaka, Li Jiming, raised concerns about Bangladesh joining the US-led Quad alliance, warning of potential damage to bilateral relations.[19] He characterized the Quad as a 'narrow-purposed' geopolitical clique, advising against Bangladesh's participation due to perceived lack of benefits. This interference by China sparked strong resentment in Bangladesh.[20]

Sri Lanka

Sri Lanka's strategic location in the shipping lanes of the Asia-Pacific makes it important for both India and China. It was among the earliest countries to establish diplomatic relations with the PRC in 1957. Even before formal diplomatic ties were established, both nations engaged in international interactions, notably signing the Ceylon-China Rubber-Rice Pact in 1952, which laid the groundwork for their early relationship.

The ascendancy of Mahinda Rajapaksa to power in 2005 marked a significant increase in Chinese influence in Sri Lanka. Rajapaksa's administration, known for its pro-China stance, reportedly received campaign funds from China and was backed by Chinese military hardware during the Civil War. Additionally, China shielded Rajapaksa from international scrutiny over alleged war crimes.

In 2013, the China-Sri Lanka bilateral relationship was elevated to a strategic cooperative partnership. China subsequently surpassed India to become Sri Lanka's largest trading partner in 2016. Under the BRI, China heavily invested in Sri Lanka's infrastructure development, financing numerous projects such as the Hambantota Port, Mattala International Airport, Narocholai Coal Power Plant, and various highway and railway projects.

These ventures positioned Sri Lanka as a strategic outpost for Beijing, alleviating some concerns regarding the Malacca dilemma, through which a significant portion of China's trade traverses. However, Sri Lanka now grapples with a severe economic and political crisis, exacerbated by a perception among locals that Chinese-funded vanity projects have burdened the nation with unsustainable debt.

Many of these projects, such as the Hambantota Port, have failed to yield expected returns, raising international apprehension about debt sustainability. Sri Lanka's request for debt restructuring has been met with Chinese reluctance, as it could set an adverse precedent for other BRI partner nations. Consequently, Sri Lanka has turned to the International Monetary Fund (IMF) for assistance.

China's preoccupation with domestic challenges, including the COVID-19 pandemic and the crisis in Ukraine, has diverted attention from Sri Lanka's plight. India has capitalized on this opportunity by extending substantial financial aid to Sri Lanka, further reshaping the regional dynamics.

In recent years, defence and military cooperation between China and Sri Lanka has flourished, particularly during the tenure of President Rajapaksa. Under his leadership, China provided defence technology and military training to Sri Lanka.[21] The growing partnership was spurred by Sri Lanka's informal request for military assistance to combat the Liberation Tigers of Tamil Eelam (LTTE) in 2006.

In response, India gifted President Rajapaksa five Mi-17 helicopters in 2006 and offered support to curb LTTE activities, albeit cautiously due to its own Tamil population concerns. This created an opening for China to expand its influence in Sri Lanka's defence sphere. Subsequently, China sealed a $37 million deal for ammunition and ordnance in 2007, followed by the provision of six F7 jet fighters, anti-aircraft guns, and JY-11 radar systems the following year. These Chinese weapons played a crucial role in eliminating the LTTE, prominently showcased during victory parades in Sri Lanka.[22]

Despite India's disapproval, Chinese nuclear submarines made visits to Sri Lanka in 2014, signaling deepening military ties.[23] In 2016, China once again extended military aid to Sri Lanka, facilitating the purchase of Chinese-made equipment and assisting in the establishment of an Aircraft Overhaul Wing (AOW) for the Sri Lankan Air Force.[24] China and Pakistan remain Sri Lanka's main suppliers of arms, and Sri Lanka values China as a countervailing force against Indian influence.

Additionally, the influx of Chinese students, migrant workers, and businesspeople has surged alongside increased Chinese activity in Sri Lanka. Chinese companies engaged in project implementation often bring in workers from China, while Sri Lanka has emerged as a popular destination for Chinese tourists. However, in recent years, India has surpassed China as the largest source of tourists to Sri Lanka, reflecting shifting dynamics in the region.[25]

Nepal

Nepal, historically aligned with India for trade, particularly for oil imports, grew increasingly concerned about its security following the 1950 military occupation of Tibet by the People's Liberation Army. This event further strengthened economic and military ties between India and Nepal. Despite the diplomatic relationship between Nepal and China being restored in 1955, significant progress was made only by 1960 when both countries exchanged resident ambassadors and signed the Sino-Nepalese Treaty of Peace and Friendship.

Initially hesitant to foster close trade and economic relations with China, Nepal's stance changed after resolving border disputes and ratifying the Sino-Nepal boundary agreement in 1960, making it the first neighbouring country of China to do so. Since 1975, Nepal has adopted a policy of balancing the influences of both China and India and has supported China's efforts to gain entry into SAARC.

For China, the presence of a large Tibetan refugee community in Nepal is concerning, as Tibet remains a restive province. Additionally, China seeks to expand into Nepali markets to sustain its export-oriented economy, with Nepal offering geographic proximity. Furthermore, China aims to extend its sphere of influence to Nepal.

The difficulties in India-Nepal relations in 2015, stemming from changes made to Nepal's constitution, created opportunities for greater Chinese involvement.[26] Nepal's transit and transportation treaties with China in 2016 and 2018 aimed to reduce its dependency on Indian ports for third-country trade.[27] However, experts suggest that significant challenges remain before Nepal's foreign trade shifts substantially towards China.[28]

Since 2008, China has invested heavily in Nepal, primarily in hydropower plants, cement factories, airports, railways, and telecommunications. These investments, along with bilateral development assistance, have facilitated key projects such as the Pokhara International Regional Airport and the Upper Trishuli Hydropower project. However, projects like the China-Nepal cross-border railway face hurdles due to their high costs.[29]

Furthermore, China's influence in Nepal has grown as evidenced by tighter border controls with Tibet, leading to a decline in Tibetan refugees fleeing to Nepal in recent years. Despite disruptions caused by the COVID-19 pandemic, Chinese tourism in Nepal has flourished since 2011 when Nepal announced free visas for Chinese nationals, with China now accounting for a significant portion of tourist arrivals in Nepal.[30]

Maldives

The Maldives, a small archipelago nation, holds strategic importance due to its central location in the Indian Ocean. Positioned along crucial SLOCs, the Maldives plays a vital role in the energy security of numerous countries, serving as a transit point for Middle Eastern oil shipments to Asia.

China and the Maldives established diplomatic ties in 1972, with reciprocal embassies opened in Beijing and Male in 2009 and 2011, respectively. However, the presence of the US military base in Diego Garcia, in close proximity to the Maldives, serves as a counterbalance to China's aspirations for greater influence in the IOR, critical for its oil and goods imports.

Traditionally aligned with India, the Maldives transitioned to a multi-party democracy in 2008, bringing Mohamed Nasheed to power. Nasheed's state visit to China in 2010 marked the beginning of increased Chinese involvement in the Maldives,[31] with a surge in bilateral trade and Chinese tourist arrivals.[32]

Subsequent leaders, such as Mohamed Waheed and Abdulla Yameen, further strengthened ties with China.[33] Yameen's presidency witnessed significant Chinese investment in the Maldives, including substantial funding for airport upgrades and infrastructure projects.[34]

Despite China's significant tourist influx, India and Britain emerged as the primary tourist-sending nations post-COVID-19 pandemic. In 2017, the docking of three Chinese naval ships in Male raised eyebrows, with former Maldivian President Mohamed Nasheed expressing concern, although the government denied any policy shift towards India.[35]

Under President Mohamed Solih, India regained some influence, yet China reasserted its presence with the election of Mohamed Muizzu in September 2023. The fluctuating dynamics between China, India, and the Maldives underscores the strategic significance of this region in global geopolitics.

Bhutan

Bhutan stands as a unique case where China has struggled to exert significant influence, despite persistent efforts to do so. The relationship between China and Bhutan has been marked by tension, largely stemming from China's annexation of Tibet in 1951. Bhutan shares historical, cultural, and religious ties with Tibet, a fact that complicates relations with China.

Territorial disputes have further strained relations between Bhutan and China, with border crises erupting in 1962 and 2014. The 2014 Doklam standoff was particularly significant, sparked by Chinese troops constructing a road in territory claimed by both China and Bhutan. Recent reports suggest that China has intensified settlement-building along its disputed border with Bhutan, heightening tensions.[36]

Despite the absence of formal diplomatic relations, bilateral trade between China and Bhutan has increased. Bhutan's economy, reliant on hydropower and tourism, has witnessed a surge in Chinese tourist arrivals.[37] In the past decade, the number of Chinese tourists visiting Bhutan has risen significantly, from fewer than 20 to over 6,000 in 2017.

Bhutan shares a complex relationship with China shaped by historical grievances, territorial disputes, and economic interests. Despite China's efforts, Bhutan remains cautious in developing its relations with its powerful neighbour, prioritizing its sovereignty and strategic interests.

Factors Driving China's Increasing Influence in South Asia

China's expanding influence in South Asia can be attributed to several key factors.

Geostrategic Considerations

Following the independence of India and Pakistan, the latter engaged in conflicts with its larger and more powerful neighbour, prompting it to seek external support both financially and militarily. Initially, the US served as an offshore balancer. However, starting from 1962, Pakistan also turned to China for assistance. Furthermore, smaller nations in South Asia view the inclusion of China in the region as a means of balancing against the dominance of India.

Weak State Institutions

Many countries in the region struggle with weak state institutions, hindering their ability to conduct thorough due diligence on investments. Uneven law enforcement, weak regulatory bodies, poor anti-corruption measures, and inefficient judicial systems exacerbate these challenges.[38]

Fragile Civil Societies

In functional political systems, civil society serves as a check on state actions. However, in South Asia, civil society often lacks the strength to effectively challenge improper actions by Chinese entities.[39]

Elite Influence and Capture

Elite capture is prevalent in the political landscapes of many South Asian countries, fostering corruption and crony capitalism. This environment provides opportunities for external powers or interest groups to buy influence. Chinese actors have capitalized on these dynamics, forming close relationships with political and business elites to advance Chinese interests. For instance, China's strong ties with the Rajapaksas in Sri Lanka have granted it significant influence in the country.

Limited Local Expertise

In some cases, the quality of local experts may be insufficient to analyse the domestic implications of Chinese involvement effectively. This lack of expertise can hinder the assessment of Chinese activities and their potential impact on local economies and societies.

Geostrategic Agenda Drives China's Approach in South Asia

China's approach in South Asia is fundamentally shaped by a geostrategic agenda aimed at safeguarding its national interests. Military security concerns profoundly influence China's relations with South Asian countries, with a clear objective of diminishing India's regional influence. Pakistan is strategically regarded by China as a crucial partner, fostering an alliance that acts as a counterbalance to India. Moreover, China's footprint in South Asia has transcended its historical ties with Pakistan, as it actively seeks closer relations with smaller South Asian nations once firmly within India's sphere of influence.

In the IOR, a significant power shift is underway. The decline of US dominance and China's ascent as a potential global power pose challenges for India, which has traditionally considered this region its sphere of influence. This dynamic has set the stage for a potential strategic contest between China and India.

Despite its burgeoning economic influence, China has encountered hurdles in building substantive security relationships in the IOR. Instances such as Myanmar distancing itself from China and Sri Lanka revisiting military facility access underscore these challenges. In the foreseeable future, China's capacity to project power into the Indian Ocean is expected to remain constrained. Efforts to establish 'Pearls' and overland transport links may yield limited impact on this scenario.

A keen contest for influence in the Indian Ocean is anticipated between China and Quad members India and the US. While China may not gain a decisive strategic edge over India in the Indian Ocean, the rivalry extends throughout the region, with India striving to preserve its advantages and China seeking to mitigate its vulnerabilities.

China primarily employs economic instruments to advance its long-term strategic interests, effectively expanding its influence in what was traditionally deemed India's strategic domain. Given China's immense size and economic prowess, its role in the region is inevitable. South Asian nations, with burgeoning economies, naturally gravitate towards China's considerable foreign exchange reserves and capital, particularly through initiatives like the BRI.

China has made substantial investments in South Asian countries, offering loans and emerging as the largest overseas investor in certain nations. However, Chinese projects face scrutiny for potential debt traps and adverse environmental impacts.

Chinese engagement in South Asia is also under the scanner for often constraining the choices available to local political and economic elites, favouring narrow interest groups. Moreover, China utilizes economic and political incentives to shape public opinion, limiting alternative narratives. The dearth of independent media and weak civil societies in South Asian countries exacerbate this issue, allowing Chinese funding to shape domestic narratives.

While China dismisses allegations of creating debt-traps, several South Asian countries, particularly in the wake of the COVID-19 pandemic, grapple with financial difficulties, with Sri Lanka serving as a prominent example where economic woes spill into political crises. On July 13, 2022, following a series of massive protests the official residence and workplace of then President Gotabaya Rajapaksa was seized by protestors. Gotabaya Rajapaksa fled the country with his spouse. Ranil Wickremesinghe was appointed interim president to succeed him who is trying to overcome Sri Lankan economic crisis. Consequently, South Asian nations have grown cautious in accepting Chinese loans under the BRI, learning from each other's experiences and adapting their approaches accordingly.

Some South Asian nations harbour skepticism regarding China's intentions and strive for a balanced approach in diplomatic relations. Balancing ties with other major powers, including the US and India, mirrors the nuanced diplomatic landscape in the region. Nonetheless, China endeavours to reassure South Asian countries, emphasizing that its improved relations with India will not compromise ties with them. South Asian nations must remain vigilant and address activities that undermine their political independence and balanced economic growth.

Future Sino-Indian relations hold significant implications for Asian and global security. China remains apprehensive about India's deepening ties with the US and its strategic positioning in the Indian Ocean. Conversely, India perceives China as encroaching upon its strategic interests, particularly in Southern Asia. China's opposition to India's participation in various international forums underscores this dynamic.

NOTES

1 J. Mohan Malik, 'South Asia in China's Foreign Relations,' *Pacifica Review*, Volume 13, Number 1, February 2001, p. 89.

2 J. Mohan Malik, 'South Asia in China's Foreign Relations,' *Pacifica Review*, Volume 13, Number 1, February 2001, p. 79.

3 'Xi's statements on the Belt and Road Initiative', *China Daily*, 15 April 2017 at https://global.chinadaily.com.cn/a/201704/15/WS59bb7a1ca310d4d9ab7e8849_6.html last accessed on 16 June 2024.

4 Pakistani President Arif Alvi said this during an interview with Xinhua in Islamabad. 'Interview: Pakistan-China relations exemplary in world, says Pakistani president,' Xinhua, 21 May 2021 at http://www.xinhuanet.com/english/2021-05/21/c_139961535.htm last accessed on 16 June 2024.

5 Suhasini Haidar, Ananth Krishnan, 'India's move on Article 370 is "illegal and invalid", says China,' *The Hindu*, 6 August 2020 at https://www.thehindu.com/news/national/indias-article-370-abrogation-illegal-says-china/article32275663.ece last accessed on 16 June 2024.

6 Tim Weiner, 'Nuclear Anxiety: The Know-How; U.S. and China Helped Pakistan Build Its Bomb,' *New York Times*, 1 June 1998 at https://www.nytimes.com/1998/06/01/world/nuclear-anxiety-the-know-how-us-and-china-helped-pakistan-build-its-bomb.html last accessed on 16 June 2024.

7 'China rules out India's entry into NSG without "consensus" on allowing non-NPT countries,' *The Economic Times*, 21 June, 2019 at https://economictimes.indiatimes.com/news/defence/china-rules-out-indias-entry-into-nsg-without-consensus-on-allowing-non-npt-countries/printarticle/69893448.cms last accessed on 16 June 2024.

8 Anand Kumar, 'Pak's Dependence on CPEC', *Deccan Herald*, 11 April 2017 at https://www.deccanherald.com/content/605722/paks-dependence-cpec.html last accessed on 16 June 2024.

9 'In major shift, China sends stern message to Pakistan on FATF', WION, 20 February 2020 at https://www.wionews.com/south-asia/in-major-shift-china-sends-stern-message-to-pakistan-on-fatf-281730 last accessed on 16 June 2024.

10 'Pakistan Army inducts China-made VT-4 battle tanks,' *The Economic Times*, 1 July 2021 at https://economictimes.indiatimes.com/news/defence/pakistan-army-inducts-china-made-vt-4-battle-tanks/articleshow/84017081.cms?from=mdr, last accessed on 16 June 2024 also see, Naveed Siddiqui, 'Pakistan Army inducts first batch of VT-4 battle tanks', *Dawn*, 1 July 2021 at https://www.dawn.com/news/1632542 last accessed on 16 June 2024.

11 Adnan Aamir, 'Pakistan alarmed by US-India information sharing pact', *Nikkei Asia*, 2 November 2020 at https://asia.nikkei.com/Politics/International-relations/Pakistan-alarmed-by-US-India-information-sharing-pact last accessed on 16 June 2024.

12 Adnan Aamir, 'China and Pakistan ink military MOU to counter US-India pact,' *Nikkei Asia*, 8 December 2020 at https://asia.nikkei.com/Politics/International-relations/China-and-Pakistan-ink-military-MOU-to-counter-US-India-pact last accessed on 16 June 2024.

13 Sameer P. Lalwani, 'A Threshold Alliance: The China-Pakistan Military Relationship,' US Institute of Peace, 22 March 2023 at https://www.usip.org/publications/2023/03/threshold-alliance-china-pakistan-military-relationship last accessed on 16 June 2024.

14 'China may be looking at setting up a military base in Pakistan's Gwadar', *The Times of India*, 12 May 2023, at https://timesofindia.indiatimes.com/world/pakistan/china-may-be-looking-at-setting-up-a-military-base-in-pakistans-gwadar/articleshowprint/100096885.cms?val=3728 last accessed on 16 June 2024.

15 Fatima Raza, 'China in South Asia: Islamabad as Lynchpin of Beijing's Strategy', *South Asian Voices*, 2 October 2017 at https://southasianvoices.org/china-in-south-asia-islamabad-as-lynchpin/ last accessed on 16 June 2024.

16 'Bangladesh fails to capitalize duty-free, quota-free benefits', *Dhaka Tribune*, 11 May 2022 at https://www.dhakatribune.com/business/270091/bangladesh-fails-to-capitalize-duty-free last accessed on 16 June 2024.

17 Anand Kumar, 'Bangladesh and its Security Relationship with External Powers,' New Delhi: KW Publishers Pvt. Ltd., 2021, p. 53.

18 Anand Kumar, 'Relationship of convenience,' *Deccan Herald*, 25 November 2016 at https://www.deccanherald.com/content/582923/relationship-convenience.html last accessed on 16 June 2024.

19 'China warns of "substantial damage" to ties if Bangladesh joins US-led Quad alliance; Dhaka calls it "aggressive"', *The Economic Times*, 11 May 2021 at https://economic

times.indiatimes.com/news/defence/china-threatens-bangladesh-says-ties-will-be-hit-if-it-joins-quad/articleshow/82544639.cms?from=mdr last accessed on 16 June 2024.

20 'Bangladesh surprised over Chinese envoy's comments on Quad', *The Economic Times*, 11 May 2021 at https://economictimes.indiatimes.com/news/defence/bangladesh-surprised-over-chinese-envoys-comments-on-quad/printarticle/82541099.cms last accessed on 16 June 2024.

21 "China to train Sri Lankan army, to provide military technology," *The Indian Express*, 31 May 2013 at http://archive.indianexpress.com/news/china-to-train-sri-lankan-army-to-provide-military-technology/1123290/

22 Hannah Gardner, China's aid revealed in Sri Lanka's victory parade, *The National*, 9 June 2009 at https://www.thenationalnews.com/world/asia/china-s-aid-revealed-in-sri-lanka-s-victory-parade-1.556125

23 Sri Lanka snubs India, opens port to Chinese submarine again, *The Times of India*, 2 November 2014 at https://timesofindia.indiatimes.com/india/Sri-Lanka-snubs-India-opens-port-to-Chinese-submarine-again/articleshow/45008757.cms, also see Beijing's nuclear subs coming again, India concerned, The Sunday Times, 19 October 2014 at https://www.sundaytimes.lk/141019/news/beijings-nuclear-subs-coming-again-india-concerned-123254.html

24 Hasitha Wijewardena, SLAF AOW repairs aircraft in SL, Ministry of Defence, Sri Lanka, 28 January 2021 at https://www.defence.lk/index.php/Article/view_article/2956

25 Meera Srinivasan, 'Chinese tourist in Sri Lanka tests positive for Coronavirus,' *The Hindu*, 28 January 2020 at https://www.thehindu.com/news/international/chinese-tourist-in-sri-lanka-tests-positive-for-coronavirus/article30670031.ece last accessed on 16 June 2024.

26 Sanjoy Majumder, 'Why India is concerned about Nepal's constitution', *BBC News*, 22 September 2015 at https://www.bbc.com/news/world-asia-india-34313280 last accessed on 16 June 2024.

27 'Nepal, China sign first-ever transit treaty; agree to have rail link to end dependency on India', *Firstpost*, 21 March 2016 at https://www.firstpost.com/world/nepal-china-sign-first-ever-transit-treaty-to-end-dependency-on-indian-sea-port-2687860.html last accessed on 16 June 2024.

28 'Nepal and China conclude protocol of TTA', *The Himalayan Times*, 8 September 2018 at https://thehimalayantimes.com/business/nepal-and-china-conclude-protocol-of-tta last accessed on 16 June 2024.

29 'China pushing trans-Himalayan rail project in Nepal with strategic aims,' *The Economic Times*, 2 April 2022 at https://economictimes.indiatimes.com/news/international/world-news/china-pushing-trans-himalayan-rail-project-in-nepal-with-strategic-aims/articleshow/90606048.cms last accessed on 16 June 2024.

30 Josie Wang, 'Chinese tourist influx to Nepal in 2020', *Nepali Times*, 31 December 2019 at https://www.nepalitimes.com/banner/chinese-tourist-influx-to-nepal-in-2020/ last accessed on 16 June 2024.

31 'President Nasheed of Maldives to Visit China', Embassy of the People's Republic of China in the Kingdom of the Netherlands, 27 April 2010 at http://nl.china-embassy.gov.cn/eng/zgyw/201004/t20100427_10042013.htm last accessed on 16 June 2024.

32 'Maldives President Mohamed Nasheed Met with Chinese Commerce Minister Chen Deming', Ministry of Commerce, People's Republic of China, 23 August 2010 at http://english.mofcom.gov.cn/article/newsrelease/significantnews/201008/20100807097814.shtml last accessed on 16 June 2024.

33 'Maldives to take control of GMR airport despite Singapore High Court order: Minister', *The Economic Times*, 3 December 2012 at https://economictimes.indiatimes.com/news/politics-and-nation/maldives-to-take-control-of-gmr-airport-despite-singapore-high-court-order-minister/articleshow/17463132.cms?from=mdr last accessed on 16 June 2024.

34 'GMR's loss is China's gain: Maldives gives airport contract to Chinese firm', *Firstpost*, 16 September 2014 at https://www.firstpost.com/business/corporate-business/gmrs-loss-is-chinas-gain-maldives-gives-airport-contract-to-chinese-firm-1990665.html last accessed on 16 June 2024.

35 Suhasini Haidar, 'Ex-president flags presence of Chinese warships in Male', *The Hindu*, 29 August 2017 at https://www.thehindu.com/news/national/ex-president-flags-presence-of-chinese-warships-in-male/article19582196.ece last accessed on 16 June 2024.

36 Devjyot Ghoshal, Anand Katakam and Aditi Bhandari, 'China steps up construction along disputed Bhutan border', *Reuters*, 12 January 2022 at https://graphics.reuters.com/CHINA-BHUTAN/BORDER/zjvqknaryvx/ last accessed on 16 June 2024.

37 'China woos Bhutan, to India's displeasure', *France 24*, 17 October 2018 at https://www.france24.com/en/20181017-china-woos-bhutan-indias-displeasure last accessed on 16 June 2024.

38 Deep Pal, 'China's Influence in South Asia', Carnegie Endowment for International Peace, Washington DC, October 2021, p. 24.

39 Ibid., p. 31.

CHAPTER 6

US's Indo-Pacific Strategy

The Indo-Pacific region, stretching from the Pacific coast of the US to East Africa, holds immense significance in global affairs, hosting over half of the world's population, a substantial portion of the global economy, and key military powers. For the US, this region is crucial for its security and prosperity. The US has deep historical ties with the Indo-Pacific dating back centuries. The Second World War reminded the US that its security is linked to the security of Asia. It recognizes the strategic necessity of its consistent role in the region, which was solidified post-World War II through alliances and commitments to organizations like ASEAN. It has long-standing treaty alliances with Australia, Japan, Korea, and the Philippines. Trade with the region supports millions of American jobs, underlining its economic importance. Successive Republican and Democratic administrations have consistently prioritized the Indo-Pacific, recognizing its growing importance.

However, regional stability in the Indo-Pacific has now been threatened by the rise of an assertive China.[1] The relationship between the US and China has evolved over different phases over the decades, from confrontation during the Cold War to cooperation during the balance of power against the Soviet Union and later economic engagement. However, since 2008, the relationship has shifted to one of 'strategic competition,' characterized by concerns over China's assertive behaviour, including economic coercion, territorial disputes, and human rights violations.

Despite these challenges, complete decoupling from China is deemed impractical due to the deep economic interdependence of the US and its allies. Apart from China's rise, the Indo-Pacific faces other challenges such as climate change, the COVID-19 pandemic, nuclear proliferation (for example, in North Korea), natural disasters, and governance issues.[2] The rise of China also necessitates bolstering relationships with other Indo-Pacific nations, ranging from regional giants like India to smaller island nations.

The Biden administration has continued and expanded upon previous initiatives in the Indo-Pacific, emphasizing the importance of alliances, partnerships, and multilateral frameworks. The Quad, AUKUS, and partnerships with ASEAN and Pacific Island nations form the core components of the US's Indo-Pacific Strategy (IPS). These are aimed at fostering cooperation and countering Chinese influence. The overarching goal is to realize a free and open Indo-Pacific that is connected, prosperous, secure, and resilient, achieved through modernizing alliances, strengthening partnerships, and investing in regional organizations to tackle twenty-first century challenges effectively. Collaboration with allies and partners remains central to achieving this vision as it was realized that it was now beyond the capacity of any one nation to handle these challenges.

Evolution of the Indo-Pacific as a Geopolitical Framework

While Asia's economic growth brought global benefits, it also drew attention to territorial disputes and challenges to international laws and norms, notably in the South China Sea. These concerns were further exacerbated by China's BRI. In response to this, the concept of the Indo-Pacific emerged as a geopolitical framework, initially proposed by Japanese Prime Minister Shinzô Abe in 2007 during his address to the Indian parliament.[3] It aimed to strengthen ties among democracies in the Indian and Pacific Oceans to safeguard sea lanes and foster prosperity. Encompassing a broader geographical scope, the Indo-Pacific construct emphasizes economic, security, and diplomatic considerations.

The Indo-Pacific framework seeks to tackle evolving challenges and opportunities, advocating for a rules-based order, freedom of navigation, and shared prosperity. It encourages enhanced cooperation among nations to address maritime security concerns, territorial disputes, and the ramifications of initiatives like the BRI.

This construct underscores the interconnectedness and growing significance of the Indo-Pacific region in global affairs. With over 65 per cent of the global GDP and crucial trade routes traversing its waters, the region's economic significance cannot be understated. Recognizing the Indian and Pacific Oceans as a cohesive area became imperative for effective policymaking, acknowledging the interdependence of countries in both regions.

During the Obama Administration, a significant power shift occurred in the Western Pacific and South China Sea region, highlighting the lack of a country capable of curbing China's assertiveness. In response, to address China's increasing assertiveness and to reassert global leadership of the US, particularly in the Indo-Pacific, President Donald Trump officially unveiled the IPS during his Asia trip in November 2017. The concept gained momentum thereafter, leading to widespread adoption by numerous countries and regional groupings, including ASEAN, France, Germany, and the European Union. The Indo-Pacific Construct has been incorporated into the US national security and defence strategies. This strategy focused on economic integration, defence cooperation, and countering China's BRI to uphold US influence in the region.

Japan, the originator of the Indo-Pacific Construct, also joined forces with like-minded countries such as Australia and India to counter shared concerns about China. The Japanese IPS has also evolved over time.

IPS of Japan

The IPS of Japan holds significant importance, especially considering that Japanese Prime Minister Shinzo Abe was the first to advocate for the concept of the Free and Open Indo-Pacific (FOIP). As a key stakeholder in the region's geopolitics and a pivotal member of the Quad, understanding Japan's approach is crucial.

Originates from Security Concerns

Although Prime Minister Abe initially introduced the concept of FOIP in 2007, Japan's IPS gained traction following the Senkaku boat collision incident in 2010. It was in 2012 that Abe proposed forming a democratic alliance comprising Japan, the US, India, and Australia, with the objective of safeguarding global public goods and ensuring freedom of navigation.

Tokyo initially prioritized maritime security in its Indo-Pacific vision because of its economic interests in upholding free SLOC and its ongoing dispute with China over the Senkaku Islands. Key goals for Japan include preserving a rules-based order and ensuring freedom of navigation. To achieve these aims, Japan envisions enhancing defence cooperation with like-minded countries across various regions, spanning Southeast Asia, South Asia, the Pacific Islands, the Middle East, Africa, and Latin America. This collaborative effort is essential for securing major SLOCs and ensuring energy security.

Japan has been actively implementing its Indo-Pacific security strategy, notably by strengthening military cooperation with regional countries. In 2012, Japan engaged in military operations with just five Indo-Pacific nations, but by 2021, this number had risen to 15. This demonstrates the deepening ties and collaborative endeavours, including joint naval exercises, military exchanges, and defence equipment and technology cooperation.

Through enhanced defence partnerships, Japan aims to contribute to the stability and security of the Indo-Pacific region. This proactive stance aligns with its economic interests and the imperative to safeguard critical maritime routes. By expanding its military engagements, Japan seeks to uphold a rules-based order, protect freedom of navigation, and foster regional security and cooperation.

Economic Concerns Take Center Stage

While Japan's Indo-Pacific vision initially stemmed from security concerns, economic considerations have now become central to its approach. Japan's IPS has evolved over time and it has transitioned into what officials and leaders now refer to as the Indo-Pacific vision. In addition to prioritizing security and stability in the region, Japan aims to foster partnerships with like-minded countries to drive economic prosperity throughout the Indo-Pacific. This renewed emphasis encompasses the importance of a rules-based order, maritime security, connectivity, and infrastructure development.

Japan acknowledges that regional economic prosperity forms a critical foundation for security and underscores the need to enhance economic connectivity to achieve shared prosperity. To support this objective, Japan introduced the Partnership for Quality Infrastructure initiative, allocating a total budget of USD 200 billion to finance connectivity infrastructure projects in the Indo-Pacific region.

Through the Partnership for Quality Infrastructure, Japan actively finances various infrastructure projects in Africa and Asia. These projects include the development of eight ports, two airports, two mega rail corridors, as well as road and power-generation projects. While Japan has not explicitly voiced concerns about the BRI, its emphasis on promoting transparency, efficiency, and sustainability, coupled with growing cooperation with the US, European Union, and Australia in infrastructure financing, suggests that the Partnership for Quality Infrastructure aims to provide Indo-Pacific countries with an alternative to Chinese infrastructure projects.

Moreover, Japan is offering financial support for quality infrastructure projects to promote inclusive and sustainable economic development while ensuring transparency and adhering to international standards.

In addition to improving physical connectivity, Japan's Indo-Pacific vision underscores the importance of trade agreements as tools for achieving greater economic integration with Indo-Pacific countries. Tokyo has played a leading role in promoting two significant free trade agreements: the Regional Comprehensive Economic Partnership (RCEP) and the Comprehensive and Progressive Agreement for Trans-Pacific Partnership (CPTPP). While these agreements remain open to China's participation, Japan's focus on free trade agreements may suggest a different underlying objective.

In the post-COVID era, there seems to be a shift in Japan's economic strategy, marked by measures to reduce dependence on China. This includes a USD 2 billion financial support package to facilitate the relocation of Japanese firms operating in China back to Japan or other countries. Additionally, in collaboration with India and Australia, Japan has launched the Supply Chain Resilience Initiative (SCRI), aiming to promote investment, facilitate buyer-seller matching, and implement trade and investment diversification measures to enhance supply chain resilience.

With this shift in Japanese economic strategy, Japan seeks to rebalance economic dynamics in the region. While remaining committed to open and inclusive trade arrangements, Japan's recent actions indicate a growing emphasis on diversifying supply chains and reducing reliance on any single country. This reflects Japan's broader strategic goal of achieving supply chain resilience and promoting economic stability in the Indo-Pacific region.

IPS of the US

The term 'Indo-Pacific' began to gain prominence in US policy circles during the Obama Presidency but saw increased usage during the Trump administration. Since then, it has become an integral part of all official documents. Several US departments have released their own IPS documents, including one by the Department of State in 2019 entitled 'A Free and Open Indo-Pacific: Advancing a Shared Vision (FOIP).'[4] This document provided a comprehensive overview of US involvement in the Indo-Pacific and outlined guiding principles for the US approach, such as respect for sovereignty and independence, peaceful resolution of disputes, free and fair trade, and adherence to international laws.

Following this, the Department of Defense published a comprehensive IPS Report,[5] and the US Strategic Framework for the Indo-Pacific was declassified.[6] The Biden administration continued this trend by releasing the IPS of the US in May 2022.[7]

The US has outlined its IPS in these publicly available documents, highlighting the region's economic and strategic significance. These documents emphasize the need for enhanced cooperation with like-minded partners to ensure prosperity and peace in the Indo-Pacific.

US documents reveal that strategic and security concerns are central to Washington's IPS. The US perceives shifting power dynamics and China's assertiveness as potential threats to the rules-based world order. To address these challenges, the US prioritizes strengthening military alliances with existing partners and expanding military cooperation with other countries in the region.

The strategy focuses on enhancing maritime security and safeguarding freedom of navigation. The US plans to bolster the defence capabilities of strategic partners in the Indo-Pacific through defence exports, joint naval exercises, sharing military technology, providing military aid, and conducting training programmes for military officials.

Development cooperation with Indo-Pacific countries is also a key aspect of the US strategy. The Free and Open Indo-Pacific vision document highlights existing financial and technical support provided by the US and aims to expand assistance further. Areas of development cooperation include skill development, trade facilitation, export promotion, energy policy, entrepreneurship development, and civil society support. Infrastructure financing, as an alternative to China's BRI, receives particular attention.

To achieve its objectives, the US has implemented three key strategies. First, it has consolidated development finance and technical assistance in the Indo-Pacific through initiatives like the Better Utilization of Investments Leading to Development Act (BUILD Act) and the Asia Reassurance Initiative Act (ARIA Act). Second, in collaboration with Japan and Australia, the US established the Blue Dot Network to certify high-quality infrastructure projects and promote transparency. Last, the US has increased coordination with other G7 countries to streamline infrastructure finance, resulting in the launch of the Build Back Better World (B3W) initiative with $40 trillion in funding to counter the BRI.

Deepening trade and investment relations with Indo-Pacific countries is also important, though the economic agenda appears less developed. Existing US initiatives such as Access Asia, Discover Global Markets, and Trade Winds have facilitated US investment in the region. The US vision emphasizes free, fair, and reciprocal trade as the basis for better trade integration, mentioning the signing of new agreements and renegotiating existing ones with Indo-Pacific countries. This approach aims to negotiate better trade and investment deals, particularly with China, addressing issues like market access and intellectual property rights (IPR) protection.

Critical technology, digital economy, and cyber security are other focal points of the US vision. The US recognizes the challenges of maintaining an open and secure internet while fostering technology cooperation. The Quad, comprising the US, Japan, Australia, and India, serves as a platform for joint investments in emerging technologies. The recent launch of the Quad Investor Network (QIN) further strengthens these collaborative efforts. The vision encourages Indo-Pacific countries to adopt a risk-based approach in evaluating technology vendors.

The launch of the Indo-Pacific Economic Framework for Prosperity (IPEF) by Washington signifies a sharpened focus on the economic dimension of its IPS. The IPEF outlines four pillars for economic cooperation with Indo-Pacific countries: trade, resilient economy, clean energy, and fair economy. It offers a range of cooperative options for countries in the region, allowing them to choose any pillar to enhance economic collaboration.

However, apart from the resilient economy pillar, which emphasizes supply-chain resilience, the other three pillars primarily revolve around setting standards rather than addressing market access, technology transfer, or finance.[8] For instance, the connected economy pillar emphasizes labour and environmental standards and cross-border data flow, while neglecting important issues such as tariff concessions, market access, and trade facilitation. Similarly, the clean economy pillar focuses on high targets for renewable energy, carbon removal, and energy-efficiency standards, but does not mention technology transfer or financing.

Considering the prevailing protectionist sentiments that led the US to withdraw from the Comprehensive and Progressive Agreement for Trans-Pacific Partnership (CPTPP), the IPEF appears to be an attempt to promote US standards without providing adequate market access.

US IPS: Some Core Components

The Biden administration has continued and expanded upon existing strategic initiatives while introducing new ones in the Indo-Pacific region. It has upheld and revitalized the Quad, strengthened strategic partnerships with ASEAN, initiated new security agreements like AUKUS, and implemented an Indo-Pacific Economic Framework. Three key elements of the Biden administration's IPS include the Quad, a non-traditional multilateral group consisting of India, Japan, Australia, and the US; the AUKUS security pact involving Australia, the United Kingdom, and the US; and Partners in the Blue Pacific, a multilateral initiative aimed at fostering closer alignment with Pacific Island nations.

The Quad and its Future

The Quad consisting of Australia, India, Japan, and the US, forms a central pillar of the Biden administration's IPS, which aims to foster a free, open, transparent, inclusive, and peaceful region. Unlike NATO, the Quad is not a formal alliance but rather an arrangement of four intersecting circles representing national interests, with growing but limited convergence in the middle. At its core, the Quad implicitly seeks to provide a counterbalance to China's influence, uniting the four major democracies in the region.

Origin and Evolution of Quad

The groundwork for the Quad was laid in 2004 following the Indian Ocean Tsunami, when US President George W. Bush initiated collaborative efforts among the four nations to coordinate relief efforts.[9] Recognizing their potential to address regional challenges, especially in light of China's rise, the group transitioned from a functional collaboration to an ideological one, driven by then-Japanese Prime Minister Shinzo Abe's proposal for an 'arc of freedom and prosperity.' This proposal was made by Abe in his 'Confluence of the Two Seas' speech in India's Parliament.

Though not a defensive alliance or a containment network against China, the Quad took on a military dimension when the US-India Malabar joint exercises expanded to include Australia, Japan, and Singapore. However, the Quad faced initial setbacks, notably when Australia withdrew in 2007 due to concerns about provoking Beijing.[10]

Despite this setback, member countries continued to strengthen bilateral relations through joint military exercises and economic integration, with the US and Japan reorienting their foreign policy agendas towards the Indo-Pacific. President Obama talked of 'pivot to Asia' in 2011 while the Japanese President Shinzo Abe in his speech in New Delhi in 2016 reiterated his commitment to a 'free and open Indo-Pacific.' As China's assertiveness grew, particularly evident during the 2017 Doklam standoff, India embraced the Quad, leading to its resurrection in 2017 with a renewed purpose to counter China's escalating influence.

The 2020 border clashes between India and China further solidified the Quad's position, resulting in its elevation to the summit level and an expansion of its scope to include vaccine diplomacy, infrastructure development, maritime security, and critical technologies.

The Biden administration intensified US commitment to Quad cooperation in 2021, extending outreach to include a 'Quad-Plus' community, incorporating countries like New Zealand, South Korea, and Vietnam. Through its endeavours, the Quad has successfully enhanced cooperation among its members, fostering closer ties and addressing common challenges in the Indo-Pacific region.

Objectives

The Quad grouping is guided by a set of clear objectives outlined in policy documents of the US and its partner nations. These objectives revolve around fostering a free and open Indo-Pacific region, promoting regional security, driving economic growth and development, addressing shared challenges like climate change, and cultivating people-to-people ties.[11] Though not framed as a direct confrontation, the Quad's strategic partnership implicitly challenges China's approach to regional influence and seeks to foster a more stable and rules-based Indo-Pacific. The core objective of the Quad is to manage China's rise in the region. While member countries have not explicitly stated this as their primary goal, their emphasis on maintaining a 'free, open, inclusive, anchored by democratic values, and unconstrained by coercion' Indo-Pacific leaves little room for interpretation that the Quad aims to be a counterweight to China's coercive projection of power in the region.

While the Quad shares a common overarching objective, each member country faces unique domestic constraints that influence their individual approaches to achieving the Quad's stated goals. Notably, the US and Australia have been more willing to openly and privately challenge China in the international arena. Due to differing interests and strategies across the various domains of the Quad's agenda, coordination and deep strategic cooperation among member nations continue to present ongoing challenges.

The Quad aims to ensure that the Indo-Pacific region is not dominated by China and that the overall balance of power remains favourable to liberal democracies. Although all four countries—India, US, Japan and Australia value their economic ties with China, they recognize the importance of maintaining a free and open Indo-Pacific region.

Challenges and Complexities in Quad

The Quad faces a number of challenges and complexities due to differing geopolitical priorities and approaches among its member nations.

Different Geopolitical Priorities and Interests of India and US: India's traditional focus on the Indian Ocean conflicts with the US's Pacific-centric strategy, potentially impacting the Quad's ability to address security issues that may not directly affect India's interests. Moreover, India and the US diverge in their views on the Indo-Pacific and how to address China's rise. While the US emphasizes upholding the rules-based international order in the Indo-Pacific, India favours a more inclusive approach, occasionally signaling openness to including China and Russia in the region's framework. Additionally, while the US adopts a more confrontational stance towards China, India prefers a model of competition-cooperation.

India's pursuit of strategic autonomy further complicates matters, as it balances relationships with various partners, including China and Russia. Some observers consider India the 'weakest link' within the Quad due to its non-ally status and nationalistic policies, such as its close ties with Russia and Iran. Concerns have been raised, particularly following India's restrained response to Russia's invasion of Ukraine in 2022, questioning its reliability as a security partner.

Despite these challenges, the evolving relationship between India, the US, and the Quad reflects a mix of shared interests and differing viewpoints. While India aims to assert itself as a major security player in the IOR, the US sees India as a potential counterbalance to China's influence in the broader Indo-Pacific. Recognizing the importance of engaging India, the US has prioritized efforts to strengthen ties through initiatives like the US-India Initiative on Critical and Emerging Technology and enhanced defence cooperation.

Challenges in the Quad's Engagement with Smaller Indo-Pacific Nations: While the Quad has successfully enhanced trade integration among its member states, it has encountered challenges in effectively engaging smaller nations and developing countries with strong economic ties to China in the Indo-Pacific region. Despite driving an upward trend in regional integration for investment and trade, the Quad's efforts have not fully extended to smaller nations outside its core membership.

The US has played a pivotal role in steering countries like the Republic of Korea and Vietnam away from heavy reliance on China, thereby diversifying trade and manufacturing hubs. However, the Quad has struggled to economically engage with smaller nations and establish trust and influence through bilateral and multilateral trade agreements. Notably, both the US and India remain outside major trade agreements like RCEP and CPTPP.

Many developing countries in the Indo-Pacific region continue to grapple with significant debts owed to China, while others experience short-term economic gains and enhanced supply chain resilience. The impact of recent economic initiatives, including the Indo-Pacific Economic Framework and the Partnership for Global Infrastructure and Investment announced in 2022, remains to be evaluated regarding their tangible effects on regional economic ties.

Moving forward, it is imperative for the Quad to prioritize efforts in building trust and engagement with smaller nations to broaden its influence and effectiveness in the region. Continued collaboration and investment in economic initiatives will be essential for the Quad to strengthen its foothold and address the diverse economic challenges faced by countries across the Indo-Pacific.

Mismatch in National and Military Interests of Quad Members: The Quad's strategic cooperation is constrained by a mismatch of national interests among its members, particularly in terms of military aspects, where challenges arise due to differences in commitments, interests, and capabilities. India's unique geography and military ties with Russia pose complexities in military cooperation. Although limited joint military exercises have been conducted among Quad members, their military interests diverge significantly.

For instance, while the US, Japan, and Australia express concerns about Chinese aggression in the Taiwan Strait, India's focus lies more on territorial disputes with China in Ladakh and Tibet, given its specific geographic position. Additionally, India's strong military ties with Russia and friendly relations with Iran raise concerns among other Quad members.

The unpredictable foreign policy of the Trump administration and China's growing assertiveness have led to increased military investments in the broader Indo-Pacific region. While these investments in indigenous military development may be perceived as safeguarding a free and open Indo-Pacific, they could also reflect a growing sense of insecurity among smaller regional powers and heightened expectations of potential military conflicts.

This escalating military investment might lead to a security dilemma, wherein China perceives it as a security threat and responds with its own military buildup. Such a situation could result in a cycle of increasing militarization and create a higher risk of miscalculation in the region.

Advance Technology and Cyber Security: The US, Japan, and Australia share significant common ground when it comes to their priorities within advanced technology and cybersecurity. The Quad Technology Business and Investment Forum, established in 2022, aims to coordinate crucial aspects such as standards, supply chain resilience, and telecommunications deployment. Notably, Australia was the first country to publicly ban Huawei's communications infrastructure following the US's call for its allies and partners to do so. Australia also maintains a strong cyber partnership with the US as part of the Five Eyes intelligence alliance. Japan's close military integration with the US further reinforces expectations of alignment on cyber issues.

India's role as an emerging secondary manufacturing hub for many US technology companies, seen as an alternative to China amid US decoupling policies, holds promise. Strengthened technology and economic relations between India and the Quad members could deepen cooperation and foster joint advancements in the fields of advanced technology and cybersecurity.

Cooperation among Quad Members in Upward Trend

The cooperation among Quad members has shown an upward trend under the Biden administration spanning key strategic areas such as military, economic, and cyber/technology domains. The US has effectively utilized the Quad to strengthen its bilateral ties with India, Japan, and Australia, with significant progress since 2018.

The US, as the leading force within the Quad alliance, has played a crucial role in shaping the extent of engagement among its members. Bilateral relationships between the US and each Quad member have been instrumental in driving closer cooperation within the group. However, it's essential to recognize that China's assertiveness has further motivated Quad members to cooperate closely, as they seek to counterbalance China's actions in the region. This dynamic has resulted in gains for the US and setbacks for China in terms of their respective bilateral relationships with Quad members.

Need to Have Realistic Expectations from the Quad

However, despite these advancements, the Quad's ability to reshape the Indo-Pacific region in line with its stated objectives has been limited. China's influence in the region remains considerable, despite some reputational damage caused by its assertive posturing under President Xi Jinping and economic challenges posed by the COVID-19 pandemic and prolonged Zero-COVID policies until early 2023.

It is important to have realistic expectations from the Quad. The Quad is a valuable tool for fostering closer cooperation among its four member powers. The Quad was never intended to be an operational force but rather a platform for developing and coordinating relations between important countries seeking to form a counterbalance to China. Its strength lies in bringing India into alignment and ensuring broad normative agreement among the largest democracies in the Indo-Pacific.

Thus despite some difference, the India-US relationship and their engagement in the Quad are likely to continue progressing incrementally, especially if the shared concern over China remains a unifying factor.[12]

However, the future trajectory of the Quad depends heavily on the individual national interests of its member countries and the development of bilateral relations between them. While the Quad has made strides in solidifying its presence, its long-term sustainability and effectiveness will be shaped by how each member prioritizes their interests and navigates their respective relationships within the group.

China's Response to the Quad

China perceives the Quad as an emerging 'Asian NATO' and a veiled effort by the US to form an anti-China alliance with a primary focus on security matters. In response to the Quad's increasing cooperation, China has taken indirect actions. It has imposed broad economic disciplinary measures aimed mainly at the US and Australia. It has escalated territorial disputes with India and Japan to assert its regional presence. It has used demarches and adopted harsh rhetoric to caution against what it views as a 'Cold War mentality.' It is also striving to strengthen partnerships in the Indo-Pacific region.

Recognizing the Quad as a perceived anti-China 'bloc,' China has embarked on efforts to build its own strategically-aligned group. This involves establishing links with other Indo-Pacific partners, including Pacific Islands and select Southeast Asian nations. Additionally, China has expanded ties with countries in Central Asia, Africa, and Latin America. Moreover, it has fostered military and trade relations with nations like Russia, Iran, Pakistan, and others, potentially seeking to create a counterweight to coordinated sanctions from countries aligned with the US.

China's response to the Quad's growing presence illustrates its concerns about being isolated or contained by a coalition of major democracies in the Indo-Pacific region. To safeguard its interests, China has proactively sought to forge alternative partnerships and strengthen ties with countries beyond the Quad's influence.

AUKUS

The US, the United Kingdom, and Australia have maintained a close relationship since World War I, which has formed the basis of an alliance between them. This alliance has grown stronger over the years, with deep cooperation based on liberal democratic values and aligned national interests. There is also an understanding that the national security of these countries is directly linked to the autonomy, freedom, and stability of like-minded partners and allies. All of this prompted these three nations to create the Australia-United Kingdom-US (AUKUS) trilateral security pact in late 2021.

The primary motivation behind forming the AUKUS was China's

significant expansion of diplomatic, economic, and military influence. This challenge from China prompted the member nations to deepen their collaboration, particularly in nuclear-powered submarine technology, highlighting their shared concerns about China's military threat. The pact aims to address strategic challenges and maintain stability amidst an evolving geopolitical landscape.

Origin and Evolution of AUKUS

In 2020, a US intelligence report stated that the Chinese navy was operating 350 ships and submarines, surpassing the US Navy's 293 vessels. The Royal British Navy and the Royal Australian Navy currently operate approximately 70 and 50 vessels, respectively.[13] This indicated a clear imbalance in naval power in the Indo-Pacific.

Following this, Australia made a request to the Biden administration in April 2021 to acquire nuclear-powered submarines. This could be seen as the genesis of the AUKUS.[14] In September 2021, the leaders of Australia, the United Kingdom, and the US jointly announced the establishment of AUKUS to support Australia's acquisition of nuclear-powered submarines for its Royal Australian Navy by 2039.

Thus, AUKUS was formed to tackle the naval power imbalance in the region. On 13 March 2023, AUKUS leaders announced Australia's plan to acquire a conventionally-armed, nuclear-powered submarine capability through the partnership.[15] This approach will be phased, involving a combination of operational American nuclear-powered submarines with Australian personnel, rotational deployments of American and British submarines in the region, the sale of US Virginia-class submarines, and the development of a new 'SSN-AUKUS' based on British and American submarine technology.

To become part of the AUKUS partnership, Australia decided to cancel its previous deal of 12 new diesel-electric submarines and instead focus on acquiring conventionally-armed, nuclear-powered submarines.[16] This shift in approach, along with the support from the UK and the US in sharing technology, was driven by the need to counterbalance China's growing naval power and assertiveness. The partnership also seeks to enhance joint capabilities in areas such as cyber, artificial intelligence, quantum technologies, and undersea capabilities.[17]

Notably, the pact marks a significant step, with the US agreeing to share its classified technology on nuclear submarine propulsion. This is only the second instance of such an agreement, the first being the 1958 US-UK Mutual Defense Agreement (MDA) that facilitated the transfer of nuclear propulsion technology to the UK.

Stated Objective and Follow-up Actions

The primary stated objective of the pact was to assist Australia in establishing the infrastructure, technical capabilities, industry, and human capital required to develop, maintain, operate, and oversee an independent fleet of conventionally-armed, nuclear-powered submarines. This was stated in the Joint statement of AUKUS leaders issued in March 2023.

To implement the objectives of AUKUS several initiatives have been taken. The US and UK are trying to work out the most suitable approach for Australia to acquire a conventionally-armed, nuclear-powered submarine capability. Besides, the partnership has announced the establishment of two initiatives: AUKUS Undersea Robotics Autonomous Systems (AURAS) and AUKUS Quantum Arrangement (AQuA). These initiatives are designed to enhance coordination on autonomous underwater vehicles and next-generation quantum capabilities, respectively.

The trilateral efforts of the partnership are concentrated on advancing cyber, hypersonic, counter-hypersonic, and electronic warfare capabilities. The leaders also emphasized on the importance of collaborative innovation and the expansion of sharing sensitive information among the member nations.

Australia Prioritizes National Security Over Trade with China

In Australia, there has been a debate regarding the prioritization of its national security alliance with the US over its economic ties with China. The establishment of the AUKUS partnership strongly signals Australia's choice to prioritize its security relationship with Washington. This decision comes amid ongoing concerns about potential punitive Chinese sanctions, which leaves Australia with little choice but to diversify its trade away from reliance on the Chinese market.

AUKUS has withstood changes in the Australian political landscape. Now, a clearer estimate of the programme's overall cost has emerged. Australia's share of the programme over three decades is projected to be between $268 billion and $368 billion. This figure provides a more quantifiable understanding of the financial commitment involved in achieving the goals set forth by the AUKUS partnership. Despite costs to Australian taxpayers, this agreement reinforces security cooperation and defence industrial information sharing between Australia, the US, and the United Kingdom for decades to come. The pact firmly establishes Australia's commitment to its security alliance with Washington and its role in strategic collaboration with like-minded partners.

AUKUS Designed to Strengthen the US's Maritime Military Superiority

AUKUS is strategically designed to bolster and reinforce the US's decisive technological military advantage over the PLA of China. Over the years, China's increased military funding and modernization under President Xi Jinping's leadership have eroded traditional US hard power advantages. The growing capabilities of the PLA Navy (PLAN), PLA Air Force (PLAAF), and PLA Rocket Force (PLARF) have raised concerns within the Pentagon.[18]

Yet, the American submarine force stands out as a significant exception to this paradigm. Given that any potential conflict between the US and China is likely to occur or be primarily fought in the maritime domain, the US retains a crucial advantage in undersea warfare. AUKUS serves as the foundation for strengthening this submarine supremacy, offering the necessary framework, incentives, and resources to further enhance capabilities.

Moreover, the partnership brings more UK SSNs (Submarines) into the theatre and includes Australia as a critical partner in a submarine warfare triad, which could pose a substantial challenge to the PLAN in the event of a conflict. It also shares the responsibility for monitoring and, if necessary, defending the vital maritime choke points within the first island chain, allowing for a more concentrated deployment of forces by individual allied navies.

Essentially, AUKUS is a strategic move to solidify and expand the US's military edge in the maritime domain, particularly in the context of potential challenges from China, and it creates a cooperative framework that enhances the collective capabilities of the allied navies involved.

Australia's decision to shift from diesel submarines to SSNs (nuclear-powered submarines) represents a significant transformation in its national security strategy and strengthens its role in deterring Chinese military aggression. While diesel submarines are suitable for coastal defence, they lack the capability for offensive operations against enemy submarines or surface combatants on the open seas. Australia's move to collaborate with the UK and the US for SSNs indicates a clear recognition that diesel submarines are insufficient as a naval deterrent against the perceived most imminent threat—the PLAN of China.

At both the tactical and operational levels of warfare, SSNs provide a far more formidable force projection platform. The shift to nuclear-powered submarines is not merely a change in propulsion but a comprehensive strategic adjustment. It enables Australia to project power effectively from vital shipping lanes like the Malacca Strait to the waters near Taiwan. Moreover, with the capacity to launch much longer-range missiles, an SSN could strike targets on China's mainland while positioned to the east of the Philippines, vastly expanding Australia's offensive capabilities.

This strategic move signifies Australia's commitment to enhancing its maritime presence and capabilities, allowing it to play a more robust and assertive role in regional security dynamics and deter potential adversaries like China. The acquisition of SSNs reinforces Australia's relevance in countering security threats and further solidifies its position as a formidable player in the Indo-Pacific region.

Challenges Facing AUKUS

The main threat to AUKUS lies in short-term domestic political considerations and incentives in both the US and Australia. In late December 2022, Senators Jack Reed and James Inhofe expressed concern in a letter to the Biden administration about the state of the US submarine industrial base and its ability to support the desired end state of AUKUS's nuclear submarine development. The senators cautioned against any sale or transfer of American submarines to Australia as it required intense operational demands. They also feared that it could put strain on the domestic industrial base. The apprehension about sustaining the domestic industrial base while meeting AUKUS requirements became more pronounced after the US announced on 13 March 2023, its decision to sell Australia at least three Virginia-class submarines, with the possibility of two more.

Another challenge stems from the massive cost of the SSN programme for Australia, estimated to be between $268 billion and $368 billion, which is five to seven times its current annual defence budget. This expenditure raises concerns about the sustained support of such a significant government investment on national defence, particularly among Australian taxpayers.

Despite AUKUS successfully navigating a government transition from the Liberal to the Labour Party in Australia, the sustainability of such a substantial commitment remains uncertain. Political dynamics and public sentiment may influence the project's trajectory in both countries, and any changes in support or funding could potentially impact the progress and realization of the AUKUS's goals.

China's Response to AUKUS

China has been critical of the AUKUS partnership.[19] It has condemned the pact as a reflection of the outdated Cold War zero-sum mentality and narrow-minded geopolitical perception. It also warned the three nations that they were hurting their own interests by forming this alliance.

China also pointed out that Australia might be in violation of its commitments under the Treaty of Rarotonga, also known as the South Pacific Nuclear Free Zone Treaty. This treaty prohibits the member nations from placing nuclear weapons within the South Pacific. The Chinese state media warned that the treaty would make Australia a potential target of a nuclear strike in the event of a nuclear war.[20]

Subsequently, China also warned the three countries that they were moving down the wrong and dangerous path for their own geopolitical self-interest. These Chinese objections clearly showed its objections to the strategic collaboration among these nations, signaling tensions and a deepening sense of rivalry in the Indo-Pacific region.

Partners in the Blue Pacific (PBP)

The Pacific Island Countries (PICs) are positioned along critical military and economic sea lanes for the US. These countries collectively hold significant diplomatic influence. Despite being historically influential in the Pacific region, the US's regional engagement in diplomatic, military, and economic matters has waned since the post-World War II era. In recent years, the PICs have become a focal point in the ongoing competition between the US and China.

Capitalizing on this decline in US engagement, China has intensified its outreach to the Pacific Island Countries, providing substantial foreign aid amounting to nearly $1.5 billion between 2006 and 2017. This increased presence of China in the region prompted a response from the US, Australia, Japan, New Zealand, and the United Kingdom, leading to the launch of the Partners in the Blue Pacific initiative. The Partners in the Blue Pacific is an informal coordination programme aimed at supporting the Pacific region and addressing its priorities collectively.

Through the Partners in the Blue Pacific, multilateral cooperation is being encouraged to streamline aid towards the Pacific Island Countries and bolster the presence of the US and its allies in the region. However, the effectiveness of this initiative in countering China's influence remains to be seen. The scale of aid provided through the Partners in the Blue Pacific will be a crucial factor in determining its success in balancing China's engagement with the Pacific Island Countries. As the competition between the US and China in the region continues, the Pacific Island Countries strategic importance is likely to remain a key focus for both nations and their allies.

India's Approach to the Indo-Pacific

The US has identified India as a crucial partner in its IPS, recognizing India's growing influence and capabilities. The deepening strategic partnership between the US and India is marked by closer defence ties, technology transfer, and joint military initiatives. This makes it essential to understand India's perspective on the Indo-Pacific.

Historically, India has prioritized its continental borders due to its geographic location, domestic political instability, conflicts with neighbouring countries, and resource constraints. However, in the twenty-first century, India began shifting its focus towards the maritime domain, recognizing its significance for trade and security.

To promote regional cooperation in the IOR, India launched the Indian Ocean Rim Association (IORA) in 1997. This initiative aimed to strengthen maritime ties among participating nations. In 2015, India further reinforced its maritime outreach with the launch of the Security and Growth for All in the Region (SAGAR) initiative.

In 2018, India officially joined the Indo-Pacific construct, acknowledging the need to address unconventional security threats and secure the eastern Indian Ocean and western Pacific Ocean. Prime Minister Narendra Modi outlined India's vision for the Indo-Pacific during the Shangri-La Dialogue in Singapore, emphasizing the importance of an open and inclusive order based on respect for the sovereignty and territorial integrity of all nations.[21]

To provide further clarity on its vision, India launched the Indo-Pacific Ocean Initiative (IPOI) in November 2019. The IPOI identified seven pillars for cooperation with Indo-Pacific countries, including maritime security, ecology, resources, capacity building, disaster risk reduction, science and technology, and trade and connectivity. India aims to leverage existing regional cooperation architecture and mechanisms to foster an open and inclusive Indo-Pacific region.

Through these initiatives and engagements, India seeks to enhance its maritime presence, strengthen regional cooperation, and contribute to the stability and prosperity of the Indo-Pacific region.

Diverse Perspectives on the IPS among Stakeholders

While the IPS, particularly championed by the US, is commonly seen as a response to China's assertiveness, there exists a spectrum of perspectives among stakeholders. Documents released by nations such as the US, France, and Canada underscore China's assertive conduct in the region. They regard China as a potential challenge to regional stability and the established rules-based order. These nations stress the importance of collective action, partnerships, and adherence to a rules-based approach to effectively tackle common challenges, including those posed by China's actions.

In contrast, South Korea adopts a more inclusive approach towards the Indo-Pacific. It recognizes China as a vital partner for achieving prosperity and peace within the region. South Korea's stance is shaped by its geopolitical context and economic interdependence with China. It seeks to balance its relationships with major powers and pursues a cooperative approach that incorporates both engagement and collaboration.

Similarly, the European Union (EU) also adopts an inclusive stance regarding the Indo-Pacific. While recognizing the necessity to address challenges and uphold a rules-based order, the EU's approach is not solely centered on great power competition. Additionally, ASEAN, a regional organization comprising Southeast Asian nations, advocates for inclusivity in terms of ideas and proposals concerning the Indo-Pacific.

China's Response to the IPS

China is acutely aware that it is the primary target of the IPS, anticipating challenges from its implementation. It foresees future expansion of economic and military cooperation among the Quad countries, which could pose negative consequences. Economically, the IPS is viewed as a competitor to China's BRI, potentially undermining its economic presence in the region. Politically, the Sino-U.S. relationship would be tested, and China's relations with Japan, Australia, India, and Indian Ocean littoral countries would be adversely affected. Strategically, China perceives threats to its national security, particularly in maritime security, with the possibility of increased US involvement in the South China Sea through the IPS.[22]

Yet, China also believes that the IPS's influence on it would be limited due to internal and external constraints. Internally, financial difficulties and personnel changes within the US administration pose obstacles to the IPS. Externally, differences in emphasis on core elements of the IPS between the US and other partners, particularly India, create additional challenges. Furthermore, small states in the region, including ASEAN countries, are reluctant to take sides between the US and China and have responded cautiously to the IPS. ASEAN seeks to maintain its centrality within the IPS and integrate China's BRI with the strategy to maximize economic benefits and minimize security threats. Nonetheless, to mitigate the risks posed by IPS, China seeks to engage with the US and other regional states.

Challenges and Considerations

The US IPS is designed to ensure regional stability by promoting a rules-based order and preventing any single power from dominating the Indo-Pacific region. At the heart of this strategy is the goal of countering China's influence, both economically and militarily, through collaboration with like-minded partners in South Asia and beyond However, the US faces the challenge of striking a balance between its strategic interests in the Indo-Pacific and avoiding direct confrontation with China. Diplomatic efforts are focused on managing competition and averting the region from becoming a flashpoint for conflict.

NOTES

1 'Indo-Pacific Strategy of the US', Washington DC: The White House, February 2022 at https://www.whitehouse.gov/wp-content/uploads/2022/02/U.S.-Indo-Pacific-Strategy.pdf last accessed on 17 June 2024.

2 Mayu Arimoto, Gabrielle Armstrong-Scott, Sophie Faaborg-Andersen, Nicholas Hanson, Chris Li with foreword by Joseph S. Nye, Jr, 'Elements of the U.S. Indo Pacific Strategy: A Qualitative Primer on the Quad, AUKUS, and Partners in the Blue Pacific,' Harvard: Belfer Center for Science and International Affairs, Harvard Kennedy School, Report, May 2023 at https://www.belfercenter.org/sites/default/files/files/publication/230526_API_IndoPacificStrategy_FINAL.pdf last accessed on 17 June 2024.

3 'Confluence of the Two Seas' Speech by H.E. Mr. Shinzo Abe, Prime Minister of Japan at the Parliament of the Republic of India, Ministry of Foreign Affairs of Japan, 22 August 2007 at https://www.mofa.go.jp/region/asia-paci/pmv0708/speech-2.html last accessed on 17 June 2024.

4 'A Free and Open Indo-Pacific: Advancing a Shared Vision', Report, U.S. Department of State, Bureau Of East Asian And Pacific Affairs, 3 November 2019 at https://www.state.gov/a-free-and-open-indo-pacific-advancing-a-shared-vision/ last accessed on 17 June 2024.

5 'Indo-Pacific Strategy Report: Preparedness, Partnerships, and Promoting a Networked Region', The Department Of Defense, 1 June 2019 at https://media.defense.gov/2019/Jul/01/2002152311/-1/-1/1/DEPARTMENT-OF-DEFENSE-INDO-PACIFIC-STRATEGY-REPORT-2019.PDF last accessed on 17 June 2024.

6 'U.S. Strategic Framework for the Indo-Pacific,' at https://trumpwhitehouse.archives.gov/wp-content/uploads/2021/01/IPS-Final-Declass.pdf last accessed on 17 June 2024.

7 'Indo Pacific Strategy Of The United States', The White House, Washington, February

2022 at https://www.whitehouse.gov/wp-content/uploads/2022/02/U.S.-Indo-Pacific-Strategy.pdf last accessed on 17 June 2024.

8 Dr. Pankaj Vashisht, 'Indo-Pacific Strategies: What Do They Entail for India?', RIS Discussion Paper Series, Discussion Paper #274, October 2022, p. 6 at https://www.ris.org.in/sites/default/files/Publication/DP%20274%20%20Pankaj%20Vashisht.pdf last accessed on 17 June 2024.

9 Soumyodeep Deb and Nathan Wilson, 'The Coming of Quad and the Balance of Power in the Indo-Pacific,' *Journal of Indo-Pacific Affairs*, Winter 2021, p. 115, please also see 'Bush Announces Tsunami Aid Coalition,' CNN, Cable News Network, https://edition.cnn.com/2004/US/12/29/bush.quake/ last accessed on 17 June 2024.

10 Indrani Bagchi, 'Australia to pull out of "quad" that excludes China', *The Times of India*, 6 February 2008, at https://timesofindia.indiatimes.com/india/australia-to-pull-out-of-quad-that-excludes-china/articleshow/2760109.cms last accessed on 17 June 2024.

11 'Quad Leaders' Joint Statement: "The Spirit of the Quad"', The White House, 12 March 2021, at https://www.whitehouse.gov/briefing-room/statements-releases/2021/03/12/quad-leaders-joint-statement-the-spirit-of-the-quad/ last accessed on 17 June 2024.

12 Lavina Lee, 'Assessing the Quad: Prospects and Limitations of Quadrilateral Cooperation for Advancing Australia's Interests', Lowy Institute, Sydney, Australia, May 2020 at https://www.lowyinstitute.org/publications/assessing-quad-prospects-limitations-quadrilateral-cooperation-advancing-australia-s last accessed on 17 June 2024.

13 'AUKUS Reshapes the Strategic Landscape of the Indo-Pacific,' *The Economist*, 25 September 2021 at https://www.economist.com/briefing/2021/09/25/aukus-reshapes-the-strategic-landscape-of-the-indo-pacific last accessed on 17 June 2024.

14 Michael R. Gordon, 'How the U.S. Agreed to Provide Nuclear Sub Technology to Australia,' *The Wall Street Journal*, 13 March 2023, at https://www.wsj.com/articles/how-the-u-s-agreed-to-provide-nuclear-sub-technology-to-australia-2b631d8f last accessed on 17 June 2024.

15 Douglas Peifer, 'French Anger over the AUKUS Trilateral Security Partnership Explained,' *Journal of Indo-Pacific Affairs*, 21 September 2021, https://www.airuniversity.af.edu/JIPA/Display/Article/2782767/french-anger-over-the-aukus-trilateral-security-partnership-explained/ last accessed on 17 June 2024.

16 Dustin Jones, 'Why a Submarine Deal Has France at Odds with the U.S., U.K. and Australia,' NPR, 19 September 2021, at https://www.npr.org/2021/09/19/1038746061/submarine-deal-us-uk-australia-france last accessed on 17 June 2024.

17 'Joint Leaders Statement on AUKUS,' The While House, 15 September 2021 at https://www.whitehouse.gov/briefing-room/statements-releases/2021/09/15/joint-leaders-statement-on-aukus/ last accessed on 17 June 2024.

18 Robert Burns, 'Pentagon Rattled by Chinese Military Push on Multiple Fronts,' AP News, 1 November 2021 at https://apnews.com/article/technology-china-asia-united-states-beijing-aea288656fab23253ee0397dc21ba68a last accessed on 17 June 2024.

19 'Aukus: China denounces US-UK-Australia pact as irresponsible', BBC News, 17 September 2021 at https://www.bbc.com/news/world-58582573 last accessed on 17 June 2024.

20 Yang Sheng, 'Nuke Sub Deal Could Make Australia "Potential Nuclear War Target."' *Global Times*, 16 September 2021 at https://www.globaltimes.cn/page/202109/1234460.shtml last accessed on 17 June 2024.

21 Ministry of External Affairs, Government of India, 'Prime Minister's Keynote Address at Shangri La Dialogue (June 01, 2018)' at https://www.mea.gov.in/Speeches-Statements.htm?dtl/29943/Prime+Ministers+Keynote+Address+at+Shangri+La+Dialogue+June+01+2018 last accessed on 17 June 2024.

22 Wu Shicun and Jayanath Colombage, 'Indo-Pacific Strategy and China's Response,' Institute for China-America Studies, October 2019 at https://chinaus-icas.org/wp-content/uploads/2020/11/Indo-Pacific-Strategy-and-Chinas-Response-Report-FINAL.pdf last accessed on 17 June 2024.

CHAPTER 7

US Attempts to Engage Smaller South Asian Nations

For the first time, the US began showing interest in the smaller South Asian nations, including Bangladesh, Sri Lanka, Nepal, Maldives, and Bhutan, in the post-9/11 era. Its aim was to play a role in resolving the deeper conflicts of these nations to prevent future incidents like 9/11. The Washington Consensus also promoted economic liberalization in the region, encouraging greater economic and trade relations among some South Asian countries. Before that, during the Cold War era, the geopolitics of South Asia were entirely defined by the India-Pakistan rivalry, where Pakistan sought to gain parity by aligning itself with the US, ostensibly opposing communism. In this phase, Pakistan played a role in bringing the US closer to China, inadvertently expediting the end of the Cold War.

However, the rise of an assertive China after 2008, making deep inroads in South Asia, has compelled the US to have broader engagement with these countries. In this endeavour, India stands as a major partner of the US.[1] The US aims to offset Chinese influence in the region through diplomatic engagement, alliance-building, and offering alternatives to Chinese investment and development initiatives. Promoting economic diversification, the US seeks to reduce dependence on Chinese financing and mitigate the risks associated with excessive debt.

Smaller South Asian countries exhibit varying degrees of engagement with China, ranging from Bhutan, which lacks formal diplomatic ties, to Bangladesh and Sri Lanka, boasting the strongest military and economic relations, respectively. The US seeks collaborative partnerships with smaller South Asian nations amidst evolving dynamics in the Indo-Pacific to maintain a balance of power in its favor.

US Adopts a Comprehensive Approach in Nepal

Nepal, a country in South Asia without a maritime border, holds significance in the IPS of the US. Geographically situated between two Asian giants, India and China, with often competing interests, Nepal endeavours to delicately balance its relationships with these neighbours. India, besides being Nepal's immediate neighbor, serves as a pivotal player in the US's IPS designed to contain China.

The geographic proximity of Nepal to India and its border with the restive Tibet makes it essential for China. Consequently, China remains wary of increasing American influence in Nepal. These unique attributes contribute to Nepal's geopolitical importance in the Indo-Pacific despite not having a maritime border.

However, amid the shifting dynamics of the Great Power competition now focused on the Indo-Pacific, Nepal maintains its own priorities and interests. The country aspires to safeguard its interests by navigating the complexities of its relationships with competing powers and engaging in newly formed multilateral partnerships and arrangements.

Evolution of US Engagement

Nepal has been a region of tertiary interest to Washington for several decades. During this period, the US primarily engaged through its embassy, providing aid for social issues. However, this approach underwent a significant transformation as the great power competition intensified.

For both Beijing and Washington, South Asia has evolved into a theatre of competition. In the last decade, Beijing's political and economic presence has seen a tremendous increase in Nepal, prompting Washington to take proactive measures. The US is now attempting to engage with Nepal in a more comprehensive manner. The current understanding is that the earlier approach of dealing with Nepal solely through aid, was too simplistic.

As a result, the US has adopted a more comprehensive approach, involving diplomacy, economic engagement, aid, and security cooperation. This shift towards a more holistic strategy signifies the recognition of Nepal's strategic importance and the necessity for broader engagement beyond social issues.

Economic Engagement through MCC Sparks Controversy

In the economic arena, the US has attempted to engage Nepal through its Millennium Challenge Corporation (MCC) Compact. Under this compact, the $500 million grant from the US government will be used for two major projects: a 400 kV electricity transmission line connecting Nepal to India (the Compact will cover the Nepal section only), and the upgrade of around 100 kilometres of roads along the East-West Highway. The projects were finalized after extensive consultation with Nepali civil society, the private sector, and other stakeholders.

Nepal signed the agreement on the MCC Compact in September 2017. However, the US desired the MCC Compact to be ratified by the Nepalese parliament to grant it the status of an international agreement for faster implementation. Some Nepalese also believed that this would bring transparency to the Compact. Interestingly, the Chinese have never sought ratification for their BRI projects by the Nepalese parliament, nor was the question of Nepal joining China's BRI ever discussed as vigorously as the MCC was debated. It is often believed that Nepal needed to join BRI urgently, and Chinese interests in bringing Nepal on board were, for the most part, ignored.

However, in the case of ratification of the MCC Compact, there was no unanimity in Nepal. Critics of the Compact claimed that it was part of Washington's IPS, which has a military component. Ratifying this Compact would imply that Nepal would have a US military presence. Some American officials had also linked the Compact to the IPS. The task force formed by the Nepal Communist Party also concluded that the Compact was a part of the IPS.[2]

To dispel doubts regarding the Compact, MCC Vice-President Fatima Sumar visited Nepal and met with parliamentarians, civil society leaders, and the business community. Nepal feared that ratification of the Compact would make it part of a military alliance and lead to its deviation from the non-aligned foreign policy. Moreover, being a close partner of China, it would also not like its territory to be used against China, which is the primary objective of the IPS. Other concerns included the belief that under the Compact, US laws would prevail over Nepal's Constitution, and the Auditor General of Nepal would not have the authority to audit the Compact.

The Chinese also attempted to draw Nepal away from the MCC and the evolving political formulation of the IPS. The Chinese Foreign Minister Wang Yi visited Kathmandu in September 2019. This visit revived debate on the evolving 'Indo-Pacific' geopolitical formulation in Nepal. At the end of this visit, the Chinese Foreign Ministry in Beijing issued a statement saying, 'Nepal firmly adheres to the non-alignment policy, disapproves of the so-called "Indo-Pacific Strategy," opposes any attempt to stop the development of China, and believes that China's development is an opportunity for Nepal and is willing to learn from China's successful experience.'[3]

This statement about Nepalese foreign policy coming from China was criticized by the US, but it also made them concerned about the growing Chinese footprint in Nepal through its BRI, where Nepal has come to be its major beneficiary. Nepal, at the same time, kept dragging its feet over the issue of ratification of the MCC Compact, which was seen as a component of the US IPS.

Nepal's Shifting Alliances

Initially, Nepal leaned towards China, criticizing IPS. However, under the Deuba government, it showed inclination towards the MCC Compact. The changing government in Nepal and internal opposition highlighted the complexities of foreign policy decisions.

In October 2021, Nepal's private sector business association called on the government to ratify the MCC Compact. They believed that the US grant of $500 million would give the fund-starved Nepali economy a boost. The Compact was expected to 'increase investment, accelerate growth, and reduce poverty'[4] by improving power supply and lowering transportation costs.

The Deuba government in Nepal also appeared to lean towards the IPS. However, protests intensified as the deadline for MCC ratification approached in February 2022. Two members of the ruling coalition—the Nepal Communist Party-Maoist Center (NCP-MC) led by Pushpa Kamal Dahal and Communist Party of Nepal-Unified Socialist (CPN-US) led by Madhav Kumar Nepal—saw the MCC as part of the US's anti-China IPS. They argued that ratification of the MCC by the Nepalese parliament would undermine the country's sovereignty.

China was also against the ratification of the MCC, and *China Daily*, in one of its editorials, suggested that this ratification would have 'far-reaching consequences economically and geopolitically' for China. It asked Nepal to 'stay out of the US' geopolitical games.' *The Global Times*, another mouthpiece of the Chinese government, considered the MCC a 'Trojan horse' designed to encircle China.[5]

At this stage, the US used coercion to push Nepal to move forward on the MCC grant issue. While the MCC Compact was debated in Nepal, US Assistant Secretary of State for South and Central Asian Affairs Donald Lu visited Kathmandu and threatened to reassess the entire US-Nepal relationship if it was not ratified. Despite significant opposition from the Communists, Dahal finally fell in line and ratified it. Despite significant domestic opposition to the MCC, the resolve of the Deuba government to get it passed showed its tilt towards the MCC Compact.

Moreover, when the Chinese Foreign Minister, Wang Yi, visited Nepal[6] towards the end of March 2022 to control the damage, Deuba told him that Nepal would now not take any loans from China and would welcome only grants. This was another indication of Nepal shifting towards the MCC Compact.[7] To address the concerns of critics and to show sensitivity to Chinese concerns, the Nepalese parliament added an 'interpretive clause' to the MCC compact. This clause stated that the MCC compact is just a development grant, is not above the country's constitution, and is not part of any strategic, military, or security alliance, such as Washington's Indo-Pacific Strategy.[8]

Diplomatic Engagement through Charm Offensive

The Deuba government was subsequently replaced by Dahal, a Maoist leader who has demonstrated flexibility in his approach towards the MCC Compact.

The Americans have also altered their approach, launching a charm offensive towards Nepal and seeking to engage Nepali policymakers actively. They are employing rapid-fire diplomacy, involving a series of high-level visits, signaling that Washington now takes its relationship with Nepal seriously.

The visit of Nuland aimed to ensure that the implementation of the MCC remains on track despite the change of government in Nepal.[9] She also announced that the US would invest more than $1 billion in clean energy, electrification, and small businesses led by women and under-represented communities in Nepal over the next five years.

During Nuland's visit, the US sought to strengthen its engagement with Nepal on democracy-related issues. She appreciated Nepalese democracy, which has evolved since 2006, in contrast to the existing authoritarianism in Beijing. Samantha Power, the administrator of the US Agency for International Development (USAID), visited Nepal in February 2023. Her focus during the visit was on economic cooperation and partnerships in priority areas. Power extended US President Joe Biden's invitation to Dahal to participate in the Summit for Democracy in March 2023.

Attempt to Enhance Military Engagement

Security has been a critical pillar of US engagement with Nepal, especially in the context of its IPS. The US is now increasingly seeking security engagement. The US and Nepali armies have been conducting joint exercises for decades for humanitarian assistance and disaster relief (HADR). However, Washington seeks to go beyond joint exercises. The US attempted to enhance its military engagement through the State Partnership Programme (SPP), an exchange programme between the US National Guard and foreign militaries.[10] Nepal has pulled out of this agreement, but the US is not likely to give up soon. The US is also looking at alternative ways to engage Nepal after the latter rejected the SPP.

China's Attempt to Bolster BRI

China has been eager to strengthen its BRI in Nepal, given the US's increased emphasis on the MCC programme, intensifying competition in infrastructure development in the region. In May 2017, Nepal and China signed a

Memorandum of Understanding (MoU) to enhance bilateral cooperation under the BRI framework, focusing on the connectivity of facilities, trade, financial integration, and people-to-people connections. Nepal perceived this as an opportunity to benefit across various sectors and overcome its status as a least-developed country.

However, progress was slower than anticipated. Initially, Nepal selected thity-five projects for implementation under the BRI but eventually narrowed it down to nine. These nine projects included the ambitious trans-Himalayan railway feasibility study, electricity transmission line extension, a technical university establishment, and various infrastructure projects. To expedite these ventures, Chinese President Xi Jinping visited Kathmandu in October 2019. Nevertheless, despite these efforts and five years since the initial MoU, no projects have been finalized yet.

Nepal has raised three main concerns with China regarding BRI projects. First, there is uncertainty about the financing method, with Nepal preferring grants over loans. Second, Nepal seeks interest rates, not exceeding 1 per cent per year comparable to multilateral funding agencies like the World Bank and the Asian Development Bank (ADB). Last, China's insistence on hiring Chinese firms for most projects is a point of contention, and Nepal wants open competitive bidding for the projects.

Nepal's concerns were communicated to China by the Sher Bahadur Deuba government which explicitly stated its inability to accept commercial loans for financing projects under the BRI. Furthermore, Nepal sought an extended repayment period of 40 years or beyond for any loans that might be taken, aiming to alleviate the financial burden and provide greater flexibility in managing the debt.

In April 2023, the Chinese Ambassador to Nepal, Hou Yanqi, reassured that Nepal remains a crucial partner in the BRI, despite some slowdowns due to the pandemic and Nepal's changing political landscape. She made it clear that China has been actively promoting its BRI in Nepal, using both grants and commercial loans for project financing. While Nepal has expressed a preference for grants, the Chinese ambassador clarified that the BRI encompasses various modalities.

Regarding the financing modality of projects under the BRI in Nepal, the former Chinese ambassador to Nepal, Hou Yanqi, stated that it includes both grants and commercial loans. She emphasized that many ongoing projects in Nepal fall under the BRI framework, illustrating the various modalities of cooperation.

Hou explained that the BRI's implementation in Nepal involves three distinct modalities. First, projects like the Gautam Buddha Airport in Lumbini have received investment from the ADB, with Chinese contractors involved in the construction. Second, in the case of the Pokhara Airport, the financing involves a combination of China's commercial loans and grants. Additionally, the construction company responsible for the project is also of Chinese origin. The third modality is exemplified by the Tribhuvan International Airport in Kathmandu. In this scenario, a Chinese company has been entrusted with the responsibility of improving the airport, while the Nepal government bears the cost of the project.

Though Nepal and China had agreed to carry out nine projects under BRI not even one has started. So China in its desperation to show that BRI was active, started claiming projects as part of BRI which were actually being implemented outside of it.

A major controversy arose in Nepal over China's BRI after the Chinese Embassy in Kathmandu unilaterally declared the Pokhara International Airport as a 'flagship project of China-Nepal BRI cooperation.'[11] This statement has raised concerns among Nepali officials and political leaders as it contradicts the fact that no project under the BRI has been formally signed in Nepal.

The airport construction in Pokhara was financed through a Chinese loan, and it was inaugurated by Prime Minister Pushpa Kamal Dahal 'Prachanda.' However, the Prime Minister did not mention the BRI during the inauguration speech, and he expressed surprise and concerns over the Chinese Embassy's sudden announcement linking the airport to the BRI.

The Pokhara airport project was not part of the official BRI project list. The negotiation of the Pokhara airport with Chinese had begun from 2010 before China launched the BRI in 2013. The BRI framework agreement was signed between Nepal and China in 2017, while the loan agreement between China's EXIM Bank and the Civil Aviation Authority of Nepal

(CAAN) for the airport construction was signed in 2016. For the construction of the airport Nepal had signed a $215.96 million soft loan agreement with China in March 2016. China's Exim Bank had agreed to provide 25 per cent of the loan free of interest and set the interest rate at 2 per cent per annum for the rest of the amount, with a payback period of 20 years.

In April 2023 at a Foreign Secretary-level bilateral diplomatic consultation mechanism between Nepal and China, both sides once again put emphasis on timely implementation of Chinese investment projects. However, in this meeting Nepal showed lack of formal interest in China's ambitious projects, such as the BRI and the Global Security Initiative (GSI), following which China sought to enhance its influence in Nepal through the Global Development Initiative (GDI), launched by President Xi Jinping. Nepal has positively received the GDI as a humanitarian aid and development programme. The GDI presents an opportunity for Nepal to foster closer ties with China and benefit from developmental cooperation. China aims to expand its influence in Nepal through the GDI, portraying it as a humanitarian aid and development programme, which Nepal has viewed positively.

China's concerns in Nepal further increased after India refused to endorse the BRI during the SCO summit in New Delhi. After that it has accelerated efforts to complete the pending BRI projects in Nepal. An agreement was reached between Nepal's National Planning Commission and China's National Development and Reform Commission to expedite the completion of previously announced BRI projects in Nepal, boosting infrastructure.

Nepal remains cautiously optimistic about the BRI's potential benefits. Now it is assertive in seeking terms that align with its economic capacity. It is also wary of Chinese attempt to include earlier negotiated projects in its flagship BRI programme.

Nepal's Evolving Foreign Policy Landscape

Nepal finds itself confronted with fresh foreign policy challenges as the stage for Great Power competition shifts to the Indo-Pacific, where both the US and China vie for influence in South Asia. In response to this dynamic geopolitical scenario, Nepal has embarked on a new foreign policy approach.

Faced with a transformed domestic and international environment, Nepal recognizes the necessity of adopting a foreign policy that allows for a delicate balance among Beijing, New Delhi, and Washington while simultaneously advancing its national interests. The contours of this new foreign policy framework aim to address these multifaceted considerations.[12]

Nepal's Reluctance to Depend on US Commitments

Despite Nepal ratifying the MCC Compact, there is a significant level of distrust towards the US. The manner in which the US withdrew from Afghanistan has instilled apprehension among smaller nations, including Nepal, about relying on the US. In Nepal, there is a prevailing sentiment that the ongoing great power competition will eventually reach a resolution. Should the US manage to find common ground with China, successfully contain China, or fail in its objectives, there is concern that the US may withdraw from its commitments in the region, leaving countries like Nepal on their own at China's disposal, as witnessed in Afghanistan.[13] A growing perception within certain circles in Nepal suggests that US withdrawal from Afghanistan underscores the notion that Nepal cannot solely depend on US aid commitments.

For Nepal today, China does not represent only a balance to India's overarching presence. The Nepalese leadership also perceives significant opportunities for mutual benefit in the context of China's dramatic rise and abundant resources.[14]

Skepticism Towards IPS and Quad

There is a prevailing sentiment in Nepal that the IPS or the Quad may not effectively manage China. Members of the Quad and the IPS are grappling with challenges in finding common ground, struggling to align their strategies and interests among member countries. In their pursuit to counter China and wield influence over smaller nations in the region, these countries have instead created various alliances and groupings, such as the trilateral security partnership or AUKUS pact involving the US, the UK, and Australia. Notably, this pact has faced criticism from close security partner France.

In the current scenario, where US influence is waning, Australia relies heavily on the Chinese economy, Japan adheres to a pacifist policy, and

India complies with UNCLOS rules while having limited military and economic power compared to China, the Quad framework and IPS are questioned as custodians of international law.[15] The future trajectories of these organizations remain unclear. In such circumstances, Nepal prefers not to align with either India or China, given their competing interests in the region. Instead, Nepal aims to maintain a low profile and derive benefits from emerging multilateral frameworks.

Regarding the India-China rivalry, some Nepalese believe that China holds a clear advantage over India in economic and military fields. They also perceive India, due to its proximity to China, faces greater risks compared to other security partners who might make India the scapegoat if tensions escalate in the course of their strategic competition. The bilateral relationship between India and Nepal deteriorated in 2015 when Nepal implemented its new constitution, though it has improved since then. Uncertain of the commitments made by Quad members post-Afghanistan, Nepal remains unwilling to take sides.

Nepal's Strategic Position

The IPS remains a source of debate and controversy among Nepalese political parties. Despite the US adopting a comprehensive approach in its foreign policy towards Nepal, the country has not officially endorsed or rejected the IPS, perceived as a counter to China's expanding influence in the region. While some Nepali leaders disapprove of the strategy, expressing support for China's BRI, Nepal is currently navigating a delicate balance among the interests of China, India, and the US to maximize benefits without compromising its sovereignty and national dignity.

The ongoing struggle for dominance in the Indo-Pacific region may culminate in a unipolar, bipolar, or multipolar global order. Nepal seeks to advance its own interests amid this geopolitical competition, aiming to derive benefits from competing powers and emerging multilateral partnerships. As a rational actor, Nepal refrains from taking sides in the ongoing great power competition, preferring a non-aligned foreign policy. By doing so, Nepal positions itself to stand with the eventual victor when the competition settles, ensuring it can reap maximum benefits.

Bangladesh Prefers an Indo-Pacific Outlook (IPO)

Bangladesh, strategically located in the Bay of Bengal within the larger Indo-Pacific region, serves as a vital bridge connecting South and Southeast Asia. The ITLOS verdict in 2012 and the subsequent UN tribunal verdict in 2014, under UNCLOS, expanded Bangladesh's maritime area, providing it with enhanced access to the Bay of Bengal.

The significance of the Bay of Bengal further escalated following China's construction of an energy pipeline through Myanmar and the establishment of a submarine base, which China financed and constructed for Bangladesh. China's naval presence in the western Indian Ocean, including a military base off Djibouti, has raised concerns among regional rivals.

As an influential player in the Indian Ocean Rim Association (IORA) and the Bay of Bengal Initiative for Multi-Sectoral Technical and Economic Cooperation (BIMSTEC), Bangladesh is experiencing economic growth. It currently ranks as the second-largest economy in South Asia. The nation's continuous economic development suggests the potential for Bangladesh to emerge as one of the middle powers. In pursuit of this objective, Bangladesh is actively strengthening its military capabilities.

Dhaka maintains amicable ties with the US, various European nations, and other members of the Quad. Bangladesh plays a significant role in Japan's vision for the Indo-Pacific, outlined in the 2019 policy document 'Towards Free and Open Indo-Pacific.' In March 2023, during his visit to New Delhi, Japanese Prime Minister Kishida Fumio unveiled Japan's new plan for a free and open Indo-Pacific (FOIP). Stressing the need for collaboration within the FOIP framework, he highlighted the potential for harnessing the economic opportunities in the Bay of Bengal region. The desire to counterbalance China's assertiveness and uphold the established global order has piqued the interest of key Indo-Pacific players in including Bangladesh in their regional strategies.

Evolving US-Bangladesh Relations

In recent years, both the US and Bangladesh have actively sought to enhance their diplomatic ties through regular partnership and security dialogues. A notable example is the third US-Bangladesh partnership dialogue in 2014, where discussions centred on the potential development of the Indo-Pacific Economic Corridor (IPEC). Even the Trump Administration, in its 2017 National Security Strategy, recognized Bangladesh as a crucial partner in the region.

While bilateral relations have seen improvement, certain challenges persist. The US has expressed concerns about the fairness of elections in Bangladesh, the human rights records of Bangladeshi security agencies, and conditions related to media freedom and labour rights in the country. Additionally, Washington has raised eyebrows over Bangladesh's expanding military-economic ties with geopolitical rivals like China and Russia.

Bangladesh has also its own set of expectations from the US. Dhaka aims for the reinstatement of Generalized System of Preferences (GSP) facilities to gain trade benefits and seeks the removal of sanctions on the Rapid Action Battalion (RAB), a Bangladeshi security force.[16] Bangladesh also desires the extradition of Rashed Chowdhury, a former Bangladeshi military officer involved in the assassination of the country's founding father, and increased US involvement in the repatriation of Rohingya refugees.

Despite these areas of contention, both nations have successfully maintained and expanded their multifaceted relationship. While challenges exist, they do not define the entirety of the US-Bangladesh relationship. The positive aspects in this partnership far outweigh the existing issues.

Recognizing the strategic importance of Bangladesh, the US has recently sent various officials and diplomats to the country, with the visit of Assistant Secretary of State for South and Central Asian Affairs, Donald Lu, being a highlight.[17] Indo-Pacific discussions featured prominently during these visits, signaling the Biden Administration's intent to strengthen ties with Bangladesh. Similarly, the UK has also dispatched its minister for the Indo-Pacific, Anne-Marie Trevelyan, underscoring the continued international engagement with Bangladesh.[18]

Diverse Perspectives on the Indo-Pacific

The Indo-Pacific region is not universally perceived solely through the lens of great power competition among all stakeholders. It is crucial to acknowledge that this vast region comprises diverse nations with distinct priorities, interests, and historical relationships. Despite a shared concern regarding China's actions and influence, approaches to addressing these concerns can vary significantly.

Some countries emphasize on cooperative engagement, aiming to balance relationships and leverage economic ties, while others prioritize collective action and uphold the rules-based order. The understanding and treatment of the Indo-Pacific region are continuously evolving as countries engage with one another and adapt their strategies based on their unique interests and objectives. As part of this process, the US has introduced the IPEF, and Japan has initiated its Bay of Bengal Industrial Growth Belt initiative (BIG-B).

Bangladesh Remains Skeptical towards the IPS

Bangladesh, however, has maintained a skeptical stance toward the IPS, a sentiment evident during the visit of US Under Secretary for Political Affairs Victoria Nuland to Dhaka in March 2022. While the US presented the trip as an opportunity to underscore its commitment to and cooperation with Indo-Pacific partners, the response from the Bangladeshi foreign ministry did not align with this narrative.[19]

Bangladesh has expressed discomfort in becoming part of any security alliance in the Indo-Pacific region. Despite the offer from US Deputy Secretary of State Stephen Biegun to sell arms to Bangladesh under the IPS,[20] Bangladesh did not agree to this proposal and instead signaled its interest in infrastructural investments.[21] Even as Bangladesh aims to diversify its arms acquisitions as outlined in its Forces Goals 2030, China remains the country's primary arms supplier. Bangladesh believes that any arms purchase under the IPS could create discomfort for China. This highlights the complex dynamics at play in the evolving landscape of the Indo-Pacific region.

Chinese Apprehensions and Bangladesh's Balancing Act

China has exhibited growing concerns over what it perceives as attempts by Washington to sway Bangladesh into aligning with the US. The Chinese ambassador to Bangladesh, Yao Wen, has accused Washington of actively pushing Bangladesh into the US camp. In an effort to dissuade Bangladesh from leaning towards the Indo-Pacific Wen outlined China's stance on the IPS, emphasizing its strong defence elements.

To exert additional pressure on Bangladesh, China's new foreign minister, Qin Gang, departed from established diplomatic norms by making a 'technical stopover' in Dhaka in January 2023, deviating from the traditional first visit to Africa. During this visit, Qin Gang held a meeting with Bangladeshi Foreign Minister Abul Kalam Abdul Momen, where Momen offered reassurances to China regarding Bangladesh's commitment to a neutral stance in the geopolitical competition between Beijing and Washington.[22]

It is crucial for Bangladesh to tread carefully, as alienating China is not a viable option. China stands as Bangladesh's largest trading partner and primary defence supplier. Bangladesh actively participates in China's BRI through its involvement in the Maritime Silk Road project. China is also deeply engaged in the infrastructural development of Bangladesh. It has constructed a submarine base where two Chinese submarines are stationed. This development has notably altered the security dynamics in the IOR, particularly in the Bay of Bengal. Balancing these relationships poses a delicate challenge for Bangladesh in the evolving geopolitical landscape.

Pivotal Role of West in the Economic Growth of Bangladesh

Western countries play a pivotal role in Bangladesh's economic development. A significant portion of Bangladesh's exports is directed toward the US and Europe. Additionally, the substantial diaspora, comprising around two hundred thousand Bangladeshi origin individuals in the US and sizable communities in Europe, plays a crucial role by contributing to remittances sent back to Bangladesh.[23]

The Bangladeshi economy relies heavily on the export of ready-made garments to the West and the remittances flowing from expatriate Bangladeshis. As Bangladesh experiences robust economic growth, the country is making a transition from a low-income to a middle-income status. While this transformation is a positive development, it presents a new challenge for Bangladesh, particularly as it loses the Generalized System of Preferences (GSP) facility. This facility had facilitated significant market penetration for Bangladeshi products in Western markets.

In this evolving scenario, Bangladesh seeks the support of Western countries to sustain its economic growth. The assistance and collaboration of these nations is vital for Bangladesh as it navigates the complexities of its economic transition and endeavours to maintain its positive trajectory.

IPO of Bangladesh

To cultivate positive relations with Western nations Bangladesh unveiled its IPO on the eve of Prime Minister Sheikh Hasina's visits to Japan, the US, and the United Kingdom. Enshrined in this document is Bangladesh's vision for a free, open, peaceful, secure, and inclusive Indo-Pacific that fosters shared prosperity.[24] Emphasizing the region's global significance, the document underscores its collective impact on the world economy, international trade, climate action, and technological advancements, identifying them as key factors for Bangladesh's long-term resilience and prosperity.

The document articulates four guiding principles and fifteen objectives. The primary guiding principle draws inspiration from Sheikh Mujibur Rahman's foreign policy mantra of 'Friendship towards all, malice toward none.'[25] It emphasizes the renunciation of force in international relations and urges adherence to relevant UN treaties and international conventions such as the United Nations Convention on the Law of the Sea (UNCLOS).

Furthermore, the document stresses on the importance of constructive regional and international cooperation as a foundation for sustainable development and international peace. The objectives derived from these principles encourage countries to build mutual trust, promote dialogue, and ensure peace, prosperity, security, and stability throughout the Indo-Pacific.

Specifically, the document advocates for the strengthening of existing mechanisms for maritime safety and security, upholding the freedom of navigation and over-flight in accordance with international law and conventions, including the UNCLOS. Bangladesh supports international efforts to combat transnational organized crimes and calls for the promotion of open, transparent, and rules-based multilateral systems that facilitate equitable and sustainable development in the Indo-Pacific. Additionally, the document places emphasis on connectivity and the free flow of commerce in the region. This strategic outlook reflects Bangladesh's commitment to actively contributing to the stability and prosperity of the Indo-Pacific.

Bangladesh's Pragmatic Approach to the Indo-Pacific

Upon the release of Bangladesh's IPO, some Western analysts perceived a potential shift toward embracing the IPS advocated by the US and its regional partners.[26] The document, emphasizing the necessity for a free, secure, and peaceful region, was interpreted as aligning with the IPS. However, a closer examination suggests that Bangladesh remains cautious in its foreign policy choices.

While discussions surrounding the IPS have risen, Bangladesh has notably refrained from engaging with the US on matters related to the security of the Bay of Bengal. This reluctance reflects ongoing mistrust and hesitance towards embracing a more active security role in the region.

The Ukraine crisis, heightening great power competition, has presented challenges for countries like Bangladesh to maintain a balanced foreign policy. Despite these pressures, it would be premature to assume a definitive tilt towards the Indo-Pacific, given the longstanding and deep ties between Bangladesh and China.

Bangladesh has been striving to maintain a balanced approach, evident in the IPO document. The document seems designed to reassure China, emphasizing Bangladesh's commitment to avoiding rivalries and disclaiming any security goals. Like several Southeast Asian nations, Bangladesh refers to its stance as an 'outlook,' conveying a softer connotation rather than a rigid 'policy or strategy.' Notably, Dhaka has not indicated any intention to join the Quad, mirroring the responses of other South and Southeast Asian nations with complex relationships with China.

Despite China's warnings against participating in the Quad and suggestions regarding the IPEF, Bangladesh has affirmed its autonomy in foreign policy matters. Dhaka has not only rejected interference from China but also decided to chart its own course, underscoring its commitment to independent decision-making.

The IPO document underscores Bangladesh's comprehensive view of security, encompassing human security and non-traditional security issues. It advocates for technology transfer to facilitate a green transition, addressing challenges such as climate change. Bangladesh and the US are already collaborating in areas such as climate change, counter-terrorism, maritime security, military training, and UN peacekeeping.

Bangladesh perceives the Indo-Pacific as an economic opportunity. The export-led economic growth has made it a trading nation. In the new economic environment Bangladesh thinks that it has to maintain positive relations with both China, its largest trading partner, and the West, whose market access and capital investment will influence future economic development. As Bangladesh aims to achieve its goal of becoming an upper-middle-income country by 2031 and a modern, knowledge-based developed country by 2041, the nation prioritizes a pragmatic and balanced approach in international relations.

Bangladesh is poised to align itself primarily with the economic facets of the IPS, steering clear of the more overtly defensive and security-oriented aspects. The country is strategically manoeuvering the competitive landscape in the Indo-Pacific by adhering to the principles of non-alignment and neutrality. To achieve this, Bangladesh is actively participating in various multilateral institutions within the region, including the Washington-led IPEF, the China-led Indian Ocean Region Forum, and the multilateral Regional Comprehensive Economic Partnership (RCEP).

In adopting this approach, Bangladesh seeks to leverage economic cooperation while avoiding entanglement in the great power rivalries that characterize the Indo-Pacific. By engaging in these multilateral forums, Bangladesh aims to safeguard its national interests.

This nuanced strategy allows Bangladesh to deftly navigate the intricate dynamics of the Indo-Pacific region, ensuring a balanced pursuit of its economic and strategic objectives. Rather than aligning itself rigidly with any one geopolitical camp, Bangladesh opts for a pragmatic and flexible stance that promotes economic growth and cooperation while avoiding unnecessary geopolitical entanglements.

Sri Lanka's Strategic Balance with the US, China and India

Sri Lanka's strategic significance in the Indo-Pacific region stems from its location in the Indian Ocean, placing it near important sea lanes of communication, including the Malacca Straits and the Strait of Hormuz. These routes witness a significant volume of naval vessels and oil tankers each year, connecting energy consumers in East Asia with suppliers in the Middle East.

Prior to 2009, Sri Lanka was primarily known for its counterinsurgency campaign against the Tamil Tigers, who claimed to be fighting for the rights of the Tamil minority. After the defeat of the Tamil Tigers by President Mahinda Rajapaksa in 2009, the world's attention shifted to the growing Chinese presence in Sri Lanka. China initiated several multi-billion-dollar infrastructure projects, largely through loans provided at commercial interest rates. Sri Lanka's growing economic and strategic ties with China have raised concerns for both the US and India. This has turned Sri Lanka into an outpost for Chinese influence, and now, with the intensification of great power competition, both the US and India are striving to gain influence in Sri Lanka. India is particularly concerned as Sri Lanka is located in its neighbourhood. The US, on the other hand, is alarmed by China's debt diplomacy and the potential militarization of Sri Lankan ports.

The relationship between the US and Sri Lanka has evolved over time, with the US providing assistance since Sri Lanka's independence. However, the relationship deepened further after the defeat of Mahinda Rajapaksa in 2015. In the subsequent Sirisena government, both the US and India had the opportunity to strengthen their positions in the country. Now the struggle for influence in Sri Lanka has intensified.

The US has come out with its IPS to keep the balance of power in its favour in the region. As part of its IPS, the US aims to provide alternative options for countries in the region, including Sri Lanka, to counterbalance China's influence. While completely excluding China from Sri Lanka may not be feasible, both India and the US are working to reduce its influence as they have a shared interest in the island country. The economic crisis in Sri Lanka that started in 2019 has provided an opportunity for them to further strengthen their positions, aided by China's reluctance to provide debt relief. However, Sri Lanka appears to be reluctant to take sides in the ongoing struggle for dominance in the Indo-Pacific.

China's Influence

The roots of the modern Sri Lanka-China relationship can be traced back to 1952, marked by the signing of the China-Ceylon Rice Rubber Pact. This agreement, negotiated by R.G. Senanayake, the Sri Lankan Minister of Trade and Commerce, emerged in response to the economic challenges confronting both nations at the time.

Sri Lanka was contending with a shortage of foreign exchange, a scarcity of rice, and a decline in commodity exports. Political upheavals had disrupted the country, and its rice imports from Southeast Asia had ceased due to a lack of foreign exchange. Furthermore, Sri Lanka's rubber exports to Western countries had diminished in the aftermath of the Korean War, resulting in reduced demand.

Conversely, China encountered restrictions on importing rubber due to sanctions imposed after the Korean War. The surplus of rubber in Sri Lanka and China's need for this commodity paved the way for the signing of the China-Ceylon Rice Rubber Pact. The primary objective was to address the economic challenges facing both nations.

It is noteworthy that this pact was formalized five years prior to the official establishment of diplomatic relations between Sri Lanka and China in 1957. This early collaboration in the economic realm laid the groundwork for the bilateral relationship, which has since flourished and expanded into diverse areas, encompassing trade, investment, infrastructure projects, and diplomatic ties.

Sri Lanka Embraces China

Sri Lanka's alignment with China saw significant growth and consolidation during the Mahinda Rajapaksa government's tenure from 2005 to 2015. Capitalizing on the Sri Lankan Civil War, China expanded its influence in the country by providing military support, including hardware, defense technology, and training. Chinese weaponry played a pivotal role in the defeat of the Liberation Tigers of Tamil Eelam (LTTE). This established China as a key defence partner for Sri Lanka and their collaboration was underscored by the display of Chinese-manufactured weapons in a victory parade celebrating Sri Lanka's triumph over the LTTE.

China also shielded Mahinda Rajapaksa from war crimes allegations on the international stage. In 2013, both nations elevated their bilateral relationship to a strategic cooperative partnership, and by 2016, China had surpassed India as Sri Lanka's largest trading partner. In a move that raised regional eyebrows, Sri Lanka permitted Chinese nuclear submarines to visit in 2014, despite concerns voiced by the Indian government.[27]

Mahinda Rajapaksa was highly popular in Sri Lanka for his role in defeating the Tamil Tigers and bringing about an investment and infrastructure boom in the country. This success fueled the aspirations of Sri Lankans to transform their nation into a trade and maritime hub. Initially, President Mahinda Rajapaksa sought military aid and investments from the US. However, he could not get this because of the war crime charges against him.[28] He also approached India for the Hambantota port development. Rajapaksa eventually accepted Chinese loans and investments when other nations showed little interest, ultimately leading to a debt trap.

During his regime, China heavily invested in large-scale infrastructure projects under the BRI, positioning itself as Sri Lanka's primary source of foreign direct investment and development assistance. These projects, while aiming to gain strategic advantage in the IOR and counterbalance India's influence, were criticized for their economic viability.[29] Mahinda Rajapaksa, strongly influenced by China, believed that these projects were in Sri Lanka's interest. There were allegations of receiving campaign funds from China during elections. China exploited Sri Lanka's economic vulnerabilities, loopholes and corrupt practices for its political and economic calculations.

During the Rajapaksa era, agreements signed by Chinese firms were shrouded in secrecy, raising concerns over their unfavorable clauses. Certain deals even ceded sovereign control over land near Sri Lanka's ports to China. However, there was a shift under the subsequent Sirisena-Wickremesinghe government. Some of these agreements were either rejected or renegotiated. This partially addressed the worries expressed by both the public and the international community.

Sri Lanka's foreign policy once again tilted towards China during Gotabaya Rajapaksa's presidency from 18 November 2019, to 14 July 2022, aligning closely with Beijing's strategic calculations. The government actively supported China and helped rebuild its image during the outbreak of the COVID-19 pandemic. Sri Lanka took a $500 million loan from China, which was labeled as a COVID-19 loan at China's request. Showing a readiness to adjust policies to accommodate Chinese interests, the government favored China over other nations in various decisions.

This shift was seen in the cancellation of a light rail project funded by Japan.[30] The Sri Lankan government also terminated a joint venture involving India's Adani Group, Japan International Cooperation Agency, and Sri Lanka Ports Authority for the development of the Eastern Container Terminal at Colombo Port. This project was subsequently awarded to the China Harbor Engineering Company.[31]

Furthermore, the passage of the Colombo Port City Economic Commission Bill by the Sri Lankan government to govern the Special Economic Zone of Colombo Port City developed by China drew criticism. It was felt that this would compromise with Sri Lanka's sovereignty. These moves by Gotabaya Rajapaksa's administration led to dissatisfaction among key partners such as India and Japan.

These Chinese-led projects transformed Sri Lanka into a strategic outpost for Beijing, addressing some of China's concerns regarding the Malacca Strait, a vital trade route. While certain projects brought tangible benefits to Sri Lanka, others faced scrutiny for their questionable economic viability. Many Sri Lankans contend that certain extravagant projects undertaken by China only exacerbated the country's debt burden, resulting in unsustainable levels of indebtedness and fostering corruption and nepotism.

Coalition Government Strives to Rebalance Sri Lanka's Foreign Policy

In a surprising electoral upset, Sirisena, once an ally of President Mahinda Rajapaksa, defeated him in the 2015 Presidential elections and formed a coalition government with his former rival, Prime Minister Ranil Wickremesinghe. During the coalition administration of President Maithripala Sirisena and Prime Minister Ranil Wickremesinghe, Sri Lanka endeavoured to rebalance its foreign policy, aiming to reduce its reliance on China. This government prioritized strengthening ties with India and the US while reassessing and revising the terms of agreements signed with China during Rajapaksa's tenure, albeit with varying degrees of success.

Prime Minister Wickremesinghe, representing the reform-oriented United National Party (UNP), sought to counterbalance the substantial Chinese loans by attracting new investments from India. During a visit to Delhi in April 2017, he inked several preliminary agreements outlining infrastructure projects for Indian companies. These initiatives included a solar power plant in Sampur, upgrades to a Jaffna airport, new railways and housing developments in the northern region, an oil tank farm and refinery in Trincomalee, and an expansion of the East Container Terminal at Colombo's main port. However, President Sirisena attempted to delay or halt these projects.

Sri Lanka faced a constitutional crisis when President Sirisena dissolved parliament and sought to appoint former President Rajapaksa as the new prime minister. Consequently, the US froze a nearly completed $500 million MCC compact for soft infrastructure investments, while the Japan International Cooperation Agency temporarily suspended a $1.4 billion soft loan for a light-railway project in Colombo. Notably, during the constitutional turmoil, Rajapaksa's shadow government finalized two multimillion-dollar contracts with Chinese firms to upgrade a container terminal at the Colombo port and procure new cranes.

Improvement in US-Sri Lanka Relations

The change in government in Sri Lanka in 2015, marked by the ousting of President Rajapaksa, has significantly contributed to the improvement of the Sri Lanka-US relationship, particularly in the defence arena. The US actively pursued closer ties with Sri Lanka, exemplified by John Kerry, then-Secretary of State's visit to Sri Lanka in 2015—the first such visit by a Secretary of State in three decades. This visit underscored a renewed commitment to strengthening the bilateral relationship.

The military cooperation between Sri Lanka and the US has a rich history, characterized by several agreements and initiatives aimed at enhancing collaboration between their armed forces. This cooperation includes port visits, joint exercises, training programmes, and logistical support, all aimed at fostering cooperation, interoperability, and bolstering the defence capabilities of both nations.

In the mid-1990s, both countries signed a status-of-forces agreement (SOFA), which established the rights and privileges for US military personnel operating in Sri Lanka. Additionally, in 2007, an acquisition-and-cross-servicing agreement (ACSA) was signed, enabling the provision of non-lethal logistics support, supplies, and refueling services between the two sides during peacekeeping missions, humanitarian operations, and joint exercises.

Following the unseating of President Rajapaksa in 2015, Sri Lanka warmly welcomed US naval visits after a five-year hiatus. Since 2016, over a dozen US Navy ships have been hosted in Sri Lanka. In a notable occurrence in 2017, the USS Nimitz, a US aircraft carrier, visited Sri Lanka for the first time in over three decades, offering Sri Lankan officials an opportunity to tour the carrier.

Since late 2018, Sri Lanka has served as a new logistics hub for the US Navy in the Indian Ocean, allowing the US Navy to utilize Sri Lankan ports and facilities for refueling, resupply, and repairs, thereby enhancing their operational capabilities in the region.

Furthermore, the US has been granted access to the Chinese-built Hambantota airport, despite concerns about China's influence. This decision highlights the growing defence cooperation between Sri Lanka and the US.

Military cooperation between the two countries has expanded beyond port visits. In 2017, Sri Lanka participated in the Pacific Partnership mission, a multinational humanitarian assistance and disaster relief preparedness mission. That same year, Sri Lanka engaged in the Cooperation Afloat Readiness and Training (CARAT) exercise with the US Indo-Pacific Command (USINDOPACOM). In 2018, Sri Lanka participated in the US-led Rim of the Pacific exercises, observing from Australian vessels.

Under the Trump Administration, Sri Lanka received financial support for its coastal maritime radar system through the Bay of Bengal Initiative. The Asia Reassurance Initiative Act of 2018 also emphasized the importance of expanding cooperation with democratic partners in South Asia, including Sri Lanka.

In 2019, the US transferred a second Hamilton-class coast guard cutter to Sri Lanka, thereby enhancing Sri Lanka's naval capabilities. Additionally, Sri Lanka regularly sends military officers for training in the US, and the air forces of both countries have initiated talks to foster cooperation.

The US is extensively involved in providing civilian aid and fostering capacity-building programmes in Sri Lanka. The US sponsors multimillion-dollar initiatives to clear landmines in Sri Lanka, contributing to the removal of these dangerous hazards and the restoration of affected areas. US hospital ships frequently visit the northern and central regions of Sri Lanka, providing crucial disaster relief and medical care.

In 2018, Sri Lanka negotiated an almost $500 million agreement with the MCC to upgrade road infrastructure and support other initiatives. Although the MCC compact was delayed during a political crisis, efforts are underway to finalize the deal.

Numerous US companies are actively engaged in various sectors of Sri Lanka's economy. US private equity firms have invested in local banking and healthcare. US-based investors, including major institutions like JP Morgan and Citibank, hold nearly half of Sri Lanka's sovereign bonds.

Gotabaya and the Economic Crisis

Sri Lanka's foreign policy once again tilted in favour of China when Gotabaya Rajapaksa became president. However, during his regime, Sri Lanka faced an economic crisis stemming from flawed government policies, the COVID-19 pandemic, and the Russia-Ukraine war. The situation was further aggravated by the Easter terror attack. The pandemic significantly affected key sources of foreign exchange, including tourism, rubber and ready-made garment exports, and remittances, leading to a shortage in foreign exchange reserves. Consequently, the country defaulted on its international loan repayments.

Amidst Sri Lanka's financial stress during the COVID-19 pandemic, China provided additional loans and support to the country.[32] China extended a currency swap to assist Sri Lanka in purchasing goods and also donated vaccines to combat the pandemic.

As the economic crisis deepened, Sri Lanka hoped for debt relief from China, considering the favourable decisions it had made in the past benefiting Chinese interests. However, there was a fundamental misinterpretation of China's policy. China did not grant debt relief to any country under the BRI to avoid establishing a precedent for other borrowing countries.

This misplaced hope prevented Sri Lanka from seeking debt restructuring from other creditors. Approaching other financial institutions such as the IMF, ADB, and World Bank could have unlocked financial assistance. Sri Lanka's initial reluctance to approach the IMF, due to concerns about China, exacerbated its economic crisis as it was unable to access assistance from alternative sources.

The profound economic crisis in Sri Lanka compelled Gotabaya Rajapaksa to step down from his position. He was succeeded by Ranil Wickremesinghe. In response to the changed circumstances and the economic crisis, Sri Lanka now aims to engage with all major powers to overcome its challenges and foster development in the country. Sri Lanka has joined China's BRI and related institutions like the Asian Infrastructure Investment Bank (AIIB) to secure financing for large-scale infrastructure projects. Additionally, Sri Lanka aims to benefit from a $480 million grant provided by the US MCC to stimulate economic growth and infrastructure development. The US has also enacted the Better Utilization of Investments Leading to Development (BUILD) Act, which establishes the US International Development Finance Corporation and doubles the US development finance capacity to $60 billion. Sri Lanka has also decided to expedite projects agreed upon with India, further demonstrating its commitment to engaging with major powers for economic recovery and development.

India's Assistance to Mitigate Sri Lanka's Economic Crisis

Amidst Sri Lanka's severe economic downturn, the nation turned to its neighbour, India, for critical support. India in line with its 'neighbourhood first' policy swiftly responded, offering substantial assistance totaling nearly $4 billion.[33] This aid encompassed various initiatives, including the delivery of 100 tons of nano fertilizers to address immediate agricultural needs.

Furthermore, India extended significant financial assistance to help Sri Lanka overcome its foreign exchange and debt crises. Measures included providing a SAARC currency swap facility of $400 million and deferring a payment of $515.2 million to the Asian Clearing Union by two months. Additionally, India offered a short-term loan of $500 million to facilitate the purchase of essential petroleum products, while a $1 billion credit facility was arranged through an agreement with the State Bank of India to procure vital commodities.

India's assistance also partly served its strategic objectives in the region. By jointly developing the Trincomalee Oil Tank Farm, both countries enhanced security interests in the Bay of Bengal.[34] Moreover, India's persuasion led to the cancellation of a renewable energy project, valued at $12 million, which mitigated potential Chinese encroachment near Tamil Nadu.[35]

The economic crisis prompted discussions between Sri Lanka and India to deepen economic ties. Both nations are considering upgrading the Indo-Lanka Free Trade Agreement and liberalizing trade norms to foster a comprehensive economic and technological partnership.[36] Sri Lanka sees this as a pivotal step towards economic stability, which could further enhance national security and political relations.

Projects delayed on the Sri Lankan side are now being expedited, including the establishment of a power grid connection through undersea cables. This infrastructure could alleviate Sri Lanka's power shortage by facilitating electricity sharing during off-peak hours. Discussions also revolve around leveraging renewable energy sources, such as establishing a solar power plant in Sampur and harnessing offshore wind energy.

Additionally, Sri Lanka aims to attract Indian higher education institutions to regions like Jaffna and develop logistics to bolster its role as a pivotal port for India and Bangladesh. While India's primary goal is to provide humanitarian aid, it also advocates for long-term assistance from the IMF to stabilize Sri Lanka's economy.[37]

By extending support to Sri Lanka, India seeks to counterbalance China's growing influence in the region, ensuring stability and security in its neighbourhood.

Geopolitical Tensions Amid Sri Lanka's Economic Crisis

During Sri Lanka's dire economic crisis, China's prioritization of its geopolitical interests over providing assistance shifted the country's focus towards other powers, notably India. While India extended significant aid during the crisis, its actions, such as convincing Sri Lanka to cancel a renewable energy project off the coast of Jaffna, strained relations with China, which perceived its influence as diminishing.[38]

In a display of influence, China insisted on docking its ship 'Yuan Wang 5' at Hambantota, leading to objections from India. India was apprehensive that the ship would be used for surveillance of its defence installations. This incident sparked tensions, with China accusing India of meddling in Sri Lanka's affairs, while India condemned China's pressure tactics.[39]

Sri Lankan President Wickremesinghe voiced concerns over the exploitation of the country's economic crisis by stronger economies to interfere in internal affairs. He sought support from political parties to thwart external influences. Wickremesinghe emphasized the non-military nature of the Hambantota port and expressed concern that the Indian Ocean was becoming a battleground for the geopolitical rivalries of Pacific powers, which could potentially lead to conflict in the region. Sri Lanka expressed its lack of interest in joining any military alliance and emphasized the need for plans that would ensure the security of the IOR and promote free navigation, allowing Sri Lanka to become a center of maritime commerce.[40]

While Wickremesinghe aimed to separate the Indian Ocean from the Pacific to avoid conflicts associated with the rivalry between major powers, the emergence of China as a global power with expanding economic and strategic interests has made it almost impossible to completely separate the two regions. China is actively seeking bases in the IOR to protect its economic and strategic interests. China insisted on docking the 'Yuan Wang 5' ship in an effort to express its dissatisfaction with Sri Lanka seeking assistance from other countries. China's intention was to provide more debt to Sri Lanka, knowing that the country would struggle to repay it, which would have allowed China to acquire additional assets such as the Hambantota port.[41] However, this strategy was hindered by the help received from other sources, especially India.

China later showed reluctance to engage in debt restructuring, which prolonged Sri Lanka's economic crisis. Despite offers from countries like India and Japan for debt relief, China's slow response raised concerns among Western nations. They urged China to cooperate with international efforts to resolve Sri Lanka's debt crisis.[42]

Sri Lanka's Strategic Vision for the Indo-Pacific Region

Sri Lanka is ambitiously positioning itself as a pivotal trading and maritime hub within the Indo-Pacific region. Central to this vision is the recognition that achieving such status hinges on fostering regional peace and stability, especially in safeguarding vital Sea Lines of Communication and strategic chokepoints. The stability of the Indian Ocean, however, faces multifaceted challenges ranging from piracy and terrorism to climate change-induced disruptions and illicit maritime activities.

In navigating these complexities, Sri Lanka has actively pursued bilateral and multilateral security collaborations with key stakeholders across the Indo-Pacific. Joint military exercises with India, China, Australia, and the US underscore Sri Lanka's commitment to regional security. Additionally, ongoing military training exchanges with the US highlight Sri Lanka's efforts to enhance its defence capabilities.

Despite engagement in various security dialogues, Sri Lanka maintains a cautious stance towards initiatives like the Quad, questioning their effectiveness in ensuring regional peace and stability.[43] The evolving nature of the US IPS further complicates Sri Lanka's strategic calculus, prompting a nuanced approach towards supporting the concept of a free and open Indo-Pacific.

Emphasizing adherence to international laws and norms, Sri Lanka advocates for the promotion of a maritime order that facilitates shared utilization of global commons. Hosting international conferences, such as the 2018 gathering in Colombo, Sri Lanka actively contributes to discussions on enhancing UNCLOS implementation and addressing issues like freedom of navigation and maritime crime.

Despite its modest role in the broader IPS, Sri Lanka strategically engages major powers to foster mutually beneficial cooperation. By leveraging partnerships in areas of common interest, Sri Lanka seeks to realize its aspirations of becoming an international financial center and a regional maritime nexus, contributing to the collective prosperity and security of the Indo-Pacific region.

Navigating Economic Crisis and Great Power Rivalries in the Indo-Pacific

Since 2016, Sri Lanka has embarked on a significant shift in its foreign policy within the Indo-Pacific region. Under the leadership of President Maithripala Sirisena and Prime Minister Ranil Wickremesinghe, the coalition government has actively expanded diplomatic ties with the US and India.

This strategic move aims to reduce Sri Lanka's previous heavy reliance on China, particularly during the presidency of Mahinda Rajapaksa.

Though Sri Lanka tilted once again in favour of China during the rule of Gotabaya Rajapaksa, the unprecedented economic crisis prompted it to seek assistance from the IMF due to its inability to secure further loans from China. While India has offered support, it advocates for Sri Lanka to undergo an IMF programme to address the crisis. Conversely, China opposes involvement from other powers or institutions, potentially seeking to exploit Sri Lanka's debt woes for strategic gains.

Despite the economic turmoil, Sri Lanka remains a crucial strategic outpost in the IOR for China, while for India, its stability is paramount. Although Chinese influence has somewhat diminished, its impact on Sri Lanka remains substantial. This dynamic underscores the complex geopolitical landscape in the region.

Recognizing Sri Lanka's strategic significance, the US has engaged with the country as part of its broader IPS. This engagement aims to promote a free, open, and inclusive regional order while also countering China's influence. Strengthening economic and military cooperation with Sri Lanka serves these objectives.

In the past, the Rajapaksas pursued policies that often conflicted with the interests of India, the US, Sri Lankan minorities, and the nation as a whole. With their absence from power, both India and the US now have an opportunity to improve relations with Sri Lanka, potentially reshaping the regional dynamics.

US-India Collaboration in the Maldives to Counter Chinese Influence

Maldives is strategically located in the Indian Ocean, adjacent to vital sea lanes of communication and in close proximity to the US military base of Diego Garcia. This underscores the importance of cooperation and information sharing with Maldives for Washington to assess maritime security threats. Maldives is also situated near India's Minicoy Island, with a relatively short distance from mainland India. This makes Maldives important for India as well.

The geostrategic importance of the Maldives has increased significantly with the emergence of China as a major power. This development has fueled great power competition, particularly in the Indo-Pacific region, which has become the primary theatre for such rivalry. In response, the US has implemented its IPS, focusing attention on the Indian Ocean. This has also elevated the Maldives to a key component of the US IPS.

Over the last decade or so, the Maldives has sought to navigate through this rivalry to maximize economic advantages without becoming entangled in great power competition. However, the situation appears to be changing following the September 2023 presidential elections, which brought pro-China Mohamed Muizzu to power.

Emerging Maritime Competition in the IOR

In the post-World War II era, the US was the predominant power in the Indian Ocean. However, this dominance is increasingly challenged by China, an emerging global power. China aims to safeguard its access to the Malacca Straits, a crucial route for its trade and energy supply. Additionally, China seeks to extend President Xi Jinping's BRI into the IOR, with several regional countries participating in its Maritime Silk Road programme. The expansion of China's trade, commerce, and economy has prompted discussions of overseas interests. This has led to expansion of China's core interests which has also necessitated changes in its naval doctrine.

To protect its expanding core interests, China is attempting a transition from a continental power to a maritime power. The Chinese defense White Paper of 2015 signaled a shift from the People's War doctrine, expressing China's desire to emerge as a maritime power.[44] Consequently, its naval doctrine shifted from offshore water defense to open sea protection. China is now increasingly concerned for chokepoints, particularly the Hormuz and Malacca Straits.

During the era of US dominance in the IOR, Western powers were mindful of Indian sensitivities. This was evident during the attempted coup against President Maumoon Abdul Gayoom of the Maldives in 1988. India's South Asian neighbours also generally refrained from providing military bases to extra-regional powers. However, this situation is likely to change with China's emergence as a major global power. Chinese diplomacy has successfully courted South Asian countries, demonstrated by its acquisition of the Hambantota port on a 99-year lease.[45] Additionally, China has constructed a submarine base in Bangladesh for the Bangladeshi navy, raising concerns about potential military use. The Chinese-built Gwadar port in Pakistan and their interest in establishing a naval base in the Maldives further exemplify China's expanding influence.[46]

As an aspiring global power, China is hesitant to rely solely on US power to secure the Indian Ocean sea lanes. Instead, it seeks a new model of military relationship with the US that aligns with the major power relationship between the two countries. Accordingly, China has significantly increased its naval power, incorporating submarines and aircraft carriers, and seeks multiple access points through overseas military and naval bases. This move aims to monitor Indian and US naval activities, potentially challenging India and US military power and containing India.

China's aspirations to project power in the Indian Ocean not only expand its strategic depth in India's backyard but also pose a challenge to India. This has added a new maritime dimension to the India-China rivalry, with both countries vying for greater influence in the Maldives. The entry of China has dramatically altered the geostrategic situation in the Indian Ocean, potentially leading to instability and conflict. China aims to establish a China-centric world order and is not interested in any cooperative security arrangements. This is reflected in its expansionist agenda and efforts to create its own institutions.[47]

The rise of China has created a convergence of interest between India and the US. Together they hope to contain China and maintain regional stability. The US IPS, advocating for a 'Free and Open Indo-Pacific,' identifies China as a key threat to regional stability.

Chinese Influence in the Maldives

The influence of China is continuously increasing in Maldives with the introduction of a multi-party democracy, which brought internal power struggles in its wake. Maldives' initial foreign policy was to elicit development support from all sides while retaining its independence of actions. However, this policy began to change in 2008 when multi-party democracy was introduced. Now, China has emerged as a major player in the region and within the Maldives.

Mohamed Nasheed was the first president to come to power after the introduction of multi-party democracy in 2008. But he could not complete his tenure and was removed in a coup in February 2012. Nasheed, while in power, claimed that he was pursuing an 'India first' policy. By this, he wanted to convey to India that after taking care of Maldivian interests, he would be mindful of Indian interests. He also claimed that his government would never do anything that would compromise the security environment in the IOR or jeopardize Indian security interests.

However, later it was revealed that some members of his cabinet were close to China. The credit for bringing China into the Maldives goes to Nasheed. It was Nasheed who allowed the Chinese to open their embassy in Malé in 2011. He also opened the doors to Chinese economic presence in the Maldives, despite Indian reservations.[48] In 2016, Nasheed, as an opposition party leader, redefined his India first policy, which means, 'not to have defense exercises with other countries, not to conduct our domestic policy in a way that creates fear in India, not to give a base to the Chinese, or indeed anyone to create strategic infrastructure, like deep-water ports and airports.'[49] This meant that a Maldivian government under him would prioritize Indian interests. It also meant that the Maldives would not do anything which could jeopardize Indian security interests.

The political crisis of 2012 in which Nasheed was removed from power created a fluid political situation and brought Mohammed Waheed Hassan to power who turned out to be anti-India.[50] The rapidly changing political situation in the Maldives also caused problems in India-Maldives relations. A pro-China tilt was seen in the Maldivian foreign policy under Waheed and his successor Abdulla Yameen.[51] Waheed canceled the contract of GMR, an Indian company ab initio immediately after taking over and it was widely believed that the Chinese were behind it. It also made India-Maldives bilateral relations frosty, leading to a downturn in defence cooperation. Waheed went on to sign a defence cooperation agreement with China. He and his Minister of Defense and National Security, Colonel (Retired) Mohamed Nazim, visited

China. During this visit, he signed three agreements with China and appreciated its policy of non-interference in their internal affairs 'unlike other influential countries'.[52]

Interestingly, even when pro-China Yameen was in power, he claimed to be following an 'India first policy' though all his policy decisions were against India. He took many steps in China's favour.[53] He made Maldives part of the BRI and a member of the AIIB. He signed a free trade agreement with China. He also enacted legislation that allowed foreign powers to buy land in the Maldives. This was meant to facilitate the Chinese buying of islands in the Maldives.[54] He engaged the Chinese in massive infrastructure development in the Maldives. Chinese have built the Friendship Bridge (the Sinamalé Bridge) that connects the capital Malé with the islands of Hulhulé and Hulhumalé in the Maldives.

During his regime, sovereign guarantees were given for private projects. According to the Chinese, the total loan given to the Maldives is $1.4 billion.[55] But this is only a government-to-government loan. The loan amount becomes 3.5 billion dollars when private loans and sovereign guarantees are also factored in. This loan becomes a burden as the Maldivian GDP is only about 5 billion dollars.[56]

Yameen made several attempts to sabotage democracy and stick to power with Chinese help. He even declared an emergency. Washington took a negative view of the Yameen administration. It expressed its concern over democratic backsliding.[57] The US also threatened to impose sanctions on Maldives if Yameen interfered with the democratic process or obstructed the peaceful transfer of power.

Beijing made deep inroads in Maldivian politics during the regime of Abdulla Yameen. Maldives grew more reliant on Chinese companies to finance key projects. To gain access to the Maldives, China is trying not only its debt-trap diplomacy, which was successful with Sri Lanka but also the fractious internal politics of the Maldives. It nearly succeeded with its game plan when President Yameen was in power. Though Yameen is now not in power, the debt taken by him, it is feared, might force the Maldives to cede important strategic space to China. China is indulging in this kind of strategy in other countries of the IOR.

The presidential elections held in 2018 brought Maldivian Democratic Party (MDP) candidate Mohamed Solih to power. Both India and the US quickly welcomed Mohamed Solih's government. MDP did well even in the parliamentary elections, and former president Nasheed now became the speaker of the parliament. The Solih government was India-friendly and the 'India first' policy followed by Solih appeared sincerer.[58] MDP was chastened by what it went through after the coup in 2012. India was given greater space and a number of projects were started by the Indians. The Solih government canceled the project signed by the Yameen government to develop a 'Joint Ocean Observation Station' on its westernmost island of Makunudhoo.[59]

Yameen's removal from power was, however, only a temporary setback to Chinese interests. China remained a powerful player in the Maldives. President Solih reviewed Yameen's trade deals with China. He declined to ratify Yameen's FTA with China. Yet, he has cooperated with the Chinese on a range of projects. The Chinese are building housing units in Hulumale. They are also building an airport in Hulhule. No Maldivian administration will risk losing China's foreign investment and economic partnership. Chinese tourists have contributed to the growth of the Maldivian tourism industry.

The pro-India alignment witnessed during the Solih government has now considerably changed with the coming to power of Mohamed Muizzu after the September 2023 presidential elections. Mohamed Muizzu and Yameen had started an 'India out' campaign.[60] They claimed that the Solih government had allowed Indian military presence in the Maldives. Though this claim was refuted by the Chief of Defence Forces Major General Abdulla Shamaal, the protestors indulged in violence against Indian symbols. There was a fire in the State Bank of India. These protests were organized with the aim to create nationalistic feelings in the Maldives. In this effort, Muizzu and Yameen were successful, and riding on this wave, Muizzu has come to power. Though after assuming charge as president he has discontinued his partnership with Yameen, his anti-India approach continues. He is strongly pro-China. He has signed a defence agreement with China. Both countries have also upgraded their relationship.

India aims to uphold its traditional geopolitical sphere of influence in

South Asia. Recognizing the constraints faced by the Maldives, India seeks to assume the role of primary security provider in the region. To achieve this objective, India has forged a close defence partnership with the Maldives. Concurrently, the US has begun to prioritize the Indian Ocean within its IPS. Both India and the US think that it is in their mutual interest to prevent the Maldives from falling under Chinese influence. However, under the regime of pro-China Mohamed Muizzu India's relationship with Maldives appears to be under stress.

India-Maldives Defence Partnership to Safeguard Regional Security

The maritime region adjacent to India holds significant implications for Indian security. It's unsurprising that India endeavours to establish itself as a primary security provider in the area. Consequently, to bolster security in the Maldives and its surrounding environs, India and the Maldives maintain a robust defence and security cooperation. This partnership endured even after the advent of a multi-party democracy in 2008, during which the UK and the US emerged as major diplomatic partners for the Maldives, while India retained its role as the principal security ally.

India actively engages in training Maldivian forces and conducts joint combat exercises, thereby enhancing maritime surveillance capabilities. Additionally, India provides military equipment to support the Maldives' defence needs. The joint training exercise, called 'Dosti,' commenced in 1991 and was later joined by Sri Lanka in 2012, aiming to foster cooperation among the Coast Guards of the Maldives, India, and Sri Lanka.

Both nations inked a defence cooperation agreement in August 2009, signifying a commitment to joint surveillance and patrolling activities in the Indian Ocean by the Indian Navy and the Maldives National Defence Force (MNDF). India further pledged assistance by providing a Dhruv helicopter and aiding in the establishment of a 25-bed military hospital in the Maldives. Despite some domestic opposition fearing encroachment on Maldivian sovereignty, the cooperation continued to advance. The annual bilateral joint Military Training Exercise, 'EKUVERIN,' initiated in October 2009, further strengthens military cooperation and interoperability between the two countries' defence forces.

The power transition following Mohamed Nasheed's departure in February 2012 led to an internal struggle in the Maldives and a cooling of bilateral relations. Nonetheless, during Waheed's tenure, the 'SENAHIYA' military hospital was inaugurated in Male with Indian assistance in September 2012.[61] Subsequently, Abdulla Yameen's alignment with China raised concerns, but India's provision of two ALH Dhruv helicopters in December 2013 demonstrated continued support.[62] Despite reservations about Yameen's proximity to China, an 'Indo-Maldivian Action Plan for Defence' was signed in New Delhi in July 2018, reaffirming India's commitment to regional security.[63]

Presently, India is expanding its coastal radar stations and recently donated a Dornier aircraft to the Maldives. Amidst the COVID-19 pandemic, India dispatched a 14-member Army medical team to set up a COVID-testing laboratory, underlining the importance of security cooperation to the Maldives, particularly for its tourism industry. India continues to assist by patrolling Maldivian territorial waters with warships and reconnaissance aircraft.

However, the incursion of China into the Indian Ocean poses a significant threat to maritime security. The Chinese challenge India's dominance in the region[64] and their influence is exacerbated by the rise of pro-China leaders like Mohamed Muizzu. Muizzu seems to be obstructing collaboration between India and the Maldives, which is crucial for safeguarding regional stability. The expanding influence of China in the Indian Ocean poses a significant threat to the region, prompting concerted efforts from both New Delhi and Washington to contain Chinese power through joint action.

The Evolving Relationship Between the US and Maldives

The bilateral relationship between the US and Maldives was established in 1966, shortly after Maldives gained independence from British colonial rule in 1965.[65] Initially, Maldives set up its embassy in Washington, but financial constraints led to its closure. Despite this setback, efforts to maintain diplomatic ties continued, culminating in the reopening of the embassy in 2007. However, due to a change in government in 2008, the embassy shuttered once more.[66]

In response to the closure, the Maldivian permanent representative to the United Nations in New York assumed the role of ambassador to the US. Despite the challenges, diplomatic efforts persisted, leading to the recent reopening of the embassy, now rebranded as the 'Embassy of the Republic of Maldives to the United States of America.'[67]

Meanwhile, the US Mission to Maldives, currently stationed in Colombo, Sri Lanka, has been actively engaged in strengthening ties with Maldives. Notably, during a visit by Mike Pompeo in February 2020, plans were set in motion to establish a physical embassy in Maldives, signaling a deepening commitment to bilateral relations.

The Maldives' relationship with the US experienced fluctuations over the years, largely influenced by the policies and behaviour of the Maldivian government. Between 2013 and 2018, the Maldives' geopolitical significance grew as it strengthened its ties with China. This also made Maldives a strategic battleground for China, India, and the US in the Indo-Pacific region.

In 2018, tensions escalated between the US and the Maldives when the Maldivian government's foreign policy alienated international bodies such as the Commonwealth, the EU, and key allies like Qatar and India. In response, the US threatened sanctions, citing concerns over democracy, the rule of law, and electoral processes. This period saw bilateral relations deteriorate, with accusations of US collusion with Maldivian opposition by state-sponsored media outlets. However, the US dismissed these claims as misinformation.

Gradually, the Maldives-US relationship saw significant improvement, potentially influenced by the Maldives' rekindled ties with India, a key US ally. This warming of relations culminated in the signing of the 'Framework for US Department of Defense-Maldives Ministry of Defence and Security Relations' in September 2022.

US-Maldives Defence Pact to Enhance Indo-Pacific Security

In pursuit of a free and open Indo-Pacific, the US and Maldives solidified their commitment by signing a defence pact on 10 September 2020, in Philadelphia. Termed the 'Framework for US Department of Defense – Maldives Ministry of Defence, Defense and Security Relationship,' the pact is a significant step towards enhancing regional peace and security in the Indian Ocean.

Representing Maldives, Defence Minister Mariya Didi signed the agreement, while Reed Werner, Deputy Assistant Secretary of Defense for South Asia at the US Defense Department, signed on behalf of the US. This pact aims to deepen cooperation between the two nations, establishing an institutional mechanism for bilateral defence and security dialogue.

Under the agreement, both countries will engage in high-level military-to-military discussions and collaborate on various initiatives, including maritime domain awareness, disaster response, and humanitarian relief operations.

Maldivian Defence Minister Mariya Didi emphasized that the framework aligns with the mutual interests of both nations and will significantly enhance their partnership.[68] She expressed optimism that the pact would bolster Maldives' defenses against threats such as piracy, violent extremism, terrorism, and illicit trafficking. Many considered the US-Maldives defence pact a crucial milestone in advancing regional security objectives and safeguarding the Indo-Pacific region.

Historically, India has harboured apprehensions regarding the presence of external powers in the IOR, particularly in close proximity to South Asia. However, the US-Maldives Defence Pact signifies a departure from this approach. Rather than discouraging Maldives from signing the pact, some believe that India has endorsed it. The pact is perceived as complementary to and aligned with India's interests. India itself advocates countering violent extremism, providing humanitarian assistance and disaster response (HADR), and supporting a rules-based order in the region, all of which are objectives of the pact.[69]

Furthermore, India and the Maldives share a special relationship. India has maintained exclusive naval presence in the Indian Ocean surrounding the Maldives archipelago for decades, conducting joint Exclusive Economic Zone (EEZ) surveillance patrols with Maldives, Seychelles, and Mauritius. India appears confident that the pact with the U.S. will not undermine its position in the islands. The pact aims to enhance engagement and cooperation in promoting peace and security in the Indian Ocean, which aligns with India's broader interests and regional stability.[70]

The Implications of the Pact for Regional Geopolitics

The significance of the US-Maldives Defence Pact goes beyond its bilateral dimension and has far-reaching implications for regional geopolitics. This pact signals a growing convergence of Indian and American strategic interests in the Indian Ocean and Indo-Pacific regions.

India has been wary of the deepening economic ties between China and the Maldives during Abdulla Yameen's tenure.[71] It was feared that the Maldives' increasing indebtedness could lead to the cession of strategic ground to China. The US-Maldives Defence Pact was expected to allay such fears, aligning the Maldives more closely with India in the strategic competition with China for influence in the region.

This pact also signifies a shift in India's relationship with the US. Historically opposed to the presence of extra-regional powers in the Indian Ocean, India had previously hindered the Maldives from signing agreements like the SOFA with the US. However, the changing dynamics, especially China's growing influence in the Maldives from 2015 to 2019, have prompted India to reassess its stance. India now supports increased US-Maldives defence cooperation as part of its efforts to safeguard its security interests.

India's reliance on the US was not deemed necessary as long as Pakistan remained the primary threat to Indian security. However, the increased assertiveness of China along India's northern border and in the IOR has significantly altered India's threat perception.

The emergence of China as a major threat, both to India and the US, has necessitated a closer partnership between the two countries.[72] India, once cautious about provoking China, now sees the need to forge stronger diplomatic and military ties with the US to counterbalance China's assertive behaviour in the region. While India is not formally aligned with the US in a security alliance, it has gravitated towards closer cooperation due to shared concerns about Chinese expansionism.

India's strategic calculus in the Indo-Pacific region has evolved as it seeks to mitigate China's growing influence. The US-Maldives defence agreement is viewed as a tool to counter China's attempts to expand its presence in the region. Despite historical skepticism about foreign military presence near its borders, India has not reacted negatively to the deal, recognizing the necessity of collaborative efforts to address common security challenges.

Maldives Approach towards the IPS Remains Uncertain

The Maldives' stance towards the IPS reflects its complex geopolitical landscape and evolving priorities. While development remains a consistent goal for successive Maldivian administrations, their international alignments have varied. This has impacted regional security dynamics and partnerships. While it's been suggested that these alignments were solely driven by development objectives, the reality is more nuanced. The differing approaches have led to diverse security partnerships potentially altering the security landscape of the Indian Ocean, raising concerns about regional stability.

During President Yameen's tenure, the Maldives deepened its ties with China between 2013 and 2018, elevating its geopolitical significance. This drew attention of major powers like China, India and the US, turning the Maldives into a strategic battleground in the Indo-Pacific. In 2018, tensions rose when the Maldives' foreign policy actions prompted threats of sanctions from the US, leading to a toxic atmosphere in bilateral relations.

Subsequent improvements in the Maldives-US relationship, particularly under President Mohamed Solih were influenced by renewed ties with India. This culminated in the signing of a landmark defence pact, the US-Maldives Defence Framework, in September 2022.

The Maldives' strategic location, near vital shipping lanes and the US military base in Diego Garcia, makes it a valuable partner for maritime security cooperation for the US. The two nations have collaborated on counter-terrorism and maritime security since 2012, conducting numerous bilateral exercises in these domains.

Despite this, the Maldives' growing alignment with China, exemplified by defence agreements under President Muizzu's leadership, poses challenges to its partnership with the US and its adherence to the Indo-Pacific vision. The country's economic ties with China, manifested in infrastructure projects under the BRI, create complexities in its relations with the US and India, who view China as a rival and a threat in the Indo-Pacific.

India and Maldives have shared defence and strategic interests. This led to a robust defence partnership between the two countries. However, the present President Mohamed Muizzu is trying to unravel this partnership. India's support in patrolling the Maldives' EEZ and countering terrorism complements the Maldives' security needs. But now Muizzu wants to do it on his own by procuring drones from Turkey. It is feared that these drones could also be used to spy on the Indian navy.

Chinese are involved in illegal fishing in Maldivian waters. Here the US, under its IPS, can assist the Maldives in combating illegal, unreported, and unregulated (IUU) fishing activities. But Maldives's engagement with China complicates the issue.

While the Maldives has aligned itself with the US Indo-Pacific vision since 2020, recent defence agreements with China, especially under President Muizzu's leadership, cast doubt on its continued commitment. As geopolitical complexities persist, navigating between competing interests and partnerships remains a challenge for the Maldives in the Indo-Pacific arena.

US-China Competition Shapes Washington's Views and Policies in South Asia and Smaller South Asian Nations

In response to the intensifying US-China competition, Washington has shifted its focus towards smaller South Asian states, recognizing the strategic importance of the region. Not only has its attention increased, but it is also offering increased security assistance and development aid to these nations as they become key players in the broader Indo-Pacific landscape. The US aims to counterbalance Chinese influence in the region by engaging in diplomatic outreach, building alliances, and presenting alternatives to Chinese investment and development projects. Economic diversification is a key strategy advocated by the US, aiming to reduce dependency on Chinese financing and mitigate the risks associated with excessive debt.

Initially, the US viewed China's projects like the CPEC with cautious optimism. However, growing concerns about the project's costs, lack of transparency, and its impact on Pakistan's debt burden have led to increased criticism. China has also managed to increase its economic influence in smaller South Asian nations, particularly through trade deals and infrastructure projects. This trend has prompted close monitoring by the US. Despite

China's increasing engagement, the US retains its importance in the economic arena for smaller South Asian countries as it remains a crucial export destination for Bangladesh and Sri Lanka, ranking second for Nepal and third for Maldives among these nations.

However, Chinese imports play a significant role in the economies of these countries, with Bangladesh and Sri Lanka heavily reliant on them, and Nepal and Maldives also seeing substantial imports from China. China's growing influence was also apparent when Maldives signed a free trade agreement with them in 2017. Yet, concerns have emerged regarding the potential drawbacks and strategic costs of Chinese financing for development projects. Sri Lanka's experience, marked by overwhelming debt and economic turmoil, serves as a cautionary tale. Similarly, Maldives faces the risk of debt distress under China's BRI. While Bangladesh and Nepal face lower risks compared to Sri Lanka and Maldives, worries persist about the long-term implications of Chinese loans on regional security dynamics. Recognizing these concerns, the US is actively encouraging economic diversification in smaller South Asian nations. India's Development Partnership aims to assist these countries in broadening their economic ties and reducing dependency on any single source of financing. This strategy seeks to mitigate risks associated with excessive debt and potential geopolitical entanglements.

In essence, while China's economic presence in smaller South Asian countries is significant, the US is addressing structural challenges within the development finance framework. By promoting economic diversification and offering alternative avenues for development assistance, the US seeks to ensure the stability and sovereignty of these nations amidst an increasingly complex geopolitical landscape.

Military relations also play a significant role in the US strategy for South Asia. The US has intensified security collaboration with South Asian nations through joint military exercises, defence partnerships, and capacity-building efforts. This is part of a broader effort to foster a robust regional security architecture to counterbalance China's military expansion and assertive behaviour.

While China's military relations with smaller South Asian nations remain relatively limited compared to India and the US, Beijing's influence is growing. Beijing's defence officials occasionally visit these nations, and vessels from the PLA Navy make port calls for goodwill or refueling purposes. However, Bangladesh is the only exception in this regard, which has a significant military relationship with China. The new government in Maldives under President Muizzu now also seems to be working to unravel India-Maldives defence partnership. Still, all five nations factor in New Delhi's strategic preferences concerning China when formulating their foreign policy stances. Consequently, none of them participate in regular joint military exercises with China. Despite China's arms sales to these countries, the dominant role exerted by India in South Asia and difficulties in the India-China relationship have ensured that military ties of these countries with China remain limited.

The competition between the US and China has prompted increased consultation and cooperation between the US and India. India recognizes the importance of balancing China's power and seeks closer ties with the US across various domains, including defence and technology. This alignment of interests between the US and India is crucial for countering China's expansionist actions and maintaining stability in the region. The rivalry between the US and China, along with concerns over Chinese activities in South Asia, has facilitated greater consultation, coordination, and cooperation between the US and India in the region. India has become more receptive to extra-regional involvement if it provides alternatives to China's initiatives. This mindset has fostered potential collaboration between the US and India in responding to agreements such as the US-Maldives defence pact and the Japan-Maldives coast guard agreement.

The US regards India as a strategic partner and a key contributor to security in the IOR and beyond. India's adherence to democratic values, its strategic aspirations, and its regional influence pose challenges to China's attempts to establish a Sino-centric order. As the competition between China and the US escalates, India finds itself in a pivotal 'swing state' position akin to China's role during the Cold War. The traditional security concerns of India, particularly regarding Pakistan and China, have become immediate concerns for Washington as well. The dynamics in South Asia are evolving rapidly, with the US-China competition playing a central role in shaping regional geopolitics.

NOTES

1 Jeff M. Smith, 'South Asia: A New Strategy,' Backgrounder, The Heritage Foundation, No. 3721, 29 August 2022, p. 7 at https://www.heritage.org/asia/report/south-asia-new-strategy last accessed on 18 June 2024.

2 By Santosh Sharma Poudel, 'Should Nepal Ratify the MCC Nepal Compact?,' *The Diplomat*, 11 October 2021 at https://thediplomat.com/2021/10/should-nepal-ratify-the-mcc-nepal-compact/ last accessed on 18 June 2024.

3 Anil Giri, 'Nepal disapproves of Washington's Indo-Pacific Strategy, Beijing says,' *The Kathmandu Post*, 11 September 2019 at https://kathmandupost.com/national/2019/09/11/nepal-disapproves-of-indo-pacific-strategy-china-s-foreign-ministry-says last accessed on 18 June 2024.

4 MCC Nepal Compact, Millenium Challenge Account Nepal at https://mcanp.org/en/mcc-nepal-compact/ last accessed on 18 June 2024.

5 Li Tao, 'MCC pact a Trojan horse disguised by Washington as "aid" to Nepal,' *Global Times*, 3 March 2022 at https://www.globaltimes.cn/page/202203/1253832.shtml last accessed on 18 June 2024.

6 Penny MacRae, 'Chinese Foreign Minister's Nepal visit puts Himalayan nation in headlights of big power rivalry in South Asia', *South China Morning Post*, 26 March 2022 at https://www.scmp.com/week-asia/politics/article/3171904/chinese-foreign-ministers-nepal-visit-puts-himalayan-nation last accessed on 18 June 2024.

7 Shrey Khanna and Aarthi Ratnam, 'As Nepal Turns to the Indo-Pacific, China Worries', *The Diplomat*, 14 April 2022 at https://thediplomat.com/2022/04/as-nepal-turns-to-the-indo-pacific-china-worries/ last accessed on 18 June 2024.

8 PIA Krishnankutty, 'Nepal okays $500 million US aid to motive country's infrastructure, adds caveat' *ThePrint*, 28 February, 2022 at https://theprint.in/world/nepal-okays-500-million-us-aid-to-motive-countrys-infrastructure-adds-caveat/851295/ last accessed on 18 June 2024.

9 Santosh Sharma Poudel, 'US Steps up Its Courting of Nepal', *The Diplomat*, 13 February 2023 at https://thediplomat.com/2023/02/us-steps-up-its-courting-of-nepal/ last accessed on 18 June 2024.

10 Hu Yuwei, 'US pushes military pact with Nepal, puts Himalayan peace at stake for geopolitical ambition,' *Global Times*, 20 June 2022 at https://www.globaltimes.cn/page/202206/1268512.shtml last accessed on 18 June 2024.

11 'Built with China's support, Nepal's Pokhara airport was inaugurated 14 days ago,' Hindustan Times, 15 January 2023 at https://www.hindustantimes.com/world-news/built-with-china-s-support-nepal-s-pokhara-airport-was-inaugurated-14-days-ago-101673764851689.html last accessed on 18 June 2024.

12 Kamal Dev Bhattarai, 'Amid Rising Big Power Tensions, Nepal Seeks a New Foreign Policy,' *The Diplomat*, 19 October 2020, https://thediplomat.com/2020/10/amid-rising-big-power-tensions-nepal-seeks-a-new-foreign-policy/ last accessed on 18 June 2024.

13 Gaurav Raja Dahal, 'The Nepal factor in the Indo-Pacific strategy', *The Kathmandu Post*, at https://kathmandupost.com/columns/2021/10/19/the-nepal-factor-in-the-indo-pacific-strategy last accessed on 18 June 2024.

14 Ranjit Rae, 'Kathmandu Dilemma: Resetting India-Nepal Ties,' Penguin Random House India, New Delhi, pp. 196-197.

15 Gaurav Raja Dahal, 'The Nepal factor in the Indo-Pacific Strategy', *The Kathmandu Post*,

at https://kathmandupost.com/columns/2021/10/19/the-nepal-factor-in-the-indo-pacific-strategy last accessed on 18 June 2024.

16 M. Humayun Kabir, 'What will Bangladesh get out of Donald Lu's visit?', *The Daily Star*, 17 January 2023 at https://www.thedailystar.net/opinion/views/news/what-will-bangladesh-get-out-donald-lus-visit-3223601 last accessed on 19 June 2024.

17 'Top US diplomat Donald Lu calls on Bangladesh Foreign Minister', ANI News, 15 January 2023 at https://www.aninews.in/news/world/asia/top-us-diplomat-donald-lu-calls-on-bangladesh-foreign-minister20230115192517/ last accessed on 19 June 2024.

18 'UK minister for Indo-Pacific eyes strengthening partnership with Bangladesh', *Dhaka Tribune*, 10 March 2023 at https://www.dhakatribune.com/bangladesh/foreign-affairs/306544/uk-minister-for-indo-pacific-eyes-strengthening last accessed on 19 June 2024.

19 Under Secretary Nuland's Travel to Bangladesh, India, and Sri Lanka, Media note, US Department of State, 18 March 2022 at https://www.state.gov/under-secretary-nulands-travel-to-bangladesh-india-and-sri-lanka/ last accessed on 19 June 2024.

20 Shafik A. Rahman, 'What should be Bangladesh's Indo-Pacific strategy?', *Dhaka Tribune*, 21 March 2023 at https://www.dhakatribune.com/opinion/op-ed/307250/what-should-be-bangladesh%E2%80%99s-indo-pacific-strategy last accessed on 19 June 2024 also see, Pranay Sharma, 'As US hones its Indo-Pacific strategy, South Asian nations come into focus', *South China Morning Post*, 18 October 2020 at https://www.scmp.com/week-asia/politics/article/3105901/us-hones-its-indo-pacific-strategy-south-asian-nations-come last accessed on 19 June 2024.

21 'Bangladesh not interested in arms purchase under US-led Indo-Pacific Strategy: Momen', *The Financial Express*, 13 October 2020 at https://thefinancialexpress.com.bd/national/bangladesh-not-interested-in-arms-purchase-under-us-led-indo-pacific-strategy-momen-1602564695 last accessed on 19 June 2024.

22 Shannon Tiezzi, 'What Was Behind the Chinese Foreign Minister's Midnight Stopover in Bangladesh?', *The Diplomat*, 11 January 2023 at https://thediplomat.com/2023/01/what-was-behind-the-chinese-foreign-ministers-midnight-stopover-in-bangladesh/ last accessed on 19 June 2024.

23 Reaz Ahmad, 'Number of Bangladeshi-Americans surges by 263% in two decades', *Dhaka Tribune*, 30 April 2021, at https://www.dhakatribune.com/bangladesh/foreign-affairs/245582/number-of-bangladeshi-americans-surges-by-263%25-in last accessed on 19 June 2024.

24 'Indo-Pacific Outlook of Bangladesh', Press Release, Bangladesh: Ministry of Foreign Affairs, 24 April 2023 at https://mofa.gov.bd/site/press_release/d8d7189a-7695-4ff5-9e2b-903fe0070ec9 last accessed on 19 June 2024.

25 Statement by H.E. Dr. A. K. Abdul Momen, MP Hon'ble Foreign Minister of Bangladesh At the Ministerial meeting of the XVIII NAM Summit Baku, Azerbaijan, 23October 2019, Ministry of Foreign Affairs, Bangladesh at https://mofa.gov.bd/site/press_release/3fb78760-073e-48b6-bfab-d467fd81923b# last accessed on 19 June 2024 also see 'Friendship to all, malice towards none,' *Dhaka Tribune*, 16 August 2023 at https://www.dhakatribune.com/opinion/longform/322647/%E2%80%98friendship-to-all-malice-towards-none%E2%80%99 last accessed on 19 June 2024.

26 Michael Kugelman, 'Bangladesh Tilts Toward the U.S. in the Indo-Pacific', *Foreign Policy*, 30 March 2023 at https://foreignpolicy.com/2023/03/30/bangladesh-us-indo-pacific-strategy-china/ last accessed on 19 June 2024.

27 Atul Aneja, 'China says its submarine docked in Sri Lanka "for replenishment"', *The Hindu*,

28 November 2014 at https://www.thehindu.com/news/international/world/China-says-its-submarine-docked-in-Sri-Lanka-%E2%80%98for-replenishment%E2%80%99/article60349022.ece last accessed on 19 June 2024.

28 C. Bryson Hull, 'War crimes heat on, Sri Lanka's Rajapaksa goes back to China', *Reuters*, 9 August 2011 at https://www.reuters.com/article/idUSTRE77816Z/ last accessed on 19 June 2024.

29 Shantanu Roy-Chaudhury, 'China, the Belt and Road Initiative, and the Hambantota Port Project,' *St Antony's International Review*, May 2019, Vol. 15, No. 1, pp. 153-164.

30 'Sri Lanka suspends Japanese-funded rail project over costs', *Reuters*, 24 September 2020 at https://www.reuters.com/article/sri-lanka-japan-railway-idUKL3N2GL3CR/ last accessed on 19 June 2024.

31 'Chinese firm gets contract to develop Colombo Port's controversial eastern container terminal', *The Indian Express*, 24 November 2021 at https://indianexpress.com/article/world/chinese-firm-contract-to-develop-colombo-port-terminal-7639883/ last accessed on 19 June 204.

32 Meera Srinivasan, 'China extends $500 million loan to Lanka', *The Hindu*, 12 April 2021 at https://www.thehindu.com/news/international/china-extends-500-million-loan-to-lanka/article34305277.ece last accessed on 19 June 2024.

33 'India-Sri Lanka ties guided by PM Modi's 'Neighbourhood First" policy, *PTI, The Print*, 11 February, 2023 at https://theprint.in/world/india-sri-lanka-ties-guided-by-pm-modis-neighbourhood-first-policy/1367071/ last accessed on 19 June 2024.

34 Meera Srinivasan, 'India inks deal with Sri Lanka to develop Trincomalee oil tank farm', *The Hindu*, 07 January 2022 at https://www.thehindu.com/news/international/india-inks-deal-with-sri-lanka-to-develop-trincomalee-oil-tank-farm/article38162574.ece last accessed on 19 June 2024.

35 'India to build Sri Lanka wind farms after China pushed aside', *The Economic Times, AFP*, 29 March 2022 at https://economictimes.indiatimes.com/industry/renewables/india-to-build-sri-lanka-wind-farms-after-china-pushed-aside/articleshow/90513780.cms?from=mdr last accessed on 19 June 2024.

36 'Keen to upgrade free-trade deal with India, says Sri Lanka President', *Business Standard*, 16 September 2022 at https://www.business-standard.com/article/economy-policy/keen-to-upgrade-free-trade-deal-with-india-says-sri-lanka-president-122091601168_1.html last accessed on 19 June 2024.

37 Aftab Ahmed and Uditha Jayasinghe, 'India plans no more funding for Sri Lanka as IMF talks progress – sources', *Reuters*, 15 September 2022 at https://www.reuters.com/world/asia-pacific/india-plans-no-more-funding-sri-lanka-imf-talks-progress-sources-2022-09-15/#:~:text=NEW%20DELHI%2FCOLOMBO%2C%20Sept%2015,loan%20agreement%20with%20the%20IMF. last accessed on 19 June 2024.

38 T. Brajesh, 'China sore over soaring India-Sri Lanka ties amid economic crisis', *The Sunday Guardian*, 23 July 23 2022 at https://sundayguardianlive.com/world/china-sore-soaring-india-sri-lanka-ties-amid-economic-crisislast accessed on 19 June 2024.

39 'India interfering in Lanka's internal affairs: Chinese scholar', Press Trust of India, *Business Standard*, 7 February 2017 at https://www.business-standard.com/article/pti-stories/india-interfering-in-lanka-s-internal-affairs-chinese-scholar-117020700627_1.html last accessed on 19 June 2024.

40 'Sri Lanka will not be part of any Indian Ocean turf war: President Ranil Wickremesinghe', Press Trust of India, *India Today*, 15 September 2022 at https://www.indiatoday.in/world/

story/sri-lanka-president-ranil-wickremesinghe-says-colombo-not-part-indian-ocean-turf-war-2000579-2022-09-15 last accessed on 19 June 2024.

41 Kaushik Basu, 'Why Sri Lanka imploded', *The Japan Times*, 27 July 2022 at https://www.japantimes.co.jp/opinion/2022/07/27/commentary/world-commentary/sri-lankan-economic-free-fall/ last accessed on 19 June 2024.

42 Srinivasan Sivabalan, 'Paris Club Piles Pressure on China to Join Sri Lanka Debt Relief', Bloomberg, 7 February 2023 at https://www.bloomberg.com/news/articles/2023-02-07/paris-club-piles-pressure-on-china-to-join-sri-lanka-debt-relief#xj4y7vzkg last accessed on 19 June 2024.

43 Nilupul Gunawardena, 'A Sri Lankan Perspective on the Indo-Pacific Concept,' Lakshman Kadirgamar Institute, Policy Briefs Series: No. 19, January 2020 at https://lki.lk/publication/a-sri-lankan-perspective-on-the-indo-pacific-concept/ last accessed on 19 June 2024.

44 'China's Military Strategy', The State Council, The People's Republic Of China, 27 May 2015 at http://english.www.gov.cn/archive/white_paper/2015/05/27/content_2814751156 10833.htm last accessed on 19 June 2024.

45 Anu Anwar, 'China's Growing Engagement in South Asia', Issue & Insights, Pacific Forum, Working Paper, Vol. 19, WP6, June 2019, p. 6 at https://scholar.harvard.edu/files/anuanwar/files/issuesinsights_vol19wp6.pdf last accessed on 19 June 2024.

46 'Maldives Could Relinquish Control of An Island As Chinese Loan & Pressure Mounts?', *The Eurasian Times*, 18 September 2020 at https://eurasiantimes.com/maldives-could-relinquish-control-of-an-island-as-chinese-loan-pressure-mounts/ last accessed on 19 June 2024.

47 Anand Kumar, 'Maldives is just another front of China's expansive policy', *The Print*, 21 February 2018 at https://theprint.in/opinion/maldives-is-just-another-front-of-chinas-expansive-policy/36988/ last accessed on 19 June 2024.

48 Indrani Bagchi, 'How "India First" turned into "China First" for Maldives', *The Times of India*, 10 February 2018 at https://timesofindia.indiatimes.com/india/how-did-india-first-turn-into-china-first-in-the-maldives/articleshow/62864889.cms last accessed on 19 June 2024.

49 Parvathi Menon, 'Maldives is sitting on a time bomb', *The Hindu*, 04 March 2016, https://www.thehindu.com/opinion/interview/Maldives-is-sitting-on-a-time-bomb/article14136769.ece last accessed on 19 June 2024.

50 'India backs Maldives leader as he agrees to early elections', *Firstpost*, 17 February 2012 at https://www.firstpost.com/world/india-backs-maldives-leader-as-he-agrees-to-early-elections-216310.html?FP_Source=FP_Hi_DT_TS_Wgt_216310&FP_Medium=FP_Hi_Topstories_160568 last accessed on 19 June 2024.

51 Azra Naseem, 'The Honeymoon is Over: Maldives as a Growing Security Threat in the Indian Ocean', *Iris Studies in International Affairs*, Vol. 26, Royal Iris Academy, p. 108.

52 Anand Kumar, *Multi-party Democracy in the Maldives and the Emerging Security Environment in the Indian Ocean Region*, New Delhi: Pentagon Press, 2016, p. 78.

53 Indrani Bagchi, 'How "India First" turned into "China First" for Maldives', *The Times of India*, 10 February 2018 at https://timesofindia.indiatimes.com/india/how-did-india-first-turn-into-china-first-in-the-maldives/articleshow/62864889.cms last accessed on 19 June 2024.

54 Anand Kumar, 'India-Maldives Relations: Is the Rough Patch Over?', *Indian Foreign Affairs Journal*, Vol. 11, No. 2, April-June 2016, p. 158.

55 'Ex-Maldives President Nasheed Returns Home, Says New Govt Will Repay $3 Bn China

Loan', *The Wire*, 1 November 2018 at https://thewire.in/south-asia/ex-maldives-president-nasheed-returns-home-says-new-govt-will-repay-3-bn-china-loan last accessed on 19 June 2024.

56 Rekha Dixit, 'Chinese debt trap not just an economic issue: Maldives speaker Nasheed', *The Week*, 13 December 2019 at https://www.theweek.in/news/world/2019/12/13/Chinese-debt-trap-not-just-an-economic-issue-Maldives-speaker-Nasheed.html last accessed on 19 June 2024 Also see, Ethirajan, Anbarasan. 'China debt dogs Maldives' "bridge to prosperity"', BBC, 17 September 2020 at https://www.bbc.com/news/world-asia-52743072 last accessed on 19 June 2024.

57 Mimrah Abdul Ghafoor, 'Beyond Realpolitik: Enlisting the Maldives into the U.S. Indo-Pacific Vision', *South Asian Voices*, Stimson Center, Washington DC, 6 February 2023 at https://southasianvoices.org/beyond-realpolitik-enlisting-the-maldives-into-the-u-s-indo-pacific-vision/ last accessed on 19 June 2024.

58 Nayanima Basu, 'Foreign Secy Shringla lauds Maldives' "India First" policy, assures Covid recovery support', *The Print*, 9 November 2020 at https://theprint.in/diplomacy/foreign-secy-shringla-lauds-maldives-india-first-policy-assures-covid-recovery-support/540699/ last accessed on 19 June 2024.

59 Jyoti Malhotra, 'Taking Russia's help on China and US on Maldives—a new Indian realism is underway', *The Print*, 15 September 2020 at https://theprint.in/opinion/global-print/russia-help-on-china-and-us-on-maldives-new-indian-realism-is-underway/503010/ last accessed on 19 June 2024.

60 Sudha Ramachandran, 'Opposition in Maldives Continues Its "India Out" Campaign as Both Countries Deepen Defense Ties', *The Diplomat*, 10 November 2020, at https://thediplomat.com/2020/11/opposition-in-maldives-continues-its-india-out-campaign-as-both-countries-deepen-defense-ties/ last accessed on 19 June 2024.

61 Vinay Kumar, 'Antony opens army hospital in Male', *The Hindu*, 17 September 2012 at https://www.thehindu.com/news/national/antony-opens-army-hospital-in-male/article3904777.ece last accessed on 19 June 2024.

62 'HAL Dhruv handed over to Maldives,' *SP's MAI*, Issue No. 24, 16-31 December 2013 at http://www.spsmai.com/aerospace/?id=2623&q=HAL-Dhruv-handed-over-to-Maldives, last accessed on 19 June 2024.

63 Dipanjan Roy Chaudhury, 'India, Maldives sign pact to expand defence cooperation', *The Economic Times*, 12 July 2018 at https://economictimes.indiatimes.com/news/defence/india-maldives-sign-pact-to-expand-defence-cooperation/articleshow/51779405.cms?from=mdr last accessed on 19 June 2024.

64 'Indian Ocean cannot be backyard of India: China', PTI, *The Economic Times*, 12 July 2018 at https://economictimes.indiatimes.com/news/defence/indian-ocean-cannot-be-backyard-of-india-china/articleshow/47891860.cms last accessed on 19 June 2024.

65 'U.S. Relations With Maldives', US Department of State, at https://www.state.gov/u-s-relations-with-maldives/ last accessed on 19 June 2024.

66 'Maldives hopes for first U.S. embassy late this year or early next', *Reuters*, 19 September 2022 at https://www.reuters.com/world/maldives-hopes-first-us-embassy-late-this-year-or-early-next-2022-09-18/ last accessed on 19 June 2024.

67 'President renames "Embassy of the Maldives in Washington" to "Embassy of the Republic of Maldives to the US of America" The President's Office', Republic of Maldives, 29 September 2022,at https://presidency.gov.mv/Press/Article/27344 last accessed on 19 June 2024.

68 Nirupama Subramanian, 'US signs defence pact with Maldives', *The Indian Express*, 13 September 2020 at https://indianexpress.com/article/world/us-signs-defence-pact-with-maldives-6594295/ last accessed on 19 June 2024.

69 Suhasini Haidar, 'India welcomes U.S.-Maldives defence agreement', *The Hindu*, 14 September 2020 at https://www.thehindu.com/news/national/india-welcomes-us-maldives-defence-agreement/article32601889.ece last accessed on 19 June 2024.

70 'Friends & neighbours', *The Indian Express*, 24 September 2020, at https://indian express.com/article/opinion/editorials/friends-neighbours-6608170/ last accessed on 19 June 2024.

71 Jayanth Jacob, 'China's growing ties with Maldives give India the jitters', *Hindustan Times*, 23 February 2018 at https://www.hindustantimes.com/india-news/china-s-growing-ties-with-maldives-gives-india-the-jitters/story-XJ1U8OXwbiTmb6Or4TqCYO.html last accessed on 19 June 2024.

72 Reuters, 'Trump spy chief labels China biggest threat to freedom since World War Two', *The Hindu*, 4 December 2020 at https://www.thehindu.com/news/international/trump-spy-chief-labels-china-biggest-threat-to-freedom-since-world-war-two/article33245042.ece last accessed on 19 June 2024.

CHAPTER 8

Balancing Act in South Asia

The US engagement with South Asia has been shaped by its global priorities of the day. The region's significance has always been evaluated based on the impact it has on other regions and the interests of the US. US interests in South Asia have shifted over time, from containment of the Soviet Union to counterbalancing a rising China. After World War II, the US initially viewed China as part of the communist bloc, which strained their relationship significantly. However, in the late sixties and early seventies, the US strategically allied with China to gain an advantage over the Soviet Union during the Cold War. In this pursuit, Pakistan, its Cold War ally in South Asia, served as a crucial bridge.

As China emerged as a major global power in the twenty-first century, the US recalibrated its South Asia policy to address the challenges posed by China's rise. The focus shifted towards managing China's growing influence. During the Cold War, US policies towards India aimed at curbing its rise, but this perception changed significantly in light of the new threat posed by China. India, as the world's largest democracy and a fast-growing economy, is now seen as a potential counterbalance to China's assertiveness. Consequently, the US is no longer opposed to India's rise and may even support it if it helps in handling China's increasingly assertive behaviour on the global stage. Presently, South Asia is a strategic tool for the US to maintain a balance of power in its favour in the broader Indo-Pacific region. The US seeks to counterbalance China's growing influence by strategically engaging with South Asian nations, particularly India, as part of its IPS.

South Asia: A Crucial Component of the Indo-Pacific Security Architecture

South Asia occupies a crucial geopolitical position, acting as a gateway between the Middle East and East Asia, making it strategically significant for global powers. Recognizing South Asia's significant geopolitical influence in shaping regional dynamics and ensuring stability, the US is deeply invested in the region.

With critical maritime arteries like the Indian Ocean and the Arabian Sea running through its waters, South Asia plays a central role in global trade and energy transportation networks. The US aims to safeguarding these vital maritime routes, protecting its economic interests, and preserving open sea lanes for all nations.

The stability and security of South Asia directly impact the broader Indo-Pacific region, influencing the geopolitical balance. Consequently, the US views South Asia as a linchpin for regional stability, essential for bolstering the overall security architecture of the Indo-Pacific.

Pakistan as a Lynchpin of US Strategy during the Cold War

Following the departure of the British from South Asia, the US did not consider South Asia as strategically important. However, the situation changed as the US recognized the crucial strategic importance of maintaining control over Gulf oil reserves, wherein Pakistan played a significant role as a neighbouring nation.

As the Cold War intensified, the US sought allies and friends to counter the spread of communism and contain the influence of the Soviet Union. In this context, the US engaged with Pakistan on an intermittent basis. The US embraced Pakistan as an ally during the Cold War due to its strategic location, proximity to communist powers, and assumptions that Islam conferred a natural immunity to communism. India because of its diversity was seen as fragile by the US policymakers whereas Pakistan was expected to emerge as a powerful country in South Asia. The US also tried to curb India's rise as it did not trust Indian National Congress and its leader Jawaharlal Nehru.

Pakistan's relationship with the US evolved as it joined two alliances, CEATO and SENTO. The US also endeavoured to support Pakistan by providing arms. American armaments served as both a source of support for Pakistan and a concern for India, as India had to match them by investing in its domestic armament industry and procuring from other sources. Pakistan emerged as a Cold War ally through alliances and military assistance, receiving substantial support that significantly influenced the regional military balance. During this period, the US served as an offshore balancer.

Pakistan was however little interested in the Cold War objectives of the US. It had joined those alliances to get support against India. It also wanted to achieve parity with its larger and better endowed neighbour. Pakistan's alliances with the US and other allied countries during the Cold War provided economic and military assistance, diplomatic support on the Kashmir issue, and opportunities for military training and interaction.

Pakistan's Strategic Partnership with China

The US-Pakistan relationship during the Cold War created a relationship of dependency. However, there was a subtle change in US–Pakistan relationship after the 1962 India-China war. After the 1962 war US provided some military and financial support to India to meet the Chinese challenge. Moreover, after the 1965 India-Pakistan war US imposed an embargo and no country was given any military assistance. It was during this period that Pakistan discovered China as a strategic ally though they never signed any formal agreement. Pakistan sorted out its border dispute with China and allied with it against the common enemy India. This was the beginning of all-weather friendship of Pakistan and China.

Though Pakistan was never wholeheartedly in alliance with the US and was gradually shifting towards China, this dynamic also benefited US. Pakistan's departure from previous alliances facilitated its role as a bridge between the US and China, hastening the end of the Cold War. The US had realized that China had its own problems with the Soviet Union and the communist movement was not a monolithic one. The US, China and Pakistan formed a balancing alliance against the Soviet Union. This completely changed the dynamic of the Cold War and was helpful in ending it in favour of US. Thus, Pakistan's alliances with the US changed over time. Initially, it was a bandwagoning alliance to counter India. Subsequently, when China joined US and Pakistan this alliance turned into a balancing alliance to counter Soviet Union.

For some time, Pakistan enjoyed benefits from both US and China. The near-alliance of Pakistan and China has lasted and only grown stronger because they share common hostility against India. Pakistan was completely disillusioned with the US after its loss in 1971 war. This also led to deepening of China-Pakistan partnership. Though the situation on arms supply front changed after 1975, Pakistan had already made its move. It had entered into a strategic partnership with China against India.

Nuclearization of South Asia and Soviet Invasion of Afghanistan

Following the 1971 war, the relationship between the US and Pakistan lapsed into a period of dormancy. In the wake of Pakistan's defeat in the conflict with India, a strategic shift was initiated. President Zulfikar Ali Bhutto of Pakistan, in pursuit of regional parity with India, made the pivotal decision to embark on nuclear weapons development, thereby reversing the nation's prior stance against nuclear armament. This initiative was sustained under subsequent leadership, notably by Zia-ul-Haq. Within a decade, Pakistan successfully acquired nuclear capabilities, aided by support from China and tacit acceptance from the US, which chose to overlook Pakistan's nuclear ambitions.

The US-Pakistan relationship was revived once again with the Soviet invasion of Afghanistan in 1979. Pakistan played a vital role in supporting anti-Soviet operations. It was used to supply weapons to jihadi fighters from Afghanistan who were considered as the most effective against Soviet forces. This brought military and financial assistance back to Pakistan. At that time, the US was too engrossed in its Cold War with the Soviet Union. It ignored the nuclear programme of Pakistan and American Presidents actually gave clean chit to Pakistan so that it can get American assistance to continue operations in Afghanistan to drive out Soviet Union. The US supply however stopped once Soviet forces left Afghanistan and the US president also stopped issuing waivers.

After the withdrawal of Soviet forces from Afghanistan in 1989, the US shifted its priorities, leading to a reduction in its involvement in the region. The end of the Cold War and the diminishing threat of communism led to a decline in US engagement with Pakistan. Pakistan, perennially in search of a patron deepened its relationship with China. Now both sides describe this relationship with various metaphors.

Interestingly, after the end of the Cold War US created the Bureau of South Asian Affairs on 24 August 1992, which has been a part of the Bureau of Near Eastern and South Asian Affairs since 1958. Now US aimed to balance its relationships with India and Pakistan, maintaining strong ties with both countries while addressing their historical conflicts. The US played a role in facilitating dialogue and negotiations between India and Pakistan, particularly in relation to the Kashmir dispute. However, achieving a lasting resolution has proven challenging, and tensions between the two countries persist. The US now also wanted to prevent both India and Pakistan from going nuclear. However, by that time things had considerably changed. First India went nuclear in 1998 and subsequently Pakistan followed suit. It is widely believed that the Pakistani bomb was based on Chinese design. The policies aimed at preventing nuclearization of South Asia failed because they did not take into account regional dynamics.

The nuclear tests conducted by both India and Pakistan in 1998 added a new imensionn to US engagement, focusing on preventing further proliferation and moderating the regional arms race, particularly regarding the contentious Kashmir issue.

As far as China was concerned, it astutely managed its relationship with the US in the 1990s. Despite massive human rights violations during the Tiananmen Square protests, American business interests ensured that China remained the most favored nation. China remained focused on its economic development and did not attempt to challenge US hegemony.

De-hyphenation of India and Pakistan

Following the 11 September 2001 attacks, the US found itself compelled to once again engage with Pakistan. The Bush administration, recognizing Pakistan's strategic importance in the global war on terror, designated Pakistan a major non-NATO ally and positioned it as a frontline state in this conflict.

Consequently, military aid to Pakistan resumed. However, a notable shift was observed in this phase. While the US sought Pakistan's assistance in combating terrorism, it concurrently pursued a constructive relationship with India, signifying a departure from past approaches. This shift had started during President Clinton's visit to South Asia in 2000. Under the Bush administration, there was a distinct de-hyphenation of India and Pakistan, with each country being assessed on its individual merits. This period coincided with the rapid rise of China, which emerged as a significant concern for the US. Pakistan's role in the war on terror was viewed as beneficial, while democratic India was increasingly seen as a potential counterbalance to China. As a result, the partnership between India and the US continued to strengthen, although notable differences persisted.

The Irregular Nature of the US-Pakistan Alliance

The irregular nature of the US-Pakistan alliance reveals that the US lacked a permanent strategic interest in the region, utilizing Pakistan opportunistically as needed. Pakistan, in turn, accepted a subordinate role in the alliance, seeing it as a means to achieve parity with India, a larger and more powerful neighbour. Pakistanis also believed that the alliance with US helped them to negotiate issues with India appropriately.

However, Pakistan also bore the consequences of this alliance. The military assumed a central role in Pakistani politics and society, portraying itself as the nation's guardian and garnering a significant share of resources. Both domestic and external actors leveraged jihadist groups, hindering the growth of liberal forces within Pakistan. The suppression of democracy went largely unaddressed by external powers like the US, contributing to the underdevelopment of democratic institutions in Pakistan.

The presence of jihadist elements fueled radicalization within Pakistani society, leading to social, political, and economic setbacks. Pakistan's economy remained turbulent, perpetuating its reliance on seeking patronage from external actors.

Shift in US Perspective on India and Pakistan

The US perspective on India and Pakistan started shifting after the 1965 war. While the US had provided substantial military assistance to Pakistan, the war showed India's military capabilities and resilience, leading to a reevaluation of its potential as a regional power. Now it was clear that even with a huge external assistance Pakistan can't be a major regional power. The Indian army had shown its ability to regenerate itself after the debacle of 1962 war and India as a country was showing prowess in science and technology. This assessment was proven right when India defeated Pakistan comprehensively in 1971 war. Actually, a section in the US believed in this even before the 1965 war, but US policymakers did not respond positively to this as they were not sure of India's positive response to their overtures.

India's image further improved after the 1990 economic liberalization when the country started making steady progress. India's software power was also displayed to the world. Indian Diaspora in US and Europe influenced policymakers in favour of India. This positive perception of India was seen during the subsequent visit of American presidents to the Indian subcontinent.

Rise of Assertive China

The turn of the century has witnessed the rise of China, and soon it was realized that the rise of China is not going to be as peaceful as was expected. Growing in economic and military prowess, China has shifted its strategy from 'hide and bide' to 'seize and lead.' The assertive behaviour of China emerged following the 2008 Asian financial crisis when it concluded that the US was in decline, prompting it to adopt a more assertive policy.

As China's economy expanded, so did its core interests. In order to protect these expanding interests, China's military doctrine began to evolve. China now seeks to project power, aiming to transform its navy from a coastal protection force to a Blue Water Navy. Chinese authorities have made expansive claims in the South China Sea and are particularly concerned about two chokepoints in the Indian Ocean, crucial for their energy supply from Gulf countries. Additionally, important communication routes pass through the Indian Ocean. These developments have led to tensions with India as both countries vie for influence in the region. India considers areas near its borders as its sphere of influence, essential for safeguarding its security. China's efforts to increase its influence in the IOR, especially in countries close to India's borders, are therefore a cause for concern. Currently, India and China are embroiled in a standoff in Eastern Ladakh, adding to existing tensions along their disputed Himalayan border.

China's assertiveness is particularly pronounced in the South China Sea, where it has laid expansive claims through its nine-dash line. It has also disregarded international rulings on disputes with the Philippines in the region. China's construction of artificial islands aims to solidify its control in the area, with militarization being a significant aspect of this endeavour. These activities have raised concerns regarding freedom of navigation, which could impact global trade. The South China Sea holds vital resources and is of strategic importance to economic powers such as South Korea and Japan. However, both nations tread cautiously in addressing China's assertive actions due to their economic dependencies on China.

Power Shift in the Indo-Pacific

A significant power shift occurred in the Indo-Pacific region during the Obama administration, marked by China's construction and militarization of artificial islands. Despite China's actions raising concerns among many countries about its expansive claims, the response from the US was perceived as lacking. The Obama administration's failure to prevent China from building islands and disregard for international rulings indicated a lack of effective counterbalance to China's growing influence.

Criticism mounted against the Obama administration for its perceived passive stance towards China's assertive actions in the South China Sea. China's unchecked expansion efforts caused tensions among Southeast Asian neighbors and highlighted the diminishing US leadership in the region. Even legal efforts by the Philippines against China's actions were rebuffed, underscoring the limitations of US influence.

The economic ties of Southeast Asian nations with China, coupled with China's increasing military strength, complicated the situation. The Obama administration navigated cautiously, balancing regional security concerns with economic realities. However, this approach was criticized for allowing China to expand its territorial claims without facing significant consequences.

Amidst these developments, the Obama administration sought to strengthen ties with India, recognizing its growing importance in the region.

The de-linking of India and Pakistan continued, acknowledging India as a key partner in managing regional power dynamics. Meanwhile, US-Pakistan relations soured due to Pakistan's ambiguous stance on terrorism, further strained by incidents like the killing of Osama bin Laden.

Initially, the Obama administration entertained the idea of a 'Group of Two' (G-2) partnership with China, but this proposal lost momentum over time. Modi's visit to Washington marked a significant milestone as both sides issued a joint statement, aligning against China and highlighting India's growing global importance. Reports even suggested discussions on joint regional patrols, indicating a potential shift in regional cooperation dynamics.

US Initiative to Restore Leadership through the IPS

During the Trump administration, US-India relations experienced significant growth, marked by increased defense cooperation, joint military exercises, and expanding economic ties. Despite the transactional nature of Trump's foreign policy, India emerged as the US's largest trading partner in South Asia, fostering a mutually beneficial relationship.

China's expanding presence in South Asia, particularly through initiatives like the CPEC, raised concerns for both India and the US. India, while cautious in its approach to China, expressed apprehensions about its growing military presence and political interference in neighbouring countries.

The revival of the Quad—a strategic grouping involving the US, India, Japan, and Australia—under the Trump administration demonstrated the growing alignment of interests in the Indo-Pacific region. This grouping, though not explicitly anti-China, aimed to address shared concerns about China's assertive behavior.

However, US-Pakistan relations deteriorated during this time, with Trump implementing a stricter policy towards Pakistan, including cutting aid and showing reluctance to assist with Pakistan's growing indebtedness due to the CPEC. Despite this, the US remained engaged with Pakistan, leveraging its influence to encourage cooperation in Afghanistan and counter-terrorism efforts.

Pakistan, in need of regular IMF bailouts, found itself in a delicate position, hesitant to solely rely on China. The US, serving as Pakistan's primary export market and a key source of foreign remittances and investment, retained considerable influence over the country's economic stability.[1]

In contrast, the US provided both moral and military support to India as a means to confront Chinese aggression. This marked a notable departure from the Obama administration's more reserved stance during similar crises.

Under the Biden administration, the US has further evolved its IPS, seeking to restore American leadership and foster a region that is open, connected, prosperous, resilient, and secure. Strengthening alliances, supporting India's rise, and enhancing the capabilities of the Quad are important elements of this strategy.

Quad largely remains a platform to discuss cooperation among the four members. Though the implicit objective of the grouping is to manage the rise of China and gain a favourable balance of power in the Indo-Pacific it has avoided getting branded as an anti-China platform. Challenges and divergences exist within the Quad, with India's non-ally status and varying approaches to the Indo-Pacific and China raising concerns. However, the shared concern over China's assertiveness continues to drive incremental progress within the grouping.

Another pivotal component of the US IPS is the AUKUS Pact, which comprises the US, Australia, and the United Kingdom. Originating from Australia's request to the US for nuclear submarine technology transfer, the alliance underscores a strategic recognition by the US that potential conflicts with China would likely occur in the maritime domain. With a focus on maintaining maritime military superiority, AUKUS members aim to bolster their capabilities, particularly through the deployment of nuclear submarines armed with missiles. Nuclear submarines armed with missiles, strategically positioned east of the Philippines, could facilitate potential offensive actions against mainland China. This will also serve the US objective of sharpening its 'military edge' to maintain its status as the most powerful military in the region and the preferred security partner.[2]

Moreover, the US is also trying to reassert influence over Pacific Island nations, where China has made significant inroads. This effort constitutes the third element of the IPS.

Rise of Assertive China Prompts a Shift in US Policy in South Asia

The emergence of China as an assertive power has led to a shift in US policy in South Asia. The US views China's strategic partnership with Pakistan, its presence in the IOR, and its BRI as challenges to its interests.

India as a Key Partner

To counter China, the US has forged partnerships with countries in South Asia, particularly India. The US views India as a key partner in its IPS to balance China and maintain stability in the region. The US perspective on India has shifted significantly. India has effectively managed its democracy and is experiencing rapid economic growth. Interestingly, the US never considered India a strategic rival, even during its alliance with Pakistan in the Cold War. Instead, it was China that perceived India as a tool of the West and valued Pakistan for distancing itself from Western alliances.

During the Cold War, US policies towards India aimed at limiting its rise. However, this perception changed markedly in response to the new threat posed by China. As the world's largest democracy, India is now seen as a potential counterbalance to China's assertiveness. Consequently, the US no longer opposes India's rise and may even support it if it helps manage China's increasingly assertive behavior on the global stage.

The US has lifted sanctions on India, signed defense and nuclear cooperation agreements, and enhanced military, economic, and technological cooperation with the country. Although Pakistan has not been completely sidelined, its importance has significantly diminished. Pakistan is not trusted after attempting to deal with both sides in the War against terror.

As China expands its influence in South Asia and the IOR, India is uneasy about Chinese intentions. India sees itself as a net security provider in the IOR, but the growing Chinese presence diminishes its position. During the administrations of President Bush and President Obama, there was an understanding in the US that India's rise was in its interest. Despite the unpredictability of US foreign policy under President Trump, the relationship between India and the US improved, and India gained access to important defense technologies that were previously denied. Even the Biden administration seeks to strengthen India's leadership in the region.

The US has not completely abandoned Pakistan, but its importance has diminished. Moreover, Pakistan's close alliance with China is viewed with suspicion. The US now regards the CPEC with skepticism.

Attempts to Engage Smaller South Asian Nations

The US is now also focusing on the smaller South Asian nations. These nations initially drew US attention following the 11 September 2001 incident. At that time, the focus was more on their internal conflicts. The US encouraged them to resolve those conflicts to bring stability to the South Asian region.

The rise of assertive China and its inroads into Pakistan and other smaller South Asian nations have prompted the US to deepen its relationship with these countries. The US has now adopted a comprehensive approach towards most of these countries.

The US actively engages in diplomatic efforts with smaller South Asian countries to build partnerships, address regional challenges, and promote shared interests. Bilateral and multilateral dialogues serve as tools for maintaining diplomatic influence and fostering cooperation.

Economic engagement and partnerships with smaller South Asian countries contribute to the overall strategic balance. The US supports economic development initiatives, trade agreements, and investments to strengthen ties and promote stability. It is trying to provide them financial help for infrastructure development under its MCC programme. Through this effort, the US is trying to provide them an alternative to China's BRI. The US also provides aid to these countries.

Security cooperation with smaller South Asian nations is a key aspect of the US strategy to ensure a balance of power in the Indo-Pacific. Military partnerships, joint exercises, and defence collaborations contribute to enhancing regional security and deterring potential threats. To enhance its defence partnership with the Maldives the US has already signed a defence agreement with it. Its defence collaboration with Sri Lanka has also increased.

The smaller South Asian nations want to take economic benefit from both the US and China. They also want freedom of navigation. But they don't want to side with either China or the US in a military alliance. They are also wary of the IPS of the US. They have adopted this strategy because in the great power competition between the US and China, there is no clear winner at present. By not siding with anyone, they want to identify themselves with the winner when the contest settles. This also protects them from the ire of the US and China in case there is some kind of compromise. Actually, the Quad, where India is a member, itself has downplayed the security component, though its objective indicates that it wants to counter China.

The US-China competition for influence in South Asia has also opened opportunities for smaller South Asian nations. Besides, it has fostered greater consultation, coordination, and cooperation between the US and India in the region. Both countries are working together to address Chinese activities and promote a rules-based order in the Indo-Pacific region. There is also a change in attitude of India. The assertive China and its rivalry with India and the US have led to a more receptive stance from India towards extra-regional involvement in South Asia.

China's Response

China is keenly aware that the US withdrawal from Afghanistan has led to a notable shift in American priorities, transitioning from combating terrorism to countering China. Consequently, South Asia has assumed a different role in the Indo-Pacific context, now expected to support US efforts to maintain a favorable balance of power to manage the rise of an assertive China. India is anticipated to play a central role in this endeavor. In response, China also aims to take steps to counter the US, India, Japan, and Australia, all members of the Quad.

China has been actively engaging with South Asian nations for some time. As part of its IPS, the US has increased its engagement with South Asian countries, excluding Pakistan. In response, China intends to enhance its own involvement with these nations. Should India choose to align itself with the US to counter China, China is likely to increase its influence with other regional states to challenge India's leadership.[3] Additionally, China has implemented economic measures against the US and Australia. It has hardened its position on the boundary settlement since November 2006.[4] It has also heightened border tensions with India along the disputed Himalayan border.

The CPEC is often viewed as a means to strengthen the 'China-Pakistan Axis,' bolstering the security and political dimensions of their relationship. Consequently, the CPEC could be interpreted as a Chinese response to a potential third phase of the US rebalance to the Asia-Pacific, coinciding with the emergence of the Indo-Pacific era.[5] Furthermore, it can be seen as China's effort to counter India's growing national capabilities and its increasing involvement in the South China Sea.

Since 2008, China has sought to establish a naval presence in the Indian Ocean to combat terrorism, facilitate economic activities, and protect its strategic interests. China's heavy reliance on the Malacca Strait for energy supplies makes it vulnerable to economic coercion during conflicts with major powers like the US. Consequently, China is focusing on securing maritime transport routes from the North Arabian Sea to the Malacca Strait and investing in infrastructure for alternative trade routes. Notably, China commenced construction of its first overseas quasi-military base in Djibouti in 2017 and is expanding its marine corps for deployments in the region. There are also indications that China is considering establishing a naval base at Gwadar Port in Pakistan.

Challenges and Considerations

The US emphasizes the importance of building strong regional partnerships in South Asia to collectively address common challenges. This will contribute to a more robust and cohesive strategy for maintaining a favorable balance of power. However, US policy in South Asia faces several challenges and must take into account certain considerations.

South Asia is characterized by diverse geopolitical and cultural complexities. Balancing various interests in the region poses a challenge. For Pakistan, balancing India has always been more important than siding with the US to address its global priorities. As a result, the US cannot expect a similar response from all South Asian countries in handling the rise of assertive China in the Indo-Pacific. On the other hand, Pakistan has chosen to partner with China, given that both countries share a common rivalry with India.

In smaller South Asian countries, foreign policy often changes with the shift of political regimes. This has been observed in the cases of Bangladesh,

Sri Lanka, Maldives, and Nepal. The fluid nature of geopolitical alliances in South Asia requires the US to adapt its strategies to changing dynamics. Shifts in alliances and partnerships among South Asian nations impact the effectiveness of US efforts to maintain a balance of power.

Moreover, China, which the US aims to balance, has made deep inroads in most South Asian countries. It is the largest arms supplier to both Pakistan and Bangladesh and has a close defence partnership with Sri Lanka. Additionally, China is attempting to engage Nepal and Maldives in defense partnerships. It has also made significant economic inroads in these countries through its BRI. China's increasing economic and military influence in South Asia poses challenges to the US strategy of counterbalancing.

India Remains Crucial for Balancing China in the Indo-Pacific

The great power competition between the US and China drives their increased engagement with South Asian nations. However, the Indo-Pacific is not perceived by all stakeholders through the lens of great power competition. Countries respond to the IPS based on their own geopolitical situations. South Asian nations navigate between US and Chinese influence, seeking economic benefits without aligning with either power. The evolving nature of the US IPS further complicates the strategic calculus of South Asian nations, prompting a nuanced approach towards supporting the concept of a free and open Indo-Pacific. No South Asian state wants to take sides in the IPS amidst the great power competition.

Though India is also careful in dealing with China, it is the only country that has consistently tried to balance China's influence since 1962. It has refrained from joining initiatives like the BRI. This makes India-US partnership in the Indo-Pacific significant for countering China's rise and maintaining a free and open region. Though the Quad has not been overtly security-oriented, both India and the US share common concerns regarding China. China remains a dominant factor influencing the India-US relationship. Both countries recognize the importance of countering China's rise and maintaining a free and open Indo-Pacific. The evolving dynamics in the region, coupled with efforts to strengthen cooperation between India, the US, and other like-minded countries, will continue to shape the future of this crucial relationship.

NOTES

1 Syed Mohammad Ali, 'The U.S.-China Strategic Rivalry and its Implications for Pakistan,' Issue Brief, Stimson Center, 1 December 2020, at https://www.stimson.org/2020/the-u-s-china-strategic-rivalry-and-its-implications-for-pakistan/ last accessed on 19 June 2024.

2 Curtis Stone, 'Voice of China: Why a Third Phase of the U.S. Rebalance to Asia-Pacific Could be Destructive,' *People's Daily Online*, 13 October 2016 at http://en.people.cn/n3/2016/1013/c90000-9126636.html last accessed on 19 June 2024.

3 Yang Xiaoping, 'Managing Leadership in the Indo-Pacific: The United States' South Asia Strategy Revisited,' *China Quarterly of International Strategic Studies*, Vol. 3, No. 4, 2017, p. 480.

4 Shivshankar Menon, 'Choices: Inside the Making of India's Foreign Policy,' Penguin Random House India, New Delhi, 2016, p. 84.

5 Yang Xiaoping, 'Managing Leadership in the Indo-Pacific: The United States' South Asia Strategy Revisited,' *China Quarterly of International Strategic Studies*, Vol. 3, No. 4, 2017, p. 473.

Index